ANYTHING, ANYTIME, ANYWHERE

The Legacy of the Flying Tiger Line
1945-89

Art Chin

To Wayne Koide,

Good luck always,

Art Chin

Tassels & Wings
Seattle, Washington

By the same author

**GOLDEN TASSELS: A History of the
Chinese in Washington, 1857-1992**

Published by Tassels & Wings Publishing
6208 S. Bangor St.
Seattle, Washington 98178

Library of Congress Catalog Card No. 93-90149

ISBN 0-9637826-8-1

Printed in the United States of America

Dedicated to Crystal,
Travis, Clinton,
and, my wife, Tami

Dreamers drift among the clouds,
Visionaries rise above them,
On wings of flight,
forever,
Inspiring others
for generations to come.

ACKNOWLEDGEMENT

I wish to extend my deepest regards to the former Seattle Flying Tigers (FT) staff for their continuous encouragement, and providing information in the preparation of the manuscript. Special thanks to Chuck Tucci, former Seattle FT Trainer, who provided helpful resource material, and Dave Palmquist, former Seattle FT Senior Supervisor, for his information regarding the changing Chicago operations during the latter 1970s and early 1980s, among other matters.

Thanks to Ann-Marie Hennessey and Mary Gonzalez, both formerly with FT Corporate Communications in Los Angeles, and Steve Grant, former Seattle FT Station Manager, for their contributing pictures of various Flying Tiger Line aircraft used in the text. I'm also very grateful to Capt. Dary Alford, former Seaboard and Tiger pilot, for offering the picture of the Seaboard 747 cargo aircraft. And, special thanks to Michele Rochester, former FT Training and Development staff member in Los Angeles, for making available complementary pictures which heartfully enhance the presentation.

Much appreciation is also extended to Ellen Toney, Bob Prescott's former personal secretary (1953-1972) for her inspiration, and to Dick Rossi, former FT pilot and one of the original former AVG\CNAC investors of the carrier, for his invaluable information about the original investors

Grateful acknowledgement to Steve Castello of the Seattle-King County Medical Disaster Team for his assistance. And the contributions of former Tiger Retirement Club President Joe Baker, current President Charles Thompson, and the Flying Tiger Archives staff in Los Angeles for usage of Tigereview pictures and material was an absolute complement to the study. Baker was the former FT Superintendant of Maintenance and Facilities, and is presently the Tiger Retirement Club historian.

With love, I thank my wife, Tami, for her extensive computer work and many sacrifices. Lastly, through all her excitement, I fulfill my promise to my Tiger-spirited daughter, Crystal Ann Chin. So let us all forever treasure this important part of our lives, and lives of many others, impressed with the historical and humanitarian achievements of the Flying Tiger Line.

CONTENTS

LIST OF MAPS

LIST OF PHOTOGRAPHS

AUTHOR'S NOTE

Writing an aviation history of the Flying Tiger Line has been of interest to me for a while, inasmuch as I've worked for the company over nineteen years. During the Thanksgiving period of 1986, there was a threat, or semblence thereof, to sell off Tigers' assets, or liquidate, had the company been unable to re-negotiate labor contracts to acquire concessions primarily from its unionized staff segment. It was a low ebb for all employees, and, at that time, I decided that I would prepare a manuscript about certain developmental facets of our air cargo company. After more than a year of procrastination, I finally started to do research on selected topics, and dedicate the writing to my daughter, Crystal, as an incentive mechanism.

This presentation , in its broadest scope, describes the experiences of a group of legendary war veterans , comrades in combat, that started a small airline which became the world's largest air cargo carrier. Flying Tiger Line, America's first cargo airlines, was originally called National Skyway Freight Corporation, and had its beginnings as a non-certificated charter air carrier in 1945, using a rented two-car garage at Long Beach Municipal Airport in California. It was formed by a group of famous former WWII Flying Tiger fighter pilots and CNAC combat cargo crew members, led by the visionary Bob Prescott. They were joined by a handful of California business venturists who shared their dream. Together, through tenacity, skill, comraderie, and sacrifice, patented into a Tiger "can do" spirit, they realized their dreams. In Prescott's words, "The difficult we can accomplish tomorrow, the impossible takes a little longer."

During its first twenty-five years, the carrier developed as a leader in the growing air cargo industry, although it struggled surviving primarily on charter and contract work, much of that being military. Subsequently, Tigers became a scheduled international air carrier, developing its extensive global system since 1969 when it was awarded the lucrative Asia-U.S. scheduled cargo route. The carrier's significant participation in the Vietnam airlift and back-haul of Asia imports to the U.S., during a period of accelerated growth, was complemented by the company's acquisition of a jetfreighter fleet.

Flying Tiger Line's primary geographic market has been Asia, developing a strong presence since 1969, and much of that may be attributed to the company's former VP of International Affairs, Madame Chennault, widow of the famous Gen. Claire Lee Chennault. The carrier acquired its name with the General's approval, and Madame Chennault, with Bob Prescott, were primarily responsible for the carrier's route acquisition and success in Asia.

In 1980, the carrier acquired Seaboard World Airlines, an established U.S.-based North Atlantic all-cargo carrier. And, finally, Flying Tigers extended its international system to service Latin America and the South Pacific, and eventually provide around-the world scheduled serice in the global economy.

The company experienced serious financial problems during the early to mid-1980's, but effected a successful "turn-a-round" in 1987 and 1988, the carrier's two most profitable years in its history. In its struggle for market share, Tigers has committed to "recapture the jungle."

In an unexpected climax, in December of 1988, **just two weeks after I finished my first draft**, Federal Express, the air courier company, tendered an offer to acquire Flying Tigers. The attractive offer "locked out" other interested parties, and both businesses awaited formal government hearings. The expected merger was effected by mid-summer, 1989.

Art Chin
August 7, 1989
Seattle, Washington

1

Building on the Flying Tiger Image: Creative Entrepreneurship as a Non-Certificated All-Cargo Carrier

The cross winds of a World War nurtured a new dimension in aviation history, borne out of necessity. During an early period of WWII in China, General Claire Lee Chennault's American Volunteer Group (AVG) comprising of some seventy young fighter pilots, volunteers drawn from the ranks of U.S. military aviation officers, performed exploits which became legendary. The three fighter squadrons formed by the volunteers became known as the Flying Tigers. From December, 1941 to July, 1942, the Flying Tiger squadrons with shark-teeth painted on their aircraft cowling, terrorized enemy aircraft and troop movements in the China war theatre, including Burma and southeast Asia. The Flying Tigers proved to be the only significant U.S. success story in Asia during the earlier period of the Pacific war.

> "During extraordinary odds, the Flying Tigers' record was impressive. In the air, they were credited with certain destruction of 299 enemy planes and the possible destruction of an additional 153. On the ground, the AVG estimated that it destroyed another 200, bringing the total number of enemy aircraft destroyed to approximately 650. In contrast, the Japanese destroyed just a dozen P-40s in the air and caught sixty-one on the ground (twenty-two of

which the AVG burned when evacuating Loiwing), for a total of seventy-three. While the AVG killed as many as fifteen hundred Japanese personnel, the group only lost ten pilots in combat and the same number in aircraft accidents. Three others were killed during air raids, and three were taken prisoner."[1]

In March, 1942, the Burma Road was closed by the encroaching enemy, cutting off the last major surface Allied supply route into China serving U.S. and Chinese forces. Then, together with an established commercial airline, the China National Aviation Corporation (CNAC), a joint Pan American-Chinese government venture, Flying Tigers provided some escort to help develop the treacherous aerial corridor route over the Himalayas between India (Assam Province area) and interior China. With CNAC providing the original pioneer flights, the historical event became known as the "Hump airlift," essentially flying air cargo, refugees, and aviation fuel supply under the most difficult of circumstances. CNAC flew the "Hump" more than 80,000 times between April, 1942 and September, 1945, carrying more than 50,000 tons of goods to China and bringing out nearly 25,000 tons. It cost the lives of twenty-five crews.[2]

As the U.S. formally entered the war, the military sought to incorporate the AVG into the new 14th Air Force, but their arrogant and threatening approach of recruitment, short of induction, alienated Chennault's individualistic fighter pilots. After the AVG formally disbanded in July 4, 1942, seventeen members subsequently contracted with CNAC. While CNAC operations were predominantly controlled by American administrators, the flight crews included an ethnic mixture of Americans, Chinese, Australians, Canadians, British, and Danes. They had served with such distinguished outfits as the AVG, the Eagle Squadron, the North Atlantic Ferry Command, the Royal Air Force, and the Royal Canadian Air Force, seeking money and adventure flying unarmed transport planes.[3]

The subsequent development of air cargo services may, in large part, be attributed to the successful learning experiences of those two organizations, and their successor, the military Air Transport Command (ATC) in "flying the Hump," and other long distance air freight operations. Valuable insight was also established concerning the role of combat cargo aircraft. The operations of the ATC and Naval Air Transportation Service carried over three and one-third billion ton-miles during the years between 1942 and 1945; this was nearly forty times the aggregate freight carried by all of the domestic airlines from 1926 and 1945.[4]

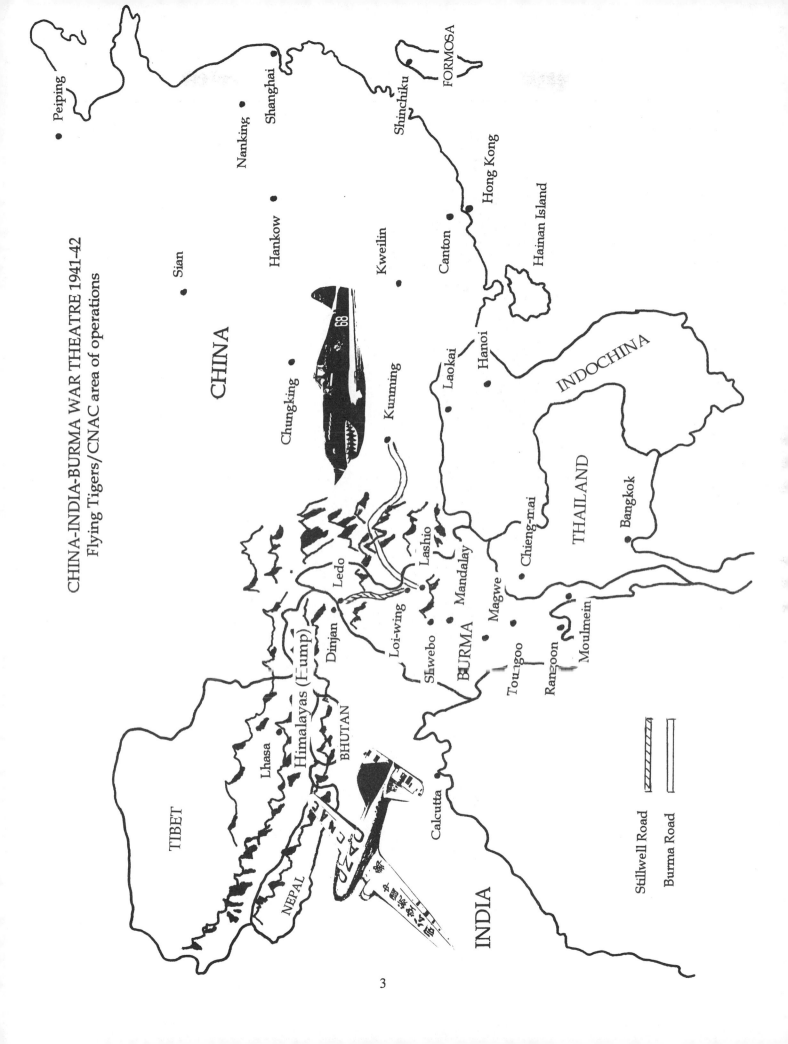

CHINA-INDIA-BURMA WAR THEATRE 1941-42
Flying Tigers/CNAC area of operations

CHINA

TIBET

Lhasa

Himalayas (Hump)

NEPAL

BHUTAN

Ledo

Dinjan

Loi-wing

Shwebo

Lashio

Mandalay

BURMA

Magwe

Toungoo

Rangoon

Moulmein

Calcutta

INDIA

Peiping

Nanking

Shanghai

Sian

Hankow

Chungking

Kunming

Kweilin

Canton

Hong Kong

Hainan Island

Shinchiku

FORMOSA

Laokai

Hanoi

INDOCHINA

Chieng-mai

THAILAND

Bangkok

68

Stillwell Road

Burma Road

3

P-40 Aerial - The single engine Curtiss P-40 with distinctive tiger shark markings was the aircraft of the American Volunteer Group, better known as the "Flying Tigers" of General Claire Lee Chennault. (1941-1942)

Robert W. Prescott with P-40 and American Volunteer Group ("Flying Tigers")

5

After WWII, hundreds of veterans military aviators took advantage of veterans' preference to purchase or lease government surplus aircraft to enter a newly emerging industry known as air cargo services. Many of the surplus aircraft were the familiar type flown during the war as military supply planes, convertible for troop movement as well. Thus, within this background, a dozen war-time pilots and mechanics, backed up by a handful of successful businessmen, enthusiastically started a new air cargo airline, which, shortly thereafter, took on the name of Flying Tiger Line, in honor of the dominating veterans who managed its operations.

The original name of the company was National Skyway Freight Corporation, formally incorporated in Delaware on June 25, 1945, a couple of months before the Pacific war had ended. The original financing of the company was by issue of 2,260 shares of $100 par value which stock was equally subscribed by a group of the company's associates and of several California businessmen.[5] In actuality, the businessmen promised to match the amount that the wartime veterans would raise themselves, in agreement by former AVG and CNAC pilot Robert (Bob) W. Prescott, who became the acknowledged founder of the organization. Most of the aviator investors were both former AVG flight leaders and CNAC pilots. Dick Rossi, an old AVG pilot, who was still flying in China with CNAC, contributed $10,000. Joe Rosbert in Hollywood, where he was acting as technical expert on a film called "Calcutta" put in $3,000, and promised to raise the rest. Other of Bob's former aviator colleagues joined in the effort, including Jules Watson and R.H. "Red" Holmes of CNAC, Jack Cornelius,

former AVG crew chief, and former AVG/CNAC pilots Duke Headman, Catfish Raines, and Link Laughlin.[6]

Bob Prescott, as expected, became the company's first president and CEO, and Sam Mosher, a commercial flower grower and co-founder of the California Fruit Growers' Exchange, became the chairman of the board. Duke Hedman was appointed a vice president, while others, including Joe Rosbert, became superintendent of operations, and Catfish Raines was the chief pilot. Bill Bartling and Tom Haywood, both former AVG flight leaders, joined the new company after it was formed, to become assistant general manager and superintendent of engineering, respectively.[7] Clifford Groh, former AVG/CNAC aviator, joined the group.

To head the legal department, Mosher hired a business acquaintance, Norman E. Meyers, a Washington, D.C. lawyer, who became the company's general counsel and director. Prescott's wife, Helen Ruth, performed the invaluable service of managing much of the office duties and handling operations personnel, among other matters, during the ongoing.

The first headquarters of National Skyway Freight Corporation was a suite in Los Angeles' Biltmore Hotel, but due to the awkward demands of the operation, it was quickly re-located to a partitioned, one-room office at the Long Beach Air Terminal in southern California.[8] The humble facilities was complemented with a usable two-car garage for maintenance operations.

The southern California location was selected in consideration that the initial contracts were with the California Fruit Growers Association, to haul fruit from the west coast to the eastern markets. Mosher also felt that flowers and produce would prove to be successful air cargo commodities. In fact, the airlines first three revenue flights totalling over 30,000 pounds, commenced on August 21, 1945, within hours of each other. On that eventful day, California flowers were flown to Detroit, Burbank grapes to Atlanta, and furniture to California from New York. But on the third day of operations, a second load of furniture crashed on takeoff at Detroit.[9] At the end of the year, Mosher and Prescott raised $2.5 million from a firm of Wall Street brokers to see them through the lean months as they scratched around for enough business to keep their aircraft busy.[10] Bond & Goodwin, a New York investment company underwriter firm issued the $2.5 million of shares at $5 par share, thus, National Skyway Freight went public on the New York stock exchange. About this time, Mosher selected Fred Benninger as the company's accountant. Benninger became, as Prescott often noted, a very key figure with the carrier in all major financial dealings for twenty years.

Budd Conestoga aircraft on field at carrier's
first terminal, Long Beach Municipal Airport, 1945.

FIRST SOLID PLANELOAD

AIR EXPRESS to ATLANTA from CALIFORNIA!!

8,000 LBS.

Thompson's Airborne Vine-Ripened Seedless Grapes

Rushed Across the Continent to You

This Giant American Airways Express Plane, owned and operated by Veterans of the famous India-China Flying Tiger Squadron.

BEING SOLD AT OUR COST

Fresh from the vine, these luscious grapes are being sold at OUR COST PRICE so that you can enjoy real natural freshness—true vineyard flavor. We gladly pass our normal profit on to our customers because it affords them the opportunity to enjoy grapes with full flavor and freshness from West of the Rockies.

ON SALE FRIDAY MORNING

★ Colonial Stores ★

BIG STAR SUPER MARKETS   LITTLE STAR FOOD STORES

Thompson's Vine-Ripened Airborne
Seedless Grapes
Lb. **43¢**

Each convenient consumer package carries the AIRBORNE SEAL ... Average weight, 2 pounds per package.

ON SALE FRIDAY MORNING

Source: Atlantic Constitution, Aug. 24, 1945

The first fleet of air cargo planes which the company acquired was the Budd Conestoga, which turned out to be "mechanically precarious," at best. The acquisition was the culmination of a learning experience in which Bob Prescott and Duke Hedman, his recruit, had scanned government agencies in the Washington, D.C. area in search of adequate aircraft for the venture. Their hope for a DC-3 became futile. However, through the War Assets Administration, Prescott learned that fourteen Budd Conestogas were available for the cost of $401,000 with a $90,000 down payment. Twenty carloads of spare parts, inventoried at $12 million, were added at no charge.[11] The Budds were peculiar specialized planes built during the war by the Edward G. Budd Manufacturing Co. of Philadelphia, known best at building stainless steel streamline railroad cars. The Budd was the first aircraft originally designed to be fabricated entirely; of shotwelded stainless steel, rather than conventional lightweight aluminum. It was designed to meet U.S. Navy specification for twin-engined cargo carrier and troop transport. The main features included a rear loading ramp which retracted upward into the sides of the fuselage to maintain an 8 ft. x 8 ft. cross section. Additional cargo could be loaded with the rear ramp closed.

The Navy awarded a contract for two hundred Budds in August, 1942, and the U.S. Army also ordered six hundred of that aircraft. However, production was short-lived due to manufacturing problems associated with the design, delays in production, higher projected costs substantially greater than the original estimates, and changing needs of the military. Consequently, the Navy cut their contract from two hundred to twenty-five, while the Army canceled their order altogether. The twenty-five aircraft produced were sold out of service, including fourteen to National Skyway, who took advantage of a veterans' preference to acquire the low price surplus equipment.[12]

Insight into this period of U.S. aviation history reveals that the "exemption for non-scheduled operators (CAB 292.5 of Economic Regulations)" enabled veteran airmen to engage in the air freight business without obtaining a certificate of public convenience and necessity from the CAB, pending final Board decision on the Air Freight Case. The exemption in combination with the availability of WWII surplus military flight equipment offered considerable leverage for wartime veterans. Consequently, the number of air cargo operators increased multi-fold shortly after the war. The proliferation of such operators, numbering over 300, became so great, and their operations so extensive that an investigation was launched by the CAB.

At the forefront, National Skyway Freight Corporation became a pioneer in

Flying Tiger Line's first aircraft was the Budd Conestoga, an all-stainless steel, rear-loading, twin-engine aircraft. Capable of lifting 7,000 pounds over a 500-mile range, the Conestogas flew at 150 miles per hour. (1945-1947)

the new air cargo industry when it virtually "put itself on the map." And the company's early operations was a gutsy "shoestring" affair using "word-to-mouth" strategies instead of advertising, employing borrowed equipment whenever needed, and never experiencing a secure paycheck. As testimony from one WWII pilot who flew under Gen. Chennault:

> "In 1945, Flying Tigers pilot Paul Kelly delivered a Budd Conestoga-load of cargo at Atlanta, George, had his uniform pressed and hit the streets, calling on anyone who might be likely source for a 'backhaul' load of freight to pay for getting the plane back home to California. Kelly's only guidelines were informal discussions with colleagues at the home office as to what industries were likely targets for the newly born airfreight business, and his ability to use the yellow pages and a telephone."[13]

And, in timely conveyance, the carrier was fortunate enough to contract with the Navy to fly 117 sailors cross country back home to New York in October of 1945.[14] Five Budds were piloted by Bob Prescott, Tom Haywood, Cliff Groh, Joe Rosbert, and Duke Hedman from the group of original AVG aviators. This event marked the carrier's first venture into passenger service.

The relatively low investment required for the purchase or lease of surplus military aircraft resulted in a substantial increase in air freight activity immediately after WWII. The entire fleet of surplus aircraft consisted of three main types: the military version of the DC-3, known as the C-47, the Curtiss Wright C-46, and the Douglas C-54. The type of aircraft employed became a highly competitive factor which encouraged National Skyway to seek a more suitable cargo aircraft than the "mechanical-plagued" Budds. From the onset, four Budds were sold off and one became mechanically inoperative in a Texas field enroute to California from its former home in Augusta, George, leaving the airline with an operating fleet of seven Budds. Thus, it has been the ensuing trend of the company to seek a more suitable and efficient fleet of cargo aircraft throughout its years.

Subsequently, the carrier either sold or discarded the Budds, including a sale of $198,000 for four Budds to Asiatic Petroleum Company. By June, 1946, the old fleet had been replaced in service by sixteen C-47s, two Convair Consolidated-Vultee single-engine aircraft, and by virtue of a CAB order allowing for veteran's privileges, they were soon able to buy a four-motored C-54, a reinforced military version of the larger and long-range DC-4.[15]

Flying Tigers relied heavily on the Douglas C-47, the cargo version of the famed DC-3. The C-47 could fly 7,500 pounds of cargo over a range of 600 miles at 150 miles per hour. (1946-1951)

The dimensional and operational statistics of the C-47 were virtually the same as those given for the Pre-War DC-3, originally produced in 1935 with production lasting for a decade. It had a payload of over 7,000 pounds. This particular type of plane became so commonly utilized that in 1945, 406 of the 457 aircraft operated by the scheduled airlines were of this type. Comparably, the C-54 had a payload of 19,000 pounds, and a cruise speed of 190 mph. Unfortunately, however, the small payload and limited range were basic weaknesses of all the early aircraft types. No serious effort to develop an all-cargo aircraft by manufacturers was made in the early years of air freight.

For an interim period in the spring of 1946, the carrier moved operations to a more spacious Mines Field (later becoming L.A. International Airport), occupying a hangar and office space previously used by North American Aviation Company. By fall of that year, the company had about 250 employees and small stations located in the Los Angeles and San Francisco areas, Chicago, St. Louis, Detroit, Cleveland, and the New York area.

To meet new commitments, on January 2, 1947, with the new fleet, the company moved again to an empty hangar with office space at Lockheed Air Terminal in Burbank, just north of Los Angeles. And by month's end, as might be expected, National Skyway Freight Corporation formally adopted the name of Flying Tiger Line. It was fitting recognition for the veteran wartime outfit which awarded the Air Transport Command (ATC) transPacific airlift contract on New Year's Day, 1947. In one stroke, it became the world's largest contract air carrier of passengers and cargo.[16]

The bid for the contract took place in the previous November when United Airlines gave up its primary ATC contract in order to concentrate on it expanding domestic passenger operations. The contract entailed twenty-eight weekly flights in support of the U.S. military forces in Hawaii, Japan and several Pacific islands, at a rate of 53 cents route mile. Half of these flights would be between Fairfield Army Base (now Travis AFB) near San Francisco, and Honolulu, Kwajalein Island, Guam and Tokyo; the other half would shuttle twice daily between Fairfield and Honolulu. ATC furnished thirty-two large Douglas C-54's, while Flying Tiger Line supplied the flight and maintenance crews, and administrative personnel. Beginning on January 1, 1947, the carrier made $500,000 profit in the first six months and was cushioned against the more severe blows of the Rate War during the immediate post-war period.[17] Established passenger lines led by American Airlines employed low-rate strategies in an attempt to neutralize newly emerging all-cargo carriers. And, very

Flying Tiger Line hangars at Burbank

importantly, the ATC contract was the start of Flying Tiger Line's long celebrated commitment to the U.S military airlift movement.

In a timely twist, it is interesting to note that during the early developmental period of the Fling Tiger Line, there is evidence to the effect that there existed a corroborative relationship among former AVG pilots who, in their new profession, flew for two commercial airlines based on opposite side of the Pacific. Claire L. Chennault, who had commanded the AVG group, became a civilian after the war, and co-founded the Civil Air Transport (CAT) in China. The mutually supportive role was suggested by the other co-founder as it read in a company bulletin:

> "By October, 1946, we had obtained an operating franchise. Our resources were dwindling fast and we knew that at least three months would have to lapse before we could have any planes. Money was needed to send pilots and crew chiefs to Honolulu and Manila to pick up the aircraft. We had figured that it would take about $250.000 of working capital to tide us over until CAT would support itself, and that was why the General (Chennault) and I and our Stateside associates had long before made a deal for financial support from the Flying Tiger Line. Louis Prescott was sent to China to survey the situation and to act as comptroller of the funds when furnished. When he was accidentally murdered (in a Manila hotel) there was no one available in the Flying Tiger organization to take his place and therefore the line backed out. I don't think either the General or I will ever forget the shock when we received the cable that the much needed financial support had been withdrawn."[18]

Fortunately, C.A.T was able to negotiate the necessary funds with Chinese bankers, and, shortly thereafter, received financial support from the United Nations and China Relief Funds. C.A.T made its inaugural cargo flight on January 31,1947, carrying relief supplies from Shanghai to Canton. In fact, the airline was originally called the Chinese National Relief and Rehabilitation Administration or CNRRA Air Transport, operating fifteen C-46s and four C-47s bought from war surplus in Hawaii and Manila. The pilots were mostly Americans with backgrounds from the AVG, 14th Air Force, the ATC, and Troop Carrier Squadrons.[19] Dick Rossi, Joe Rosbert and Catfish Raines also flew for C.A.T. for a period of time while associated with the Flying Tiger Line.

And, at the time when C.A.T. was making its inaugural cargo flight, Flying Tiger

FTL C-54 refueling on Wake Island enroute to Tokyo.

Line began its military commitment island-hopping across the Pacific. Industry-wise, while the multitude of air freight carriers struggled in the new and growing air cargo industry, the acquisition of the Pacific airlift proved to lucrative. The company received three times as much revenue from the military contracts as from common carriage freight during 1947 and 1948.[20]

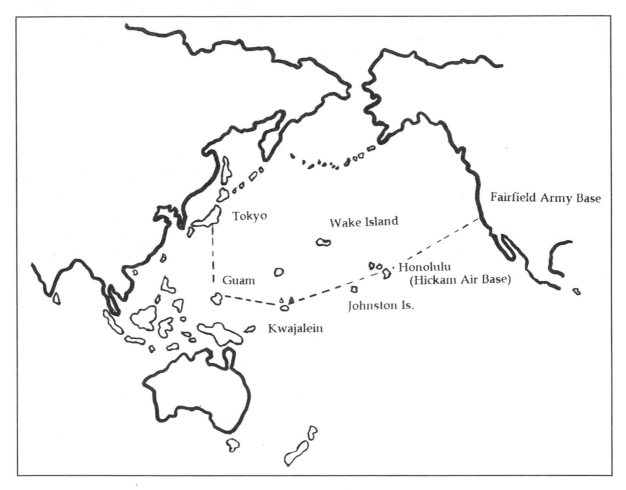

Routing of FTL's Pacific ATC airlift

Meanwhile, the right to engage in scheduled transportation of air freight for two of the largest operators in the field, Slick Airways and the Flying Tiger Line, was under study by the Civil Aeronautics Board from the time they began operations until July 29, 1949, when they were awarded temporary certification. Collectively, the upsurge of air cargo carriers after WWII had a significant impact detrimental to the combination carriers (both passenger and cargo). In fact, during the first two years after the war, statistics reveal that the air cargo carriers carried more tonnage than the established combination carriers, many which were re-organizing and utilizing limited space on their aircraft, if at all, for cargo.

Year	Combination Carriers	All-Cargo Carriers	Total Freight Ton-miles
1946	46,103	26,389	72,491
1947	38,871	45,300	84,171
1948	70,438	45,524	116,750
1949	96,347	50,804	147,050
1950	115,789	76,712	192,500
1951	103,928	95,112	199,040

Source: Civil Aeronautics Administration, **Statistical Handbook of Civil Aviation** (Washington:Government Printing Office, 1954) p. 85, and, CAB, **Air Freight Case, Docket 810, July 29, 1949** (Washington:Government Printing Office) p. 580.

Understanding the competition has always been a key factor in the underlying development of air cargo business. In October, 1944, American Airlines established the first commercial air scheduled service. And after the war, other major airlines went into the air freight business, but displayed little interest in actively promoting air cargo, except for United Airlines and TWA, who were also re-organizing their fleets. They began intensive efforts to generate traffic through solicitation, additional cargo flights, and using extra space on their scheduled aircraft to compete with the newly emerging all-freight carriers. The leader in this action was American Airlines, the carrier which had lost volume leadership to Slick Airways in the early Post-War Period.[21] Perhaps the most effective strategy instituted was the (tariff) rate war which, subsequently, as it ran its course through 1947, eliminated all but a handful of the independents. Large numbers of all-freight carriers went bankrupt in 1947 and 1948. Double trouble came in the form of high cost of aviation gas due to scarcity and post-war inflation.

In an unprecedented move, on May 5, 1947, the CAB promulgated a regulation which permitted most of the applicants to engage under certain conditions as scheduled air cargo carriers pending final decision on their respective applications. The nine applicants included California Eastern Airways which had an entire fleet of large C-54s, Flamingo Air Service, Globe Freight Airline, U.S. Airlines, Willis Air Service, Mutual Aviation, Air Cargo Transport Corp., Slick Airways and Flying Tiger Line. These carriers were required by the regulation to provide data and other information to the CAB for a detailed study which, coupled with the regular hearings, formed the basis for the Board's decision making in route and service allocations.

Under CAB ruling, Flying Tiger Line was one of the three air cargo carriers offered the opportunity to fly a scheduled trans-continental route temporarily. Tiger's authorized air traffic markets included Los Angeles (Burbank) and San Francisco in the California area; Seattle and Portland in the Northwest; Cleveland, Chicago, Detroit, Kansas City, St. Louis and Dayton in the North Central region; Dallas, Oklahoma City in the Southwest; and New York, Philadelphia, and Allentown in the Northeast. Also, due to extensive lobbying on the part of Flying Tiger Line and Slick Airways, and leading all-freight carriers, the nine applicants were allowed to fly "demand" points. Under the "demand" or "area" concept, the carriers were offered the right to provide air freight service to unspecified markets of opportunity. In other words, a carrier may adjust routing to serve cities not originally specified under the CAB authorization to help develop the air cargo market as well as enhancing the carrier's revenues.

In actuality, CAB records for the period of May 5, 1947 to September, 1948, revealed that neither Slick or Tigers operated any service of any consequence to other than a select few major population centers. For that period, Slick supplied over ninety percent of its service between ten large cities, operating only thirty-seven flights to "demand" points while Flying Tiger operated absolutely no "demand" service, and confined its entire service to eight cities - New York, Los Angeles (Burbank), San Francisco, Detroit, Cleveland, Chicago, Kansas City, and St. Louis.[22] Other than New York, no east coast point was served although operational facilities were available.

The reason for serving only select points already adequately served by other carriers was that strictly flying only domestic air cargo was an unprofitable business. Other sources of revenue were needed. In fact, this was a pattern which was to haunt Flying Tiger Line for years to come.

During the CAB study period, it was noted that all the freight carried by the three major non-certificated applicants who had supplied data had been carried at an average loss of 4.23 cents for each ton-mile. The three carriers included Slick, Tigers, and California Eastern, the latter which went bankrupt in May, 1948, after flying a regular scheduled transcontinental route using a straight DC-4 fleet. Slick lost about 3 cents on every ton-mile of traffic during the first 9 months of 1948, while Flying Tiger lost about 2.5 cents per ton-mile for the same period.[23]

An over-view of the competitive rate war is provided in a sampling of air freight carriers, both all-cargo and combinations, engaged in trans-continental service in September of 1948:

Carriers	Number of Shipments	Tons carried	Freight revenue	Revenue per ton mi.
American	26,484	2,625	$406,859	20.5¢
Northwest	4,363	330	65,127	20.2¢
United	16,991	1,696	331,105	17.3¢
TWA	11,061	918	188,756	19.9¢
Flying Tiger	2,464	548	161,212	15.3¢
Slick	6,196	1,158	316,185	16.3¢
Total	67,559	7,275	1,469,244	18.0¢

It was noted that after two years of operations since June, 1947, none of the nine all-cargo carriers operated at a profit in domestic service, only four were still in operation, while the others were in some form of bankruptcy or re-organization. An analysis revealed that the marginal success of Slick and Tigers may be attributed to their "creative entrepreneurship" which supplemented their domestic scheduled service with aircraft leasing, maintenance services, and commercial and military charters. In 1949, Slick owned twelve C-46 aircraft and had an additional ten C-46s leased from the Military Air Transport (MATS), which formed in 1948 merging the Army and Navy air forces.

Flying Tiger Line was awarded the short-term Pacific airlift in 1947, and, in October of that year, inaugurated its C-54 Sky Tiger service. The carrier was also indirectly engaged in commercial passenger charter through the means of leasing its aircraft to so-called "irregular" passenger carriers. During the CAB study period, Tigers operated six C-54s for its domestic route and operated a number of C-47s for supplemental or shuttle service, including leasing to other air carriers on short-term agreements. And, Flying Tigers, like Slick, profited by maintenance, servicing and aircraft modification work which explained their disproportionate representation of maintenance personnel in their work force:

        50 in flight operations
        31 in ground operations
     114 in maintenance
        31 in traffic and sales
        22 in executive and administrative positions

"Creative entrepreneurship" proved to be the successful survival strategy for that period among the independent air freight carriers as only four of the original applicants in the **Air Freight Case** were in condition to render the service envisioned by the CAB at the time that the decision of certification was given in July of 1949. As an added factor, on the human side, Joe Baker, formerly the President of the Flying Tiger Retirement Club, noted that the employees were "exceptionally skillful and dedicated" at their jobs, which, collectively, made Flying Tiger Line outstanding.

Meanwhile, as the rate war was taking its toll, the CAB conducted an investigation of air freight rates, sensing a need to protect the interest of the new air cargo industry. As a result, minimum rates for general commodities were established at 16 cents a ton-mile for the first 1,000 ton-miles in any one shipment, and 13 cents a ton-mile thereafter, not including low "back-haul" rates. Consequently, while both Slick and Flying Tiger continued to experience limited financial loss from common carriage activities, they both enjoyed corporate profits for the last half of 1948, owing mostly to their supplementary services.

It was reported that for the first 9 months of 1948, Slick grossed over $1,200,000 from its aircraft sales and service operations, equivalent to over 40 percent of its common carriage revenues. During the same period, Flying Tiger reported approximately $350,000 from supplementary revenues, most of which came from the leasing of its fully manned aircraft to so-called irregular passenger carriers. Total revenues from its common-carrier freight operations amounted to about $1,175,000 for that period. Thus, an analysis suggests that the diversified revenue base accounted for their gainful financial portfolio. Their respective balance sheet reflected their financial status on Sept. 30, 1948, according to the CAB study:

Item	Slick	Flying Tiger
Cash	$165,439	$182,544
Accounts receivable	703,045	365,720
Material & supplies	427,713	77,346
Operating property & equip	915,581	774,902
Total assets	2,497,112	1,408,456
Total liabilities	2,130,323	496,397
Net Worth	366,789	1,002,059

For the Flying Tiger Line, in fiscal year 1948-49, the company had the first profitable year of any major American-based carrier operating without a subsidy. And a decision was handed down in the **Air Freight Case** in July 29, 1949, temporarily certificating four all-cargo airlines for a five-year period. Those certificated were Slick Airways, United States Airlines, Airnews, and the Flying Tiger Line. Airnews commenced with operations for a period, and the United States Airlines later had its certification revoked. The balance of the non-certificated cargo carriers were left out. Thus, the large post-war group of short-term opportunists were largely out of operation due to rate-war competition and governmental action, leaving the most resourceful.

Bob Prescott, the visionary aviator, conveyed the promise of the future in writing James M. Landis, Chairman of the CAB during the hearings in 1947:

> "Perhaps some of us are overly optimistic. Certainly I will say to you that optimism and an almost blind faith in the future have been two requisites to us who have persisted in this business. But I visualize great fleets of cargo planes moving about our country in the not too distant future. Surely it is true that in every other form of transportation the volume of freight movement has far exceeded that of the passengers."[24]

Notes

1. Charles R. Bond, Jr., and Terry Anderson, **A Flying Tiger's Diary** (Texas A & M University Press) 1984, p. 214.

2. William M. Leary, Jr., **The Dragon's Wings** (Athens: The U. of Georgia Press) 1976, p. 172.

3. Ibid., pp. 157 & 172.

4. John H. Frederick, **Commercial Air Transportation**, 4th ed. (Homewood, Ill.: Richard D. Irwin) 1955, p. 432.

5. Civil Aeronautics Board, **Air Freight Case, Docket 810, July 29, 1949** (Wash., D.C.: Government Printing Office) p. 645.

6. Frank J. Cameron, **Hungry Tiger: The Story of the Flying Tiger Line** (New York: McGraw-Hill) 1962, p. 46, and letter to author from Dick Rossi, dated May 7, 1991.

7. Ibid., p. 47.

8. Ibid., p. 50.

9. **Tigereview**, October 1, 1980 issue, p. 2.

10. R.E.G. Davis, **Airlines of the United States Since 1914** (London: Putnam) 1972, p. 431.

11. Ibid., p. 432, and op. cit., **Hungry Tiger**, p. 45.

12. **Jane's All the World's Aircraft** (London: Sampson, Low and Marston Co.) 1945-46, pp. 215c-216c.

13. **Tigereview**, Vol.33, No. 1, January, 1979, p. 2.

14. Flight Attendants Diana Smith Nagatani and Sharon Schleis, "Flying Tigers Passenger Operation '45-'89," **Tiger Tracks**, Los Angeles, March, 1989, p. 5.

15. Op. cit., **Hungry Tiger**, p. 86.

16. Ibid., p. 82.

17. Ibid., pp. 91-93, and, op. cit., **Airlines of the United States Since 1914**, pp. 432-33.

18. Malcolm Rosholt, **Flight in the China Airspace**, 1910-1950 (Rosholt, Wis.: Rosholt House) 1983, p. 70, and, Robert Hotz., edit., **Way of a Fighter: The Memoirs of Claire Lee Chennault** (New York: G.P. Putnam's Sons) 1949, pp. 351-361.

19. Ibid., **Way of a Fighter: The Memoirs of Claire Lee Chennault**, p. 358.

20. Elbert Newell Dissmore, **A Trenchant Analysis of Post-War Developments in Air Freight Transportation** (Unpublished M.A. Thesis, Business Administration, U. of Washington) 1955, p. 72.

21. Ibid., p. 52.

22. Op. cit., **Air Freight Case**, p. 576.

23. Ibid., pp. 624, 628 and 645.

24. Ibid.

2

Flying Tiger Line Earns Its Wings: Route 100

The July 29, 1949, CAB certification, in effect, delineated geographic areas and service points for the operations of four selected all-freight air carriers. It may be surmised that the rationale for the selective routes strategy was established to broaden the geographic coverage of air cargo services to complement defined economic regions conducive toward developing air freight traffic. As such, Air News was assigned to operate largely in the Texas area. U.S. Airlines was given a certificate to operate North-South routes east of the Mississippi. Slick Airways was given a southerly transcontinental route from California extending to the Eastern terminals through points in the south and mid-west, and duplicating half of the Flying Tiger service points. And Flying Tiger Line was awarded transcontinental Route 100 from the Pacific Coast to the North Atlantic Seaboard, extending on a northerly arc through the mid-west area. **Flying Tiger Line had earned its wings!**

THE BIG DAY · · · WE GET OUR CERTIFICATE · SCHEDULED SERVICE STARTS · '49

Slick Airways was a friendly co-leading competitor with Flying Tigers throughout the five-year certificated period, sharing considerable amount of similar routing patterns and cargo aircraft types. U.S. Airlines operated regularly in 1949 and 1950, then suspended operations in July, 1951. It operated only intermittently thereafter, finally ceasing operations entirely in 1953. U.S. Airlines became somewhat competitive with Riddle, an all-cargo carrier which emerged in 1951. After being certificated for an overseas all-cargo operation between New York and San Juan Island via Miami, Riddle began to use its authority under a letter of registration and entered the New York domestic airfreight market, eventually shifting its geographic coverage to include much of the U.S. Airlines network.

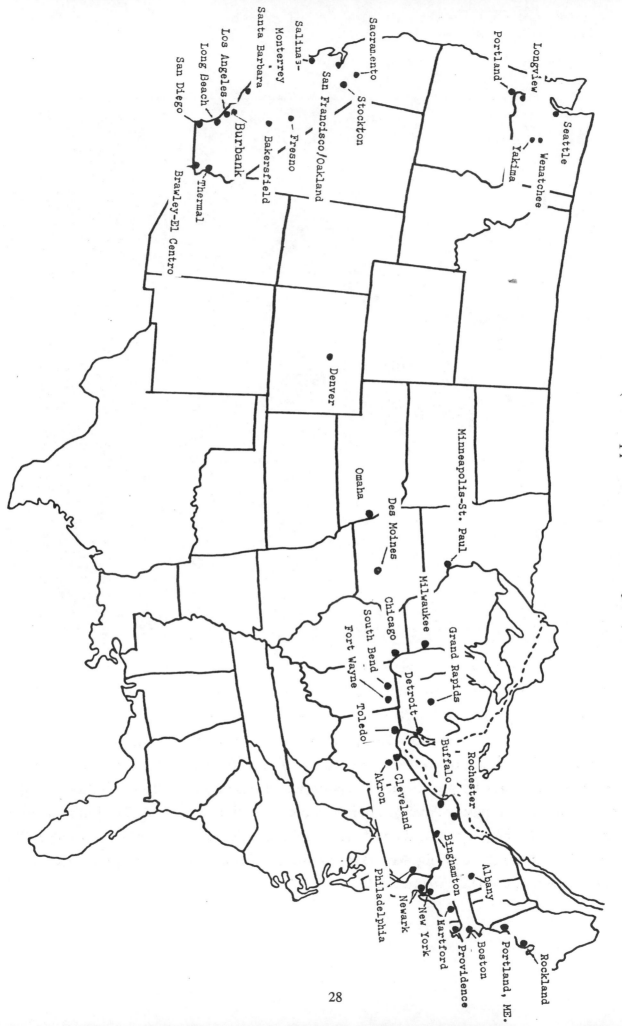

FLYING TIGER LINE'S AUTHORIZED AIR SERVICE POINTS
(CAB approved commencing July 29, 1949)

28

Flying Tiger Line, itself, was given a temporary five-year period to operate as a scheduled air cargo carrier to serve the California areas of Los Angeles (through Burbank), Bakersfield, Brawley-El Centro, Fresno, Long Beach, Oakland, Sacramento, Salinas-Monterey, San Diego, San Francisco, Santa Barbara, Stockton, and Thermal; the northwest areas of Longview, Portland, Seattle, Wenatchee, and Yakima; the central points of Minneapolis-St. Paul, Denver, Des Moines, Omaha, Akron, Chicago, Cleveland, Detroit, Fort Wayne, Grand Rapids, Milwaukee, South Bend, and Toledo; and the northeast points of Albany, Binghamton, Boston, Buffalo, Hartford, New York, Newark, Philadelphia, Providence, Rochester, Rockland, and Portland, Maine.[1]

At the inception of its certificated operations, Tigers served San Francisco, Burbank (Los Angeles area), San Diego, Chicago, Cleveland, Detroit, South Bend, Rochester, and Newark, serving the New York area. In 1950, Tigers expanded its services to Oakland, Denver, Milwaukee, Toledo, Akron/Canton, Buffalo, Philadelphia, Hartford, Providence, and Boston. In August, 1950, it had schedules operating from New York to Los Angeles via Philadelphia, Rochester, Buffalo, Akron/Canton, Cleveland, Detroit, Chicago, and Burbank. Tigers also had schedules operating between Newark (New York area) and Boston via Hartford, and it operated schedules from San Diego to Burbank. In 1951, Binghamton and Oakland were added. In 1952, Rochester, Providence, South Bend, Grand Rapids, Portland, Seattle, and Albany were added. But in that same year, service to Denver was terminated due to operational problems and the schedules were routed through Salt Lake City and North Platte. Bob Beckman, Sr., former FTL General Manager of Portland, and 37-year veteran, noted that the Seattle-Denver route, employing C-46 aircraft, was not profitable at the time. The carrier began using Salt Lake City as a stop for crew changes, refueling and transloading at that time, and North Platte as a fuel stop point. In 1953, Sacramento was added, but discontinued service shortly thereafter. In 1954, Tigers began service to Minneapolis-St. Paul through a mid-west routing.[2]

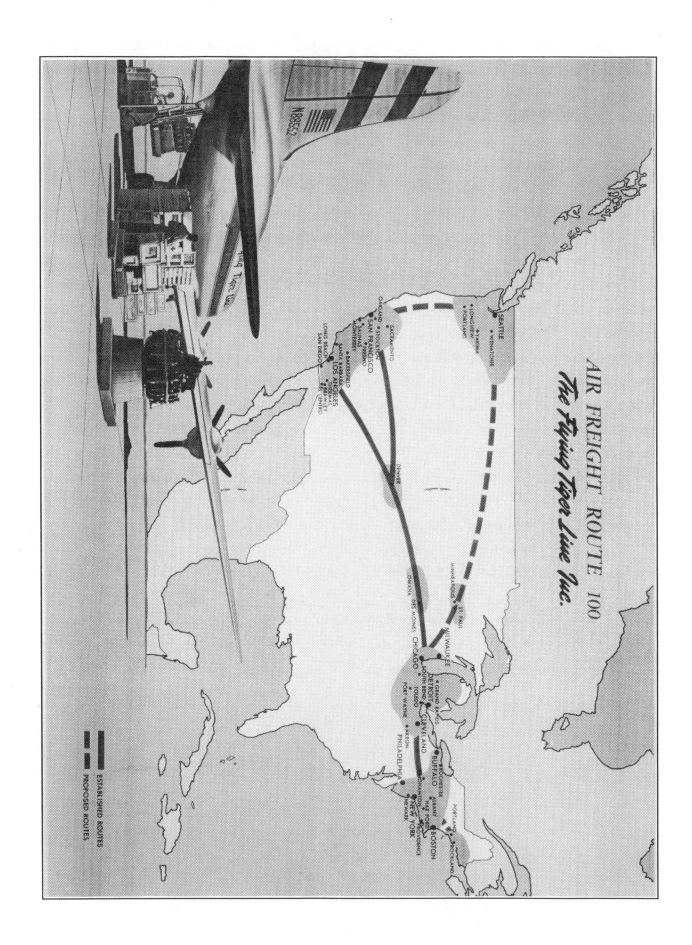

AIR FREIGHT ROUTE 100
The Flying Tiger Line Inc.

ESTABLISHED ROUTES
PROPOSED ROUTES

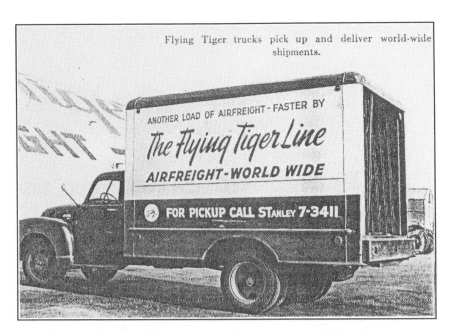

Vehicle of FTL's extended truck network

Flying Tiger Line served seventeen points in 1950 and increased its service each year to where, in 1953 and 1954, it was serving twenty-three cities, of which seven were served through the nearest airport by means of truck, under a truck hub system.

In a similar pattern, Slick served twenty-two cities directly and served eight through their truck hub system. Slick was authorized to serve certain points in the southwest. To differentiate, Tigers served Portland, Oregon and Seattle during the period 1952 through 1954 without any all-cargo competition, and it served Binghamton, Albany, Rochester, and Grand Rapids during all or part of the period 1951 through 1954. But other than these points, Slick and Tigers competed with the passenger combo-carriers or between themselves at all points served by all-cargo service, numbering forty-three in 1954.

Slick had its greatest geographical coverage in its certificated existence in 1952, employing C-46s since it began service, and DC-6A aircraft, which it acquired in June, 1951, to serve the major transcontinental markets. In similar fashion, throughout the five-year certificated period, Tigers used the Curtis Wright C-46s to handle the bulk of its common-carriage services. The C-54s were flown sparingly in scheduled services in 1950 and 1951, then not flown in scheduled services throughout 1952 and 1953. However, the Company maintained an average of seven C-54 aircraft on the Pacific airlift for the period.

In a continual move to upgrade to more efficient air cargo aircraft, Prescott became interested in acquiring a fleet of C46s at some time late in 1949. Subsequently, the C-46s became Tiger's "workhorse" for the ensuing decade. Nicknamed the **Commando**, the C-46, along with the C-47, were the common cargo planes used in the "Hump airlift" during WWII, and very familiar to Flying Tiger/CNAC veterans. The cargo capacity of the C-46 was twice that of the C-47, and in 1949, Tigers replaced the C-47s with the Commandos.

While some questioned Prescott's strategy, his decision proved to hold considerable insight backed with an ounce of good fortune. After WWII, the Commandos became something of aviation's stepchild, used chiefly for freight. In January, 1947, the War Assets Administration still had about 625 of them available, with few bidders, at a time when the less economical DC-3 (C-47) was commanding a market price of about $10,000. The DC-3s were more popular with the passenger and combo airlines. The Flying Tiger Line held high interest in eighteen surplus Commandos moth-balled at Pyote, Texas, at some point late in 1949. None had more han ten operational hours being moth-balled and cannibalized. Yet Tigers outbid Slick and American Airlines considerably at $509,000 to acquire the entire lot.[3]

By July 9, 1950, the last of the Commandos had been overhauled and re-conditioned in Burbank. Each plane had been stripped of some 4,000 pounds of excess military gear, only one of the ways its payload was increased. All this, including the installation of new radios, jumped the cost of each Commando from $28,000, which was Curtiss-Wright's market estimate, to $55,000. There was motivation to quickly complete the overhauls. The last of the eighteen Commandos was eventually ready for service by summer of 1951, being deployed in domestic operations and auxiliary flights from the United States to Alaska, Canada, Mexico and Puerto Rico.

Meanwhile, on June 25, 1950, the Korean conflict began. Within twenty-four hours after the Military Air Transport Service had requisitioned commercial aircraft, Tigers beat all competition and placed the first civilian plane in MATS service from the west coast to Hawaii and Japan.[4] Tiger's seven planes were made available to MATS by mid-August accounting for ten per cent of the commercial lines' contribution to the Tokyo airlift portion of the Korean logistical line. The mission involved eighteen commercial carriers, including Chennault's C.A.T. Many established passenger combo's with cargo aircraft also committed primarily four-engined C-54s. For instance, Eastern Airlines operated several C-54s from 1947 to 1950, but suspended its all-cargo service because of the Korean airlift, while Capital diverted its four C-54s and Northwest Airlines had to cancel its cargo services in February, 1951, for the duration

The Curtiss C-46 "Commando" that Flying Tigers flew on supply missions over the Hump during WW II came home for civilian duty, joining Tigers' fleet in 1949. It flew at 200 mph, carried 13,000 pounds of cargo and had a range of 900 miles. (1949-1961)

The C-54, first of the four-engine airfreighters, was used by FTL in the largest, longest airlift ever flown by a private contractor - supplying the American Occupation Forces in Japan. It flew 200 mph, carried 20,000 pounds with a 2,000 mile range. (1947-1957)

34

of the Korean conflict which ended in summer, 1953.[5] The airlift to Tokyo followed two primary routes; one from McChord Air Force Base near Tacoma, Washington, from which planes flew the shorter Great Circle route, following the arc of the Aleutian Islands to Tokyo, and, the more important one, from Fairfield-Suisan AFB to Tokyo by island-hopping the central Pacific via Hawaii and some of the island air bases developed during WWII. One third of the Tiger flights accommodated passengers, while two-thirds hauled freight.

FTL's C-54 aircraft, first acquired in late 1947, were deployed primarily in overseas operations. Don Downie, a FTL pilot during the Pacific airlift to Tokyo, discussed his experiences:

> "Long overwater flights at night during that period were still regarded with a certain amount of trepidation, particularly over the vast expanse of the Pacific, where landmarks were nonexistent and friendly airports few. It took a reliable aircraft like the C-54 to make intercontinental overwater flight in variable weather, at night, a near non event. The C-54 had a maximum 20,000 lb. payload, and the fast turn around and short on-the-ground time made the C-54 so efficient on those Pacific airlifts. At Haneda Airport in Tokyo, it was impossible to park even a percentage of the additional aircraft that came in and out during the Korean war. Things got so bad that one runway was closed down and used for temporary parking.
>
> Crews flying in and out often spent 230 hours in the air during a single month, although the pilots were only allowed to fly 120 hours during the same time period. To get enough pilots for the long transPacific trip, Flying Tigers had their crews make a full round trip, San Francisco-Tokyo and return, a total of 74 hours, and then fill out the remainder of their 120 monthly hours flying freight between Burbank and Denver or, Chicago and Newark."[6]

The program in which the commercial airlines were committed to the military air transportation system was initiated during the Korean crisis and was known as the Civil Reserve Air Fleet (CRAF) program. The government program embraced the concept that volunteer commercial aircraft, meeting specific guidelines, may be deployed to augment the U.S. military fleet should the need arise, such as national emergencies and war time. Those commercial carriers subscribing to such a commitment, depending on type and number of aircraft with support factors, were eligible to bid for certain military contract work. Since that time, Flying Tigers has committed all its aircraft to CRAF, and being eligible for military contracts, at that time, was assigned to primarily MATS' Pacific Division (others being the Atlantic or Continental Division.) As such, Tigers was committed to a basic annual contract with MATS to provide air transportation services for personnel and cargo from the west coast of the U.S. to various military bases throughout the Pacific area. The basic contract was subject to expansion by MATS as the need arose on a day-to-day basis, thus the monetary rewards made the contracts lucrative for Tigers.[7]

Korean veterans homeward bound leave
Tokyo for a speedy flight stateside.

In fact, from 1951 to 1953, the company received 48.1%, 42.5%, and 48% of its revenue, respectively, from the Pacific airlift, alone. In fiscal year, June 30, 1952 to June 30, 1953, the airline reported operating revenues of over $9.2 million from the Pacific airlift. With the increased activity, the total FTL roster increased from 528 employees in January, 1951, to 1337 by year's end, and 1650 by June, 1952, including over 1300 covered by unions.

Tiger stewardesses help on the long trips across the Pacific.

       The contract was renewed July 2, 1952, involving about fifty round trips monthly for MATS flying over the transPacific route between Travis AB and Tokyo. The following fiscal year, operating revenues increased to over $12.3 million for the Pacific airlift, and subsequently dropped to almost $4.7 million for fiscal year 1954. In glaring reality, the limited contribution of domestic common-carriage revenues compared to the other more profitable income accounts for the airline, became even more apparent during the Korean crisis airlift period:

Year	Common Carriage	Pacific Airlift	Rentals, Charters & Sale
1951	$3,578,863	$7,492,469	$4,510,727
1952	4,532,742	9,278,571	8,026,183
1953	6,037,356	12,358,940	7,339,401
1954	4,557,660	4,689,452	9,395,807
1955	5,104,790	1,043,996	9,214,504
1956	7,833,598	--------	14,097,722
1957	8,448,604	--------	16,202,542

Source: Statistics compiled from Moody's Transportation Manual, 1958

In analyzing continuous studies of the Flying Tiger Line since it began, the CAB noted in 1956 that "the history of Tigers' operations demonstrates that its common carrier scheduled services received only about one-fourth of its corporate attention and efforts and that its main force has been diverted to more profitable military contract operations, maintenance work, and other miscellaneous undertakings. In short, **the tail has been wagging the Tiger!**"[8]

Sources of revenue

	% from freight	% from charter sales, rental	% from Pacific
1949	58.6	41.3	—
1950	43.7	56.3	—
1951	22.9	28.9	48.1
1952	20.7	36.7	42.5
1953	23.4	28.5	48.0
1954	24.5	50.4	25.2
1955	33.2	60.0	6.8
1956	35.6	64.4	—

In another military defense contract the Air Material Command, Flying Tiger Line received an air freight contract worth more than $2 million, flying engines and other aviation equipment between Kelly Field, near San Antonio, Texas, and three bases in the midwest and on the Pacific coast. The six month contract, which started July 1, 1952, specified a maximum of 78,000 miles of flying per month for the duration.

During this period, the airline also negotiated a contract with the U.S. Navy involving two daily transcontinental freight flights between New York and Oakland, California. The domestic Navy freight charter added approximately $200,000 to $300,000 a month to their domestic traffic revenues for charters. And, having developed a good reputation for overhauling and maintaining Commandos, in July 9, 1953, the company announced the receipt of a U.S. Air Force $2½ million contract for maintenance work on about one hundred Commandos. The contract lasted for over a year.[9]

With a fleet of thirty-five aircraft, Flying Tiger Line also developed eight separate charter operations at the same time, in addition to the regular transcontinental air-freight service and the Korean airlift. These included transporting summer students to Europe; displaced Europeans to Australia and America; farm laborers from Puerto Rico to the U.S.; illegal Mexican entrants in the U.S. back to Mexico; U.S. Air Force

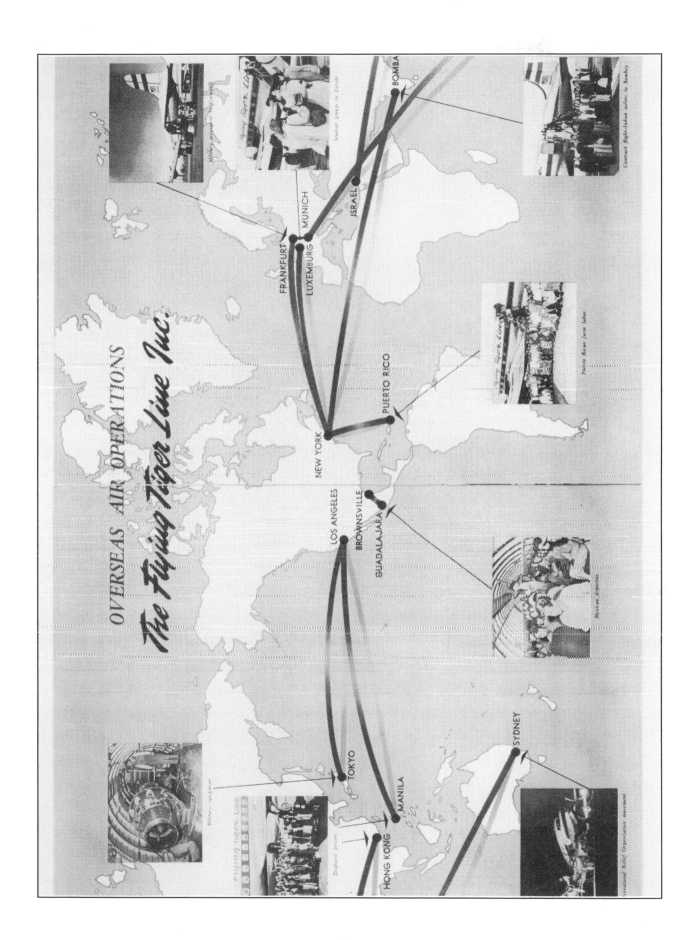

OVERSEAS AIR OPERATIONS

The Flying Tiger Line Inc.

trainees to various training bases; airplane maintenance and overhaul in the company's own Burbank shops for independent air-coach operators and industrial concerns.[10]

To enumerate some of their charter activities, in the summer of 1951, Tigers began airlifting Mexicans as seasonal laborers (farm hands and pickers) when the demand for harvest labor was needed in California and the Southwest during the Korean crisis. Brownsville, Texas, became the Tigers' Eastern base for the migrant airlift, while El Centro, California, served as the Western base. Meanwhile, during the same period, in another geographic area, Tigers was also participating in another labor airlift entailing 153 flights. The company flew 11,000 Puerto Ricans north to work on the farms of New Jersey, Pennsylvania and other Eastern states.

In the European front, on Christmas Day, 1951, two Tiger Commandos arrived in West Germany for what was scheduled as a three-month **Baby Berlin Airlift**. West German government contracted Pan American, who sub-contracted part of its share to Tigers, to quickly airlift the stockpile of goods from Berlin to intra-national points for protection and distribution in view of the threat of the Soviet occupation of eastern Germany with Berlin situated in the central zone. With FTL's C-54s committed to the Korean airlift, the carrier deployed two Commandos, which was not commonly used for the long distance flying across the north Atlantic route. The mission entailed six daily flight involving twelve hours a day, an extraordinary feat at the time.

In 1955, the U.S. Air Force contracted with commercial lines to set up an aerial pipeline of engines from such points as Wright-Patterson Air Field at Dayton, Ohio, to bases in England, France and Morocco. With Flying Tiger Line's experience in the past moving engines for Boeing's Aircraft Company of Seattle, it was a suitable and profitable venture. In addition, by April of that year, twenty Tiger planes were on contract work in Asia, Europe and the Caribbean, while eight more Tiger planes were flying domestic troop movements for the Army in a program known as the **Civilian Army Movement System** (CAMS).[11]

Flying Tiger Line also engaged in interline (joint airline) agreements with most of the major carriers, both domestic and international, and had approximately two hundred agency representatives in various geographic areas as booking and sales agents. Agents and temporary facilities were provided at London and Frankfurt to accommodate Tiger charters. The company offered contract passenger business, aircraft leasing, and provided full maintenance and overhaul services for many other carriers.

However, the leverage for profitability found in contract, charter, leasing and maintenance work was not noticeable in Tigers' competitive scheduled common-carriage operation. In large part, as will explained, there were problems of limitation inherent in the usage of the costly and inefficient military surplus aircraft employed for air freight. Despite this assumption, Flying Tiger Line clearly became one of the leaders in the air cargo industry as time progressed.

While the total airfreight movement among the all-cargo carriers revealed a certain parity among six or more companies prior to 1949, beginning with 1950, only three airlines shared significantly in this market. Slick and Tigers divided the east-west business, and U.S. Airlines was the sole north-south airfreight carrier until Riddle entered the picture in 1951. Slick and Tigers statistically dominated the common carriage market for all-freight carriers:

Year	Slick	Tigers	Other all-freight carriers	Total American, TWA & United
1950	37,796	21,435	5,027	77,140
1951	47,580	29,173	6,385	72,676
1952	48,580	37,868	4,966	87,217
1953	43,589	37,741	4,664	98,873
1954	34,883	27,467	4,407	108,877

* all above (000) ton miles

As early as 1951, Tigers began using the Commandos to offer a regional overnight air freight service from Newark (NY area) and Chicago terminals. The westbound flight from New York gave next-morning delivery to Detroit, Chicago, Milwaukee and other mid-western cities. The eastbound flight from Chicago did the same for the Newark (NY area) and New England destinations. Both these overnight flights were in addition to the Tigers' six daily transcontinental flights serving twenty-four cities. Between the coasts, the planes followed a flexible flight pattern by which the Tigers utilized "plane efficiency" rather than a strict schedule. This meant that for its way-stops (demand points) the aircraft landed only at those cities along Route 100 that happened to be offering the most revenue freight that particular day. This tactic developed the biggest available daily payload.[12] By 1954, FTL's scheduled domestic operations included ten to twelve daily flights between L.A., San Francisco, Seattle, and Newark (NY area) and the northeast, and involved twenty-five intermediate points.

Despite low rates, Tigers managed to achieve net incomes from its common-carriage services in 1951 and 1952, reportedly being $658,000 and $326,000 for those respective years. As an influencing factor, competing passenger/cargo combo's operating cargo aircraft at the outset of the Korean airlift suffered severe decline in their common-carriage business as their cargo aircraft became committed to the airlift. In effect, those affected either severely cutback or suspended their all-cargo flights for the duration, and confined the cargo loads to pre-dominantly passenger aircraft belly compartments only. During that period in which Tigers committed part of their fleet to the airlift, the company experienced increased domestic traffic and high load factors on their aircraft.

Year	Domestic ton miles	Dom. rev. yield ton mile	Load factor (% domestic)
1951	28,137,979	14.82¢	83.4
1952	31,788,962	15.81¢	80.7
1953	51,324,134	16.75¢	79.0
1954	45,152,383	18.11¢	76.3

Source: Moody's Transportation Manual, 1957

Towards Consideration of a FTL-Slick Merger

In retrospect, until the end of the hostilities in Korea, FTL and Slick were fully occupied with their common-carriage business, maintenance and charter business, and the military contracts they secured. At the end of this period, however, they faced an appreciable decrease in revenues. The MATS contract with FTL, for a portion of the Pacific airlift, was canceled October 31, 1953, with the implications noted:

> "Shorn of most of their military revenues and restricted against the carriage of mail and express, and further confronted with sharply increased costs, it has become apparent by looking at the balance sheets of the Flying Tiger Line and Slick Airways that they have not been making money from freight traffic for over a year."[13]

Another perspective needed to be explored being that Flying Tigers and their friendly competitor, Slick Airways, duplicated their services in many areas of the country, except for the Northwest and the Southeast. They shared the heavier traffic lanes from points such as Newark and New York, Burbank, Detroit, Philadelphia, Chicago and Boston, and both companies used C-54's and Commandos. Slick acquired a DC-6A transcontinental freighter in 1951, when Tigers placed theirs on order for 1953 delivery.

In the early part of 1953, the management of Slick and Tigers agreed upon a plan to merge the two airlines; and on March 26,1953, they filed with the CAB a joint application for approval. The terms of the merger provided that Slick would be merge into Tigers and that Slick, as an entity, would cease and become part of Tigers. The purpose of the merger was to strengthen the financial condition of the surviving corporation and give it the benefits to be derived from consolidation of separate facilities operated by both companies at many locations. A significant factor in the proposed merger was the reduction in operating costs possible for the surviving corporation through consolidation of their facilities. This plan would have made it possible to reduce the total amount of personnel required by nearly 40 per cent. This was due to the fact, as forementioned, that the operations of the two companies were contiguous in many places.

On January 7, 1954, the CAB issued its order No. E-8022 approving the merger and making the surviving company, the Flying Tiger Line, subject to certain labor protective provisions. These provisions called for integration of seniority lists and made the surviving company liable for any adverse effect on employees as a result of the merger for a period of three years from its effective date, including providing 60% of each person's current pay once he or she were laid off because of the merger. Remaining employees would absorb some of that cost through lower wages and other benefit adjustments. And because of sagging revenues, about nine hundred employees were projected to be laid-off by mid-summer 1954, increasing the severance pay liability.

The actual merging of the two companies began about the first of February, 1954, and the planes of each carrier were integrated into a single fleet for transcontinental operations. This integration involved moving of employees of each company from one place to another in order to carry out an exchange of freight between the two companies. For example, the accounting section of Slick's general office was moved into Tigers' general office, and Tigers' control moved over into the Slick offices due to the fact that the latter had more space. At the time of the merger the two companies had three DC-6As operating in transcontinental service-two by Slick and one by Tigers. The records within the merged companies were kept on an interline basis under interline agreement since every effort was being made to correctly account for the expenses of the merger.[14]

One of the problems concomitant with the merger was the matter of termination compensation of dismissed employees. Both Slick and Tigers were reluctant to terminate employees because of potential liability under the protective provision of the

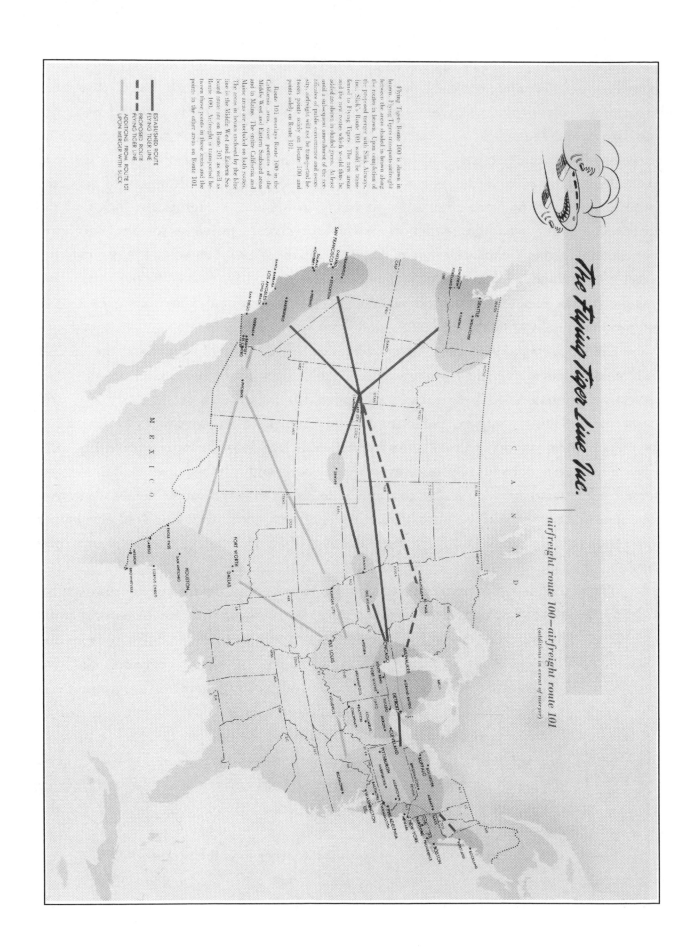

The Flying Tiger Line Inc.

airfreight route 100—airfreight route 101

(additions in event of merger)

Flying Tiger Route 100 is shown in brown. Flying Tigers transports airfreight between the areas shaded in brown along the routes in brown. Upon completion of the proposed merger with Sick Airways, Inc., Sick's Route 101 would be transferred to Flying Tigers. The new areas and the new routes which would thus be added are shown in shaded green. At least certificates of public convenience and necessity, airfreight will not be transported between points solely on Route 100 and points solely on Route 101.

Route 101 overlaps Route 100 in the California areas, over portions of the Middle West and Eastern Seaboard areas and in Maine. The entire California and Maine areas are included on both routes. The areas in brown enclosed by the line are the Middle West and Eastern Sea-board areas are on Route 101 as well as Route 100. Airfreight is transported between these points in these areas and the points in the other areas on Route 101.

ESTABLISHED ROUTE
FLYING TIGER LINE

PROPOSED ROUTE
FLYING TIGER LINE

ADDITIONS FROM ROUTE 101
UPON MERGER WITH SICK

44

merger established by the Board. They could not determine the number of employees, particularly pilots, who should be dismissed, and of other employees, who should be dismissed, and Slick soon found that it was badly overstaffed with pilots. The retention of these pilots drove its costs for the C-46 aircraft inordinately high since, in some months, pilot costs were over 20 cents a mile and the average for the year was approximately 19 cents as contrasted with about 14 cents before the merger. There was a surplus of accountants in the company, and Slick's internal auditor was auditing the books of Tigers and making special studies of Tiger' accounts. As Slick employees were aware of the fact that the surviving company would be Tigers and as the salesmen's calling cards were printed in the name of Tigers, they did not push the sale of freight in the name of Slick.

In August, 1954, because of management's belief that a potential liability of an estimated $3 or $4 million existed as a result of the employee protective provisions, Slick and Tigers requested the Board to modify the labor protective provisions. Due to the uncertain profitability of air freight at that time, the management of both carriers decided the risk was too great. But on September 20, the Board denied this request, and the merger collapsed.

Bob Prescott, President of Flying Tiger Line expressed the situation as follows in the company's 1954 Annual Report:

> "Undoubtedly many will still be puzzled as to why the merger agreed to by the parties in March, 1953, could not be consummated promptly and must be found in the prolonged hearings before the Civil Aeronautics Board and the extended, fruitless, negotiations with the unions."

Subsequently, when the merger plans of the Flying Tiger Line and Slick Airways failed, the management of FTL was of the opinion that labor conditions were too unfavorable for that company to remain in the air freight business. In June 1, 1954, the company reported to have 2500 employees, and not enough projected business activities to justify that size a labor force. As a result, it sought permission from the CAB to enter the equipment leasing field and to sell its air freight rights to Slick Airways. However, when the employees heard of this plan, the majority agreed to reductions in pay to help the company stay in the air freight business.

Facilities at Burbank were to be integrated upon merger with Slick Airways, Inc.
The Tiger office was located just outside the airport directly above the FTL hangar.

The two companies finally separated in November, 1954, and one time after November, Slick's management decided to liquidate, but the Slick employees offered to take pay cuts, thus reassuring management of their faith in the company's future. However, Slick had started their steady decline which would eventually drive them out of the domestic common-carriage business in 1958.

During the summer of 1955, Tigers' machinists and maintenance personnel went on strike for 114 days. Although the company lost some revenue through the strike period, it recovered from the effects of the dissolved merger as well as the strike by year's end, and showed a profit.

And, as expected, on March 12, 1956, the CAB renewed Flying Tiger's U.S. Route 100 certificate on a temporary basis for another five years, effective May 11 of that year. The company indicated that they would have preferred a permanent certificate, or at

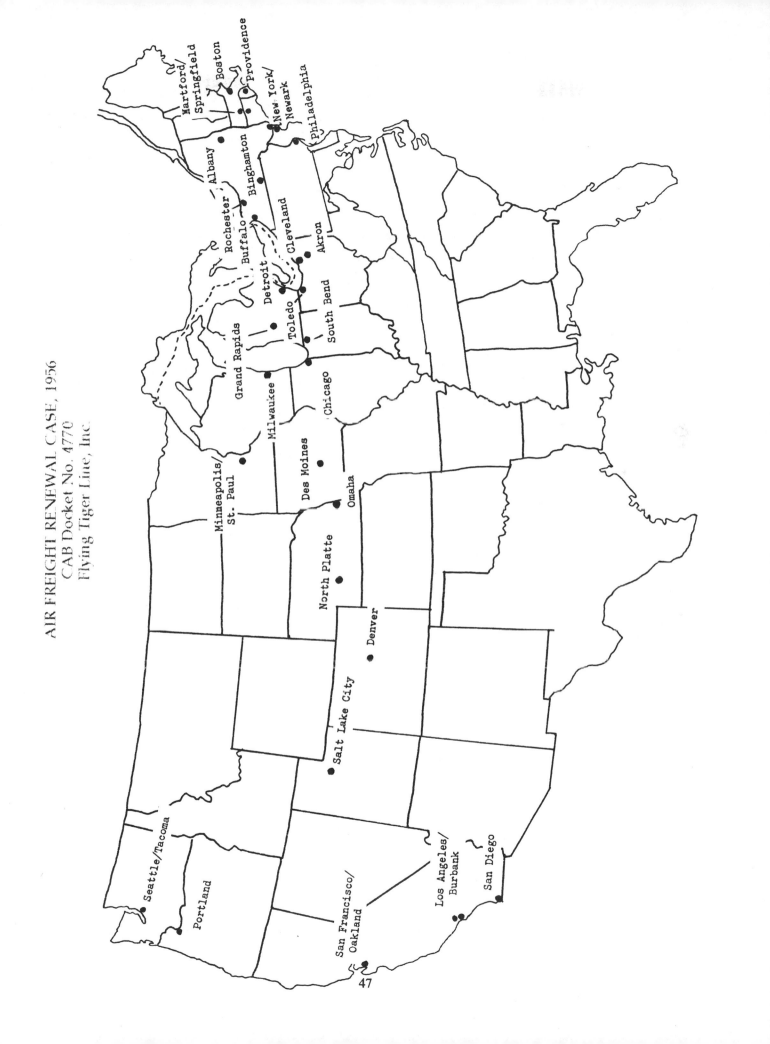

AIR FREIGHT RENEWAL CASE, 1956
CAB Docket No. 4770
Flying Tiger Line, Inc.

Hartford/Springfield

Boston

Providence

New York/Newark

Philadelphia

Albany

Binghamton

Rochester

Buffalo

Cleveland

Akron

Detroit

South Bend

Toledo

Grand Rapids

Milwaukee

Chicago

Minneapolis/St. Paul

Des Moines

Omaha

North Platte

Denver

Salt Lake City

Seattle/Tacoma

Portland

San Francisco/Oakland

Los Angeles/Burbank

San Diego

47

least, a 10-year grant, arguing that freight carriers should be given the same opportunity to obtain the more favorable 10-year term financing for equipment, namely aircraft, that was available to other carriers. Continuing authorization on an inter-area basis, Tigers experienced a decrease in specific service points from forty-three in the 1949 authorization to twenty-five. The carrier was also permitted to serve Salt Lake City, Denver, Omaha, and Des Moines on a demand basis, and to serve Providence, Albany, Rochester, Akron, Toledo, South Bend, Grand Rapids, and San Diego under a truck hub system to the nearest regularly served Tiger station, making economically possible all-cargo service points having a limited freight-generating potential.

Slick Airways was also given a five-year renewal of temporary Route 101 on the inter-area basis, and permitted to serve Phoenix, Wichita, Kansas City, Oklahoma City, Pocatello, and Nashville on a demand basis, and six other points on a truck hub system.

In an unprecedented move, the CAB also decided to permit FTL, Slick, Riddle, and another emerging cargo line, the American Air Export and Import Co. (AAXICO) to carry nonpriority first-class mail and post cards as air mail, on a nonsubsidized basis for a one-year period, at rates comparable to air freight charges. AAXICO, like Riddle, operated primarily east of the Mississippi with a north-south orientation in routing. Flying mail was a privilege that the combination carriers had been enjoying on an experimental basis for a couple of years, as a result of a proposal made in the 1947 **Air Freight Case** by the all-cargo carriers. With recent approval, Flying Tiger Line carried their first consignment of mail by air on May 28, 1956.

At the time of re-certification, the all-cargo airlines were also given authority to transport air express offered by the Railway Express Agency (REA), previously the exclusive right of the combination carriers. Consequently, Tigers was able to develop a stronger revenue base to complement common-carriage, though not as lucrative as the high-rate air mail subsidies afforded combination carriers.

The oscillations of the Flying Tiger Line was tempered by the echoes in Bob Prescott's often quoted remark:

> **"We're unique, so let's not imitate. Imitation let's you catch up to the guy ahead, but never lets you pass."**

Notes

1. Civil Aeronautics Board, **Air Freight Case, Docket 810, July 29, 1949** (Wash., D.C.: Government Printing Office) p. 572.

2. CAB, **Air Freight Certificate Renewal Case, Docket 4770 and 5016, March 12, 1956** (Wash., D.C.: Govt. Printing Office) pp. 234-35.

3. Frank J. Cameron, **Hungry Tiger: The Story of the Flying Tiger Line** (New York: McGraw-Hill) 1962, pp. 122-23.

4. Ibid., pp. 123 & 125.

5. Op. cit., **Air Freight Case, Docket 810, July 29, 1949**, pp. 223-225, and Frank J. Cameron, p. 125.

6. Don Downie, "Long Ranger," **Wings**, April, 1990, Vol. 20, No. 2, pp. 11, 50-54., and FTL Annual Report, 1951, p. 6.

7. Stanley M. Ulanoff, **MATS: The Story of the Military Air Transport Service** (Franklin Watts, Inc.: New York) 1964, p. 57, and Moody's Investors Service, **Moody's Transportation Manual**, New York, 1966.

8. Op. cit., **Air Freight Certificate Renewal Case, Docket 4770 and 5016, March 12, 1956**, p. 244.

9. Moody's Investors Service, **Moody's Transportation Manual**, New York, Aug. 30, 1952, pp. 1085, 1135, 1158, 1172 and 1958.

10. Op. cit., Frank J. Cameron, pp. 133-141.

11. Ibid., p. 183.

12. Ibid., p. 137.

13. T.W. Holmgren, "The Case For the All-Freight Airlines," **Pacific Air and Truck Traffic**, Vol. X (Feb., 1954) p. 5.

14. Op. cit., **Air Freight Certificate Renewal Case, Docket 4770 and 5016, March 12, 1956**, p. 238.

3

Enter the Super-Connie

The precarious financial posture of Flying Tiger Line in the first decade of operation was characteristic of all the all-freight carriers. Competition resulted in low rates and consequently, compounded by the use of inefficient piston-powered military surplus aircraft and inadequate ground handling equipment, produced low revenue yields for common-carriage traffic. The basic problems of piston-powered aircraft were low productivity and high operating costs, associated with slow turn-around (off load/on load) times, limited aircraft capacity, speed and range. Being their main asset, Flying Tiger Line well understood the need for the improvement of air cargo planes, as they were dependent on such equipment. As early as 1950, Bob Prescott noted in the company's Annual Report that **"the key to the future of the airfreight industry is to found in the development of a more efficient cargo plane."**

However, the all-cargo carrier difficulties in securing new flight equipment during the late 1940s and early 1950s had centered around their relatively insecure financial position at the time. The financial problems of those carriers, together with the manufacturer's marginal risk in producing cargo aircraft, precluded any equipment purchases other than military surplus planes, especially in consideration of favorable financing terms for veterans.

At the time that Tigers received its certificate for Route 100 in July, 1949, it had an organization employing approximately 250, and was operating six C-54 Skymasters and three C-47s, and anticipating the acquisition of C-46 Commandos. The company also had some aircraft on lease.

The C-54 Skymaster had thrice the load capacity of the C-47, and had a large cargo-loading door cut in the fuselage aft of the wings. However, the cargo door was located about ten feet or more from ground level, rather than the five feet of the C-47 with an inclined floor. The C-54 also featured a separate crew entry door forward of the wing, whereas with the C-47 and C-46, the crew cabin door led to the main cargo section behind the crew pit. Thus, an aisle way free of cargo was needed for crew members. On the C-54, a twin-boom hoist and winch was installed for loading or off-loading heavier pieces of freight in the labor-intensive process of bulk handling the cargo. In summation, the Skymaster was considered the most adequate cargo aircraft at that time.

By early 1951, while enjoying the transPacific airlift contract, Tigers moved their headquarters offices from the Lockheed hangar to their own new, two-story office building two blocks away. The company also owned 100,750 sq. ft. of land adjacent to the 16,000 sq. ft. terminal at Burbank. The facility became the fleet headquarters for the newly acquired C-46 twin-engined Commandos.

FTL's new Burbank headquarters, 1951

By June 30, 1951, the company was operating a fleet of thirty-four surplus military aircraft of which twenty-two were owned and twelve were leased. The fleet mix included mostly C-46s as the "workhorse," and a few C-54s and C-47s. With the lucrative Pacific airlift contract and other positive revenue accounts, Tigers positioned itself to acquire more capital to upgrade its fleet.

In a 1952 transaction, Chennault's Civil Air Transport in Hong Kong arranged to ship about fifty-odd C-46s, and some C-47s and Convairs to the U.S. With the Communist takeover of mainland China in 1949, the aircraft used by the Nationalists sought refuge in Hong Kong, a British possession. C.A.T. airlines opened an office at Burbank to handle the sales of the aircraft under a new salvage company named Aviation Parts and Equipment, Inc.[1] Subsequently, a large number of these arrived at the Tigers' Burbank hangars for assembly and overhaul. Flying Tiger Line promptly purchased thirteen from Chennault's fleet, rebuilt them for U.S. commercial use, and sold them to Riddle Airlines, an east coast freight operator, and Intercontinental Airways of Burbank for a profit of over $350,000.[2]

At the close of 1951, a contract was entered into between FTL and the Douglas Aircraft Corp. for the delivery of seven DC-6A aircraft, with delivery dates in 1953. It was the biggest commercial aircraft ever built up to that time, and the $7 million invested made this the largest single order ever placed for new cargo planes. The Flying Tiger Line 1951 Annual Report noted that, "Carrying nearly twice as much cargo as the C-54, the DC-6A flies 100 miles an hour faster and represents the modern version of today's cargo aircraft."

It is significant to note that the purchase of the DC-6A represented FTL's first acquisition of a non-military surplus cargo aircraft. This aircraft was first available and utilized by Slick in 1951 for transcontinental service. The DC-6A Liftmaster represented an important milestone in the development of air freight transportation since it was the first aircraft produced as a cargo transport for commercial use, and fully pressurized with reinforced flooring. By producing the DC-6A in the same configuration as the DC-6 series passenger aircraft, and off-setting developmental costs to the passenger design, the manufacturer was able to reduce the selling price of this aircraft from $2,660,000 to $1,100,000, and in this way the technological gains of the passenger aircraft were made available to the air freight industry. And the payload of the DC-6A at 30,000 lbs. maximum capacity exceeded the Curtiss-Wright C-46 at 12,000 lbs., and the Douglas C-54 at 20,000 lbs. The DC-6A was also considerably faster than the other two types of aircraft.[3]

The freight carrying version of the standard DC-6 featured a new cargo designed fuselage and was five feet longer. There were two large doors forward and aft of the wing, with the larger in the aft serving as the main cargo door. There was a self-powered loading elevator which folded up for storage within the aircraft. It could be

Flying Tigers acquired the Douglas DC-6A cargo aircraft, carrying 32,000 pounds of cargo at 275 miles per hour with a 2,000-mile range. At the time, the DC-6A carried more freight, cheaper and faster than any aircraft then flying. (1953-1958).

attached to either the front or rear cargo door with a lift capability of 4,000 lbs. from truck-bed height to cabin floor level, with the main cargo section being sixty-eight feet long. The main drawback of the DC-6A was that the cargo floor height was high relative to truck-bed height, thus, the loading and unloading process was more difficult, resulting in slow turn-around times and increased handling costs.

By mid-summer, 1953, the DC-6A was on a seller's market, while at the same time, the Korean conflict airlift was at a decline, impacting the Flying Tiger revenue base. For approximately $9 million, FTL arranged to lease four of its yet undelivered DC-6As to Northwest Airlines for seven years, with a three-year extension option. Consequently, the cost was $8,8000,000 to $9,880,000, depending on the length of the contract. With foresight, the company had four of the DC-6As outfitted for passenger utilization so that they could be leased to combination carriers.[4]

Almost simultaneously, Flying Tiger Line sold outright to Japan Air Lines delivery rights on two more of the new planes for $1.2 million, plus the $250,000 down payment the company had already committed. At the same time, the company re-ordered two more DC-6As for delivery in December, 1954, and January, 1955.

On February 13, 1955, the Flying Tiger Line inaugurated its DC-6A transcontinental service. It provided overnight delivery for certain high traffic lanes including, subsequently, daily San Francisco-Chicago service, and Burbank-Newark transcontinental routing through Chicago and Detroit. On June 30, 1955, the Tiger fleet included seven C-54s with one on lease, seven DC-6As with four on lease, and twenty-three C-46s. Increase fleet capacity for Tigers was reflected in their proportionate increase in domestic freight volumes from 1954 to 1956.

By 1956, three cargo carriers in domestic operation accounted for 42% of the total air freight ton-miles. However, individual carrier growth was highly variable. Slick, Flying Tiger, and Riddle increased 1956 ton-miles over 1955 figures by 22%, 36%, and 48% respectively, proportionate to their individual base figures. In a graphic representation, one may notice that with the continuance of the growth pattern, Flying Tiger Line and Slick (before the decline) would soon surpass all the individual combination carriers, including American Airlines, the leader since 1949, in the hauling of air freight.[5]

The nature of all-freight carrier operations was considerably different from cargo operations of passenger-cargo combination carriers. The marketing strategy was expectedly different, of course, since passenger revenues constituted more than 80% of total revenue for the combination airlines. Their aircraft would be operated for the prime purpose of passenger transportation, and all-cargo flights would be offered only

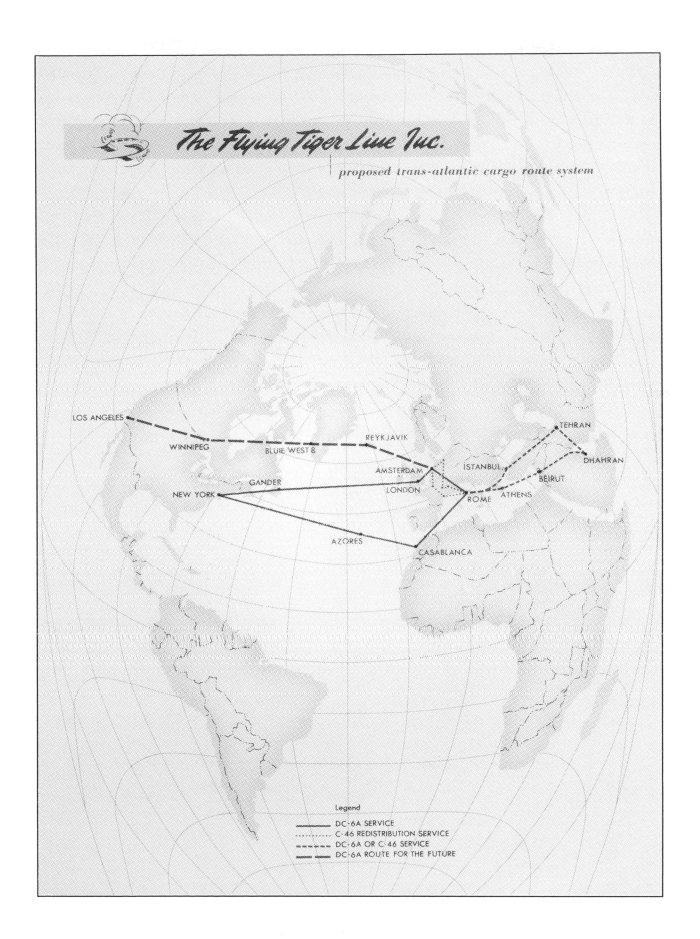

The Flying Tiger Line Inc.

proposed trans-atlantic cargo route system

LOS ANGELES
WINNIPEG
REYKJAVIK
BLUE WEST 8
AMSTERDAM
TEHRAN
ISTANBUL
DHAHRAN
GANDER
LONDON
BEIRUT
NEW YORK
ROME
ATHENS
AZORES
CASABLANCA

Legend
DC-6A SERVICE
C-46 REDISTRIBUTION SERVICE
DC-6A OR C-46 SERVICE
DC-6A ROUTE FOR THE FUTURE

when and where a high load factor and profit margin could be maintained. Nevertheless, they were, in effect, limiting their all-cargo service to the most lucrative routes more than were the all-cargo carriers. The advantage of the all-cargo carriers was that they could fly at night, on non-specific routing, and not be concerned with passenger needs. A disadvantage was the one-way traffic and limited back-haul traffic at times. The passenger-demographic patterns differed from some of the city-paired routing of air cargo markets.

Flying Tiger Line and American Airlines were the leaders of their respective groups in cargo ton-miles carried in 1956, and operated over substantially the same territory. Total freight ton-mile volume had more than tripled for Tigers from 1949 to 1956, while American Airlines had little more than doubled its cargo traffic. American's increase had been steady and cargo revenues had not dropped below 7% of total revenue. Flying Tiger's increase had been greater, but much more erratic growth, with a sharp decline in 1953 and 1954, due partly to an unsuccessful merger attempt by Flying Tiger Line and Slick Airways.[6]

DOMESTIC TON-MILES OF FREIGHT FLOWN ON SCHEDULED FLIGHTS BY MAJOR CARRIERS, 1948-56
(in millions of ton-miles)

Carrier	1949	1950	1951	1952	1953	1954	1955	1956
American	31.8	35.1	35.4	44.9	52.3	53.9	67.0	71.4
United	23.6	27.8	22.2	26.6	27.6	33.6	39.5	50.1
TWA	12.0	13.7	15.0	15.6	18.9	21.3	24.3	23.7
Eastern	8.5	9.9	5.3	6.8	8.1	10.3	13.9	14.7
Northwest	4.6	6.9	3.7	3.6	3.7	4.5	6.6	7.8
Capital	7.0	8.1	5.2	3.9	4.1	4.2	4.0	Unk
Braniff	1.2	2.0	2.0	2.3	2.8	2.9	3.4	Unk
Delta	1.9	3.1	3.6	4.3	5.5	5.7	6.6	7.2
FTL	3.6	19.4	27.9	37.2	35.6	25.3	46.9	67.6
Slick	6.4	35.7	44.1	44.6	38.9	32.8	41.9	63.6
Riddle						14.9	14.3	21.2

Source: CAB, Recurrent Reports of Mileage and Traffic Data for Domestic Trunk Lines; Domestic Nonmail Carriers, Certificated All-Cargo Lines.

Perhaps the greatest tactical move for the Flying Tiger Line in the mid-1950s was their decision to discard most of their inefficient piston-engined military surplus aircraft, and acquire a more potentially profitable fleet to expand their markets and revenue base. Instead of acquiring more DC-6As, however, the company decided to invest in another cargo aircraft, the Lockheed 1049-H.

In 1955, Tigers placed a $20 million order for ten new Super-H Constellations, the cargo version of the 1049-G, later increasing the order to twelve. At the outset, Tigers ordered ten of the first nineteen Super-Connies in production, with Quantas Empire Airways ordering two, United States Overseas Airlines ordering two, and Seaboard and Western Airlines ordering five. The new aircraft would have a load capacity about 25% greater than the DC-6A, and also had the capability of quick conversion for passenger use.

In 1957, the Flying Tiger Line took delivery of the ten Super-Connies to supplement its fleet of three DC-6As, eight C-54s and fifteen C-46s. Two more Super-Connies were added at year's end. However, not all the airlines were as progressive as Tigers. The change-over from old to newer and more efficient cargo aircraft in the late 1950s was a very slow process.

In fact, a study of aircraft in operation in the mid-1950s noted that a substantial amount of older equipment was brought back into use in 1956.[7] The number of all-cargo flights being offered at the time increased by 10% in 1955 and 1956, and to provide for the additional service, the airlines made use of older, uneconomical passenger aircraft. DC-4s increased from 145 to 147, C-47s from 40 to 48, and C-46s rose from 85 to 129 between those two years. These aircraft were just as uneconomical when transporting cargo. The continued utilization of the older airplane at the time, with extremely high operating costs, prevented an earlier reduction in the air freight rates.

The downgrading of older passenger equipment to cargo services was a manifestation of the status cargo held in the airline business. Freight was the stepchild of the passenger carriers, seen as supplementary revenue rather than a business in itself. Very few aircraft had been purchased by the passenger operators for the expressed purpose of moving freight only. This basic weakness in air cargo was partly the fault of the aircraft manufacturers who expressed little confidence in the future of air cargo. All-freight carriers had little lobbying power and, at times, had to be innovative.

The Super-Connies were long range four-engined aircraft with much promise in its time, and, after Tiger modification, represented a substantial increase in speed and

The Lockheed Super H Constellation, airlifting 43,000 pounds of freight at 300 miles per hour over a 2,500-mile range, helped Flying Tigers revolutionize the marketing map of the United States with the first nonstop, transcontinental airfreight schedules. (1957-1967)

productivity over the other cargo aircraft in their fleet, including the DC-6A. The additional speed and carrying-capacity enabled the newer planes to operate more economically and profitably. From the fully-allocated cost standpoint, operation of the old C-47, C-54, and C-46 cargo aircraft allowed marginal profit at best for the cargo carrier on an individual flight basis. In comparison, even the per-hour earning ability of the DC-6A was about two-and-a-half times that of the C-54, and over seven times that of the C-47, while the earning ability of the Super-Connie 1049-H was one and-a-half times that of the DC-6A:[8]

Aircraft	C-47	C-46	C-54	DC-6A	1049-H
Payload(tons)	3.95	6.75	9.25	15.20	21.25
Direct Cost Per Hour	$72.56	$142.63	$156.13	$252.29	$384.55
Indirect Cost Per Hour	$24.19	$47.54	$93.68	$100.92	$153.82
Total Cost Per Hour	$96.75	$190.17	$249.81	$353.21	$538.37
Per Hour Earning Ability	$77.07	$163.90	$231.71	$503.82	$737.26
Gross Profit or Loss( ) Per Hour	($18.68)	($26.27)	($18.10)	$151.61	$208.89
Avg. System Block Speed	150 mph	170 mph	190 mph	265 mph	352 mph

Source: Stanley N. Brewer, **Vision in Air Cargo** (U. of Washington, 1957) p. 7.

Bill Bartling, the Flying Tiger VP in charge of Research and Development is credited with boosting the pay-load design of the Super-Connie to almost 23 tons rather than the 16½ ton maximum for the DC-6A. Thus, the Lockheed 1049-G was redesignated the 1049-H, and eventually seventy aircraft of that model were built for other airlines. The Super-Connie had a normal range of 4540 miles with an added three hours of reserve fuel. This translated into fewer fuel stops and less airport costs. And

Lockheed's "lead time" between order and delivery of that aircraft was a full eighteen months shorter than that of the DC-6A.[9]

The Super-Connie also featured a forward cargo-entry door 5 ft. wide and 6 ft. high, and a main double rear cargo door 9½ ft. wide and 6¼ ft. high. However, the Super-Connie suffered the same drawback for cargo operations as the DC-6A in that the main cargo deck floor was situated about ten ft. off the ground, thus, using forklift and pallet or pallet box techniques was very time consuming. More efficient cargo operations awaited the introduction of adaptable roller systems and the application of a scissor-type loading mechanism which would elevate unitized freight loads to the main cargo deck height.[10] However, a distinct advantage of the Super-Connie was that it had a lengthy cargo compartment of 83 ft. as compared with the C-46 with 48 ft. length, the C-54 with 57 ft. length, and the DC-6A with 68 ft. length.[11] The Super-Connie also had two lower compartments to accommodate freight.

As an added feature, it was noted that six men could convert the Super-Connie to a 114-passenger configuration in just four hours, seating five-abreast, thus opening the door to a new overseas mass-travel market. On October 10, 1957, Flying Tiger Line inaugurated a 7 hour-55 minute non-stop service with a fleet of 331 mile-an-hour air freighters, transporting an almost 23-ton payload from the West Coast to the East. Subsequently, Tigers implemented the largest transcontinental all-cargo airlift program ever initiated connecting fifteen air cargo-generating cities on both coasts and in the Midwest with a daily close-of-business pickup and next-morning delivery. With the Super-Connies placed into the transcontinental route and military contract work, Tigers' revenues soared almost 80%.[12]

Dewline Project 572

Besides placing orders for the Super-Connies and starting the DC-6A transcontinental service in 1955, that year Tigers also embarked on what may have been physically and logistically the most challenging mission to date. That entailed the carrier's role in transporting supplies and equipment into remote sites in the construction of the Dewline (Distant Early Warning System) between 1955 and 1957, providing a series of radar outposts that was designed to signal the alarm for approaching enemy aircraft deployed via the polar route. Named **Project 572**, fifty radar installations were built along a barren 3,000-mile frontier from Alaska to Baffin Island in 32 months. It has been noted as "one of the world's unsung technical accomplishments," a Cold War phenomena.[13]

The Dewline was a part of the extensive North American Air Defense Command (NORAD) system providing surveillance and warning from Midway to Iceland, and involving sea, land, and air systems. Radar stations of the Ballistic Missile Early Warning System (BMEWS) were added in the early 1960s in Greenland and Alaska. South of the Dewline is the Mid-Canada line, and roughly along the U.S.-Canada border is the Pinetree System.

Project 572 was a joint venture employing fifty Canadian and thirty-one American commercial airlines working in lightly mapped Polar areas under the extreme Arctic conditions, sometimes reaching 55 degrees below zero. Then, sometimes, temperatures reaching 80 degrees in the summer shade would quickly melt the ice, jeopardizing the stock of equipment and supplies in place. Compass deviations and visual "white- out" and upside-down mirages often appeared above the horizon.

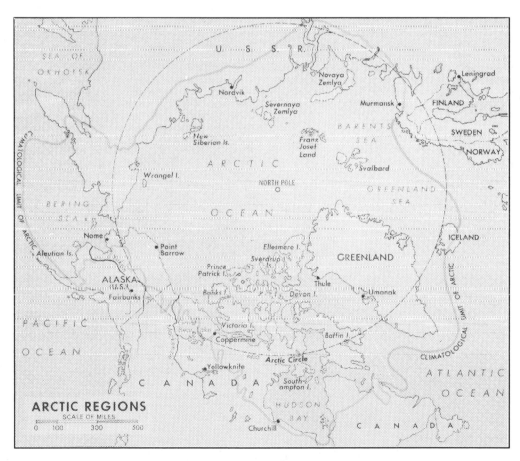

Dewline's Polar Area south part of Circle

"Baby, It's Cold Up Here!"
Flying Tigers Draw Dewline Duty... 1956.

Tigers assumed the largest role of any American airline on the project, using C-46s, C-47s and C-54s. The first U.S. commercial plane to fly into Dewline's polar area was a C-46 in February, 1955. Shortly thereafter, the carrier deployed a fleet of seven planes operating out of Churchill for the eastern sector, and eleven planes under the name of Queen Charlotte Airlines for the western sector. In Hay River, Tiger flight crews and maintenance personnel lived in a small hotel built over the perma-frost, and at Churchill, sixteen Tigers lived in one large room at the Royal Canadian Air Force base, sometimes working twelve-hour shifts, seven days a week. At both the Western and Eastern sites in the beginning were rudimentary outposts, using a collection of white tents. Throughout the project, no Tiger personnel received serious injury. However, seven Tiger planes became disabled or lost, which provided a most memorable story for the participants who gathered for a reunion in 1978.[14]

"On the morning of April 6, 1956, a Tiger DC-4 numbered 010, crashed-landed in inclement weather at Site 31, and although the crew walked away from it, the airplane was judged a total loss. An insurance adjuster traveled to the crash site where he confirmed the verdict and settled for $500,000.

At Burbank, John Dewey, the experienced executive mechanic, and the airline's management shared ideas about the matter. As a result, Flying Tigers bought the crippled aircraft back from the insurance company for parts and scrap value of $115,000, and Dewey headed north again with a team of crack mechanics. Armed with parkas, snow glasses, survival kits and ingenuity, the team set up accommodations in small portable huts and went to work on 010. Ten days later the 'total loss' was towed to a landing strip and flown home to Burbank.

In the Tigers' hangars, it was given a full renovation at a cost of $65,000. Then put in the market, it fetched a sale price of $700,000."[15]

By July, 1957, the Dewline was completed and operational as a result of the "can do" teamwork.

In 1958, Tigers had the greatest share of the MATS Pacific airlift, a contract that amounted to $18 million or, roughly, three-fourths of the company's income from all sources. The mission involved one Super-Connie flight daily between Travis AB to Tokyo. Unfortunately, in September, 1959, MATS ordered $37 million in total overseas contracts, and made the awards to the very lowest bidders. Tigers refused to bid at the unrealistic prices, and subsequently, some of the successful bidders went bankrupt from the experience. This led to a CAB response which led to the enactment of minimum rates for military charters on October 1, 1960, allowing Tigers back into that market.

Meanwhile, new civilian contracts and increased common-carriage business compensated, in part, for the lost in MATS business.[16] Other all-freight carriers also experienced disappointments at that time.

For the year ended March 31, 1958, Slick and Riddle lost approximately $2,600,000 and $1,080,000, respectively in their overall operations, including both certificated and noncertificated services. These losses forced Slick to abandon its certificated services on February 22, 1958, leaving the transcontinental all-cargo route entirely to the Flying Tiger Line. In that year, the company broke the 100 million ton-mile figure for air freight, being the first airline to accomplish that feat.

Scheduled and nonscheduled operating revenues of all-cargo carriers

	Scheduled Amount (000)	% of Total	Nonscheduled Amount (000)	% of Total	Nontransport Amount (000)	% of Total	Total
AAXICO[a]	$579	8.6	$6,131	91.4			6.710m
Flying Tiger[b]	$9,569	28.9	23,504	71.0	$19	0.1	33,092m
Riddle: Domestic[b]	3,953	44.2	4,682	52.4	308	3.4	8,944m
International[b]	1,914	97.3	51	2.6	1	.1	1,966m
Slick[b]	6,499	40.1	9,600	59.2	114	.7	16,213m

[a] Year ended June 31, 1958
[b] Year ended March 31, 1958

Source: CAB Reports, **Riddle Airlines et. al. Exemptions**, 1958, pp.16 and 22

North Atlantic Passenger Service

With the fleet of Super-Connies, Flying Tiger Line also broadened their revenue base by stepping up the group-charter business that they had pioneered. This modification of the air passenger business, conforming to CAB rules, allowed such a noncertificated passenger carrier as the Flying Tigers to transport clubs and groups on a charter basis. The CAB denied Tigers certification to carry passengers on a scheduled basis, which left Tigers free to deal with certain approved groups who would charter the entire plane for their membership only. Until 1955, each such European contract had first to be offered to a certificated American trans-Atlantic carrier, which was to say to Pan American or Trans-World Airways. When they refused, Tigers accepted, and dozens of contract carriers followed the Tigers into this bargain basement. In summer of 1955, the CAB ruled this "right of first refusal" was no longer necessary, but it continued to insist that each charter be flown under an individual exemption obtained through its offices. Tigers quickly booked fifty groups to Europe on a round-trip basis. Eventually, by the end of 1956, they were flying 20,000 passengers to London, Paris, Frankfurt, Rome, Tel Aviv, and other places, making Tigers the largest independent air carrier across the North Atlantic. Flying Tiger bases opened up at Frankfurt and Gander, and a Tiger passenger agency blossomed in Geneva.[17]

It is interesting to note that Tigers became competitive with Seaboard Airlines (known as Seaboard and Western then) which began as a U.S.-based passenger charter airline to Europe in 1946. Seaboard, like a number of other charter carriers, profited from the Berlin and Pacific airlift. Then facing intensive competition, applied for and received CAB authority to operate scheduled all-cargo service between the U.S. and Europe in 1955.[18] (Tigers would ultimately acquire Seaboard a quarter of a century later.)

FTL used the DC-6As for their earlier European charters, but with the advent of the Super-Connies in 1957, they carried 70,000 group travellers by year's end. During one month, Tiger planes averaged one trans-Atlantic crossing daily. By late August and early September, all groups were west-bound, and Tigers filled the east-bound flights with military equipment to help meet official U.S. policy commitments during the crisis in Lebanon. By the end of the 1960 season in the continual pattern, over 300 Tiger round-trip charters had provided lifts for 30,000 passengers, all being bona fide members of clubs, church groups or employee organizations.[19]

For the summer time European charters, Flying Tigers applied and received

CAB permission to fly temporary trans-Atlantic charter passenger flights from July to the end of September, 1961.[20] This was the process which the company continued to use until a couple of decades later when Tigers started a subsidiary passenger line named Metro International, serving both scheduled and charter flights.

Notes

1. Malcolm Rosholt, **Flight in the China Airspace, 1910-1950** (Rosholt, Wis.: Rosholt House) 1983, pp. 71-73.

2. Frank J. Cameron, **Hungry Tiger: The Story of the Flying Tiger Line** (New York: McGraw-Hill) 1962, p. 148.

3. Moody's Transportation Manual, 1954.

4. Elbert Newell Dissmore, **A Trenchant Analysis of Post-War Developments in Air Freight Transportation** (M.A. Thesis, Business Administration, U. of Washington) 1955, pp. 13-14.

5. Robert Lee Day, **The Present Competitive Position of Air Cargo** (M.A. Thesis, Business Admin., UW) 1958, p. 57.

6. Ibid., pp. 57 and 60.

7. Ibid., p. 20, as quoting:
   Preble Stover, "Air Cargo Booming, Looks Ahead to Better Planes," **Aviation Week** (March 12, 1956) p. 135; and, 1956 data from **Aviation Week** (Feb. 11, 1957) p. 45.

8. Stanley H. Brewer, **Vision in Air Cargo** (UW, Seattle, 1957) p. 7, citing: **Moody's Transportation Manual, 1956**, statistics used for computation, and **American Aviation**, (April 23, 1956) p. 131, and, **Air Freight Rate Case, Docket 1705 et al CAB**, Appendix A.

9. Op. cit., Frank J. Cameron, pp. 231, and **Jane's All the World's Aircraft, 1956-57**, completed and edited by Leonard Bridgman (London: Sampson, Low and Marston Co.) p. 302.

10. Ibid., **Jane's All the World's Aircraft, 1956-57**.

11. L.R. Hackney and Walter Tydon, "Dimensional and Loading Data-Military and Commercial Cargo Transports," **National Security Industrial Assn.** (Dec. 3, 1952) pp. 1-4.

12. Op. cit., Frank J. Cameron, p. 232.

13. "Remembering the Dewline," **Tigereview**, Sept./Oct., 1978, pp. 2 & 3.

14. Op. cit., Frank J. Cameron, p. 204-218.

15. Op. cit., "Remembering the Dewline."

16. Op. cit., Frank J. Cameron, p. 233.

17. Ibid., p. 251.

18. Nawal Taneja, **The U.S. Air Freight Industry**, (Lexington: D.C. Heath, Lexington Books) 1976, p. 37.

19. Op. cit., Frank J. Cameron, pp. 251 & 254.

20. **Moody's Transportation Manual, 1961**, p. 1304.

4

Tiger Comes of Age

Throughout most of the 1960s, Flying Tiger Line experienced extraordinary growth as the lone survivor of the 1949 Air Freight Case, and emerged as the foremost all-cargo carrier. Among other attributes, it received its permanent certification of U.S. Route 100 in 1962, and by 1969, had upgraded its propeller-driven piston-engine fleet to an entire pure jet freighter fleet allowing for more extensive geographic capability and cargo capacity. Inter-relatedly, the period was dominated by the Pacific airlift centering on the Vietnam crisis which lasted from 1964 to 1975, or thereabouts, being Tigers' primary revenue activity. The decade of events translated into "avenues of opportunities" for the carrier.

Heavily involved, the emergency airlift MAC contracts and mail contracts provided Flying Tigers with generous revenues which enabled the company to acquire the modern cargo fleet to sustain its leadership in the industry, establish and upgrade selective terminals, ground equipment, and introduce containerization for more efficient and speedy cargo handling.

In June, 1958, the Tiger aircraft fleet comprised of thirteen Super-Connies, including two on lease, and eleven C-46 Commandos, of which nine were held for sale. That year, the company entertained thoughts of ordering the soon-to-be produced jet freighters, or, perhaps, the multi-functioned convertibles. The combination carriers were ordering the passenger configuration jetliners which, in themselves, constituted a competitive threat to all-cargo carriers. In conjuncture with the intensively competitive schedule offered by combination carriers, the "belly" compartments of the new Boeing 707s, and later DC-8s, were capable of carrying from 14,000 lbs. to 20,000 lbs. of freight, besides a full load of passengers.

However, during 1958, Tigers elected to order the less expensive turbo-props which they felt were better suited to their medium-range operations and the company's budget. The cost of the CL-44D cargo aircraft produced by Canadair, Ltd., was about $3.8 million at the time as compared with an estimated $7 million projected for the upcoming Boeing 707 cargo jet freighter. During the decision-making process, FTL's Art Seymore, senior aviator, spent eight months test flying the CL-44D model before the acquisition, being that the Canadian manufacturer did not have available, at the time, any test pilots to perform the same.

The CL-44D aircraft had a load capacity of near 65,000 lbs. with a continental range, and used four Rolls-Royce Type engines. It was calculated to have a 40% operating cost advantage over the Super-Connies. With a prominent swing-tail design, the aircraft was an adaptation of the Bristol Britannia, and initially built to meet Royal Canadian Air Force (RCAF) requirement for long range troop and freight transport. Of twenty seven produced, the first delivery of the CL-44Ds went to FTL starting May 31, 1961, on an initial order of ten aircraft. Seaboard, the trans-Atlantic all-cargo carrier, ordered five CL-44Ds with first delivery on June 20, 1961, and Slick Airways ordered four with the first delivery on June 17, 1962. Thus, all-cargo carriers were the predominant interested parties of the CL-44Ds.[1]

For cargo carriers, the CL-44Ds offered attractive features besides the price tag. The maximum payload was 63,272 lbs. as compared with the 42,500 lbs. maximum for the Super-Connie, and the cruise speed of 400 mph was about 100 mph faster. The CL-44D had a 3,100-mile range with full payload, or a 5,660-mile range with 37,300 lbs. using reserve fuel. In total, it was calculated to have a 40% operating cost advantage over the Super-Connie for the cargo operator.

The structural advantages of the CL-44D for cargo operators was also readily apparent. The main cargo cabin was 98½ ft. long, 11 ft. wide, and almost 8 ft. high. The noticeable feature was the hinged tail section which could open and swing aside in a minute-and-a-half for direct (straight-in) loading, accommodating freight up to 84 ft. in length. Not only did it allow straight-in loading near ground level, but it also offered a palletized set up which could allow for considerable time savings. A pallet

The Canadair CL-44, acquired by Flying Tigers in 1961, had a cruising speed of 375 mph over a range of 3,000 miles. With its unique swing-tail design, which permitted straight-in loading, it was capable of carrying up to 65,000 lbs. of cargo. (1961-1969)

handling system was developed by Douglas Manufacturing Company for the U.S. Air Force using **Mac pallets**.[2] However, Flying Tiger Line utilized primarily the "bulk load" technique on their common-carriage flights.

The first CL-44D arrived at Tigers' Burbank terminal on June 2, 1961, from Montreal, Canada via New York. At this time, the old company insignia of the open-mouth tiger shark was formally changed to a giant encircled "T", which was painted on the tail sections. And, on July 16, FTL made its first trans-Pacific flight from Travis AFB to the Far East. As the carrier's mid-west hub, Chicago Tigers opened a new $1½ million freight terminal in March of 1962, featuring fourteen loading docks. Anticipating a fully automatic operation, the "turn-around" time of off-loading and loading the CL-44D was projected to be a little over one hour for a 62,500 lb. maximum payload. The Super-Connie best turnaround time, with the 46,000 lb. maximum, was three to five hours, as it was entirely bulk loaded.[3]

Flying Tiger Line essentially followed a leap-frog strategy in cargo aircraft acquisition. By acquiring the relatively inexpensive four-engine turbo-prop freighter, it secured a competitive cost advantage over the piston engine freighters flown by the combination carriers. But when the combination airlines finally introduced the Boeing 707 and DC-8 freighters after 1963, the Tiger's cost advantage vanished.[4]

Following a chronology of Tiger's fleet acquisition, in April, 1962, the company reportedly had ten Super-Connies and eight CL-44Ds, with two more on order. A year later, the carrier's fleet comprised of eight Super-Connies, ten CL-44Ds, and had placed an order for two DC-8F Traders, jet freighters, for $17 million with Douglas Aircraft Co., with an early 1964 delivery. Tigers was moving toward the pure jet age.

After viewing the performance of a new Lockheed version jet cargo plane at a Georgia air show in October, 1964, Prescott became impressed enough to consider an acquisition for the Tiger fleet. Shortly thereafter, the company placed an order for eight Super Starlifters, the Lockheed 300, at $64 million with delivery starting late 1967. The fanjet freighter version was identified as the C-141, and is today still popular in the Air Force fleet.

With an impressive showing, the Flying Tiger Line and Slick Airways quickly ordered a proposed normal growth version, the Lockheed 300B. The high-speed aircraft featured straight-in, truck-bed level, rear loading, a special 18-ton maximum loader, and thirteen pallets of up to 70,000 lbs. payload, following the advent of the roller system in jet freighters. The Starlifter was similar to but larger than the CL-44D, which accommodated thirteen MAC pallets (military size at 108" x 88") on its roller system. The Starlifter also offered the option of side or rear loading.

Flying Tiger Line placed an order of eight Starlifters with a $500,000 deposit, and a clause indicating that the order was subject to modification and elongation of the fuselage to better meet Tiger's needs for the commercial cargo aircraft. Unfortunately, though, the order was also contingent upon Lockheed Manufacturing Company having a minimum of fifty commercial orders of that aircraft in order to proceed with production, which never materialized.[5]

In 1965, Flying Tiger Line had considered the possible acquisition of the Mercury General American Corporation, a helicopter company based at Torrance, California, staffed with thirteen full-time employees operating a fleet of six helicopters, including one leased from Flying Tiger. The acquisition objective, as reported to the CAB, was to "obtain valuable knowledge and experience in helicopter operations which would have future application to (Tigers') scheduled air cargo services, and the possible use of the trade name, **Flying Tigers Helicopters**,"[6]

Mercury General was a contract firm involved in providing aerial photography services for the motion picture industry, in geophysical survey operations in Canada, and in meeting the needs for transportation of personnel in connection with a large water development project in central California. In operation since 1958, the helicopter company had experience in the use of helicopters for fish spotting and drone retrieval activities, the transportation of personnel and cargo for large construction projects, in offshore oil-drilling activities, and in fire suppression work for the U.S. Forest Service. Mercury General officers were, also at the time, providing consultant services on an interim basis to Flying Tiger in connection with the establishment of a Lear Jet dealership in San Francisco.

However, according to current Flying Tigers Retirement Club President Joe Baker, the CAB proposal never materialized. What'smore, Ellen Warner Toney, Prescott's personal secretary (1953-72) noted that Peter Prescott, the only son, died in a Lear jet crash about this time. Later, the Peter Prescott Memorial Hospital in Taipei, Taiwan, was named in his memory, as well as a scholarship fund.

At the end of 1965, FTL had a mixed fleet of sixteen CL-44Ds, eight Super-Connies, and two B707-349Cs, leased from Boeing in October-November, 1965. Furthermore, the company contracted with Boeing to lease two B707 convertible aircraft for June and December, 1966, deliveries. Their mission was for deployment in the trans-Pacific airlift serving the Vietnam crisis.

During the following year, Tigers entered into a purchase agreement to acquire ten DC-8-63F "stretch" jetfreighters, including engines and parts, from Douglas Manufacturing Company. Meanwhile, at the end of 1967, Tiger's mixed fleet

B-707 Aerial - Flying Tigers met the challenge of the jet age with the Boeing 707-349C Intercontinental jets. The Boeing 707s carried 72,000 pounds of freight at 550 miles per hour over a 3,000 mile range.

comprised of eleven CL-44Ds owned and three leased, two Boeing 707s owned and four leased, and ten Super-Connies owned but held for sale. The Super-Connies were grounded in anticipation of acquiring the upcoming DC-8-63Fs, of which the company acquired two by purchase in early 1969, and acquired three by lease agreement at the same time. Meanwhile, the airline also negotiated for the lease of four additional "stretch 8s," including toward an almost pure jet cargo fleet."[7]

The financial and operational ability to update Tiger's cargo aircraft fleet to jetfreighters may be understood, in large part, from its expanded revenue base and domicile focusing primarily on military charters, which will be discussed later. However, the other all-cargo carriers were in financially precarious positions during the late 1950s and early 1960s, which were highlighted in CAB studies considering their applications for domestic re-certification.

The CAB decisions advanced on May 3, 1962, in the **Domestic Cargo-Mail Service Case**, addressed the request by four individual major all-cargo carriers for re-certification of their domestic routes, in addition to expanding their geographic domicile. As an innuendo of their financial status at the time, all of the all-cargo applicants requested subsidy eligibility except for Flying Tigers, who in a qualifying position, stated that it did not want subsidy unless its competitors were subsidized. Tigers was the only all-cargo carrier operating regularly scheduled domestic common-carriage as certificated in 1956. In general, the four all-cargo airlines, including Slick, Riddle, and American Air Export and Import Company (AAXICO), as well as Flying Tigers, had sought permanent renewal and some selective geographic extension of their existing authority to carry property, express freight, and nonsubsidy mail.

AAXICO, who had suspended common-carriage freight operations in 1959, had requested cargo and mail routes under Route 121 from Houston to Detroit and Chicago in the midwest spurs, and to New York on the eastern seaboard, all via New Orleans and other intermediate points. AAXICO had some significant military contracts in their charter service, but did not have convincingly promising assets to operate a dependable scheduled common-carriage operation, thus, the CAB denied their request for renewal of Route 121.

Riddle, another regional carrier, received re-certification of Route 109, New York to Miami, and re-certification of Route 120, geographically east of the Mississippi, extending from Boston to Miami, and from Chicago and Detroit to Miami on other north-south routes. The CAB amended but renewed Riddle's request for another temporary five years, commencing on July 2, 1962. The temporary rather than permanent certification was justified in view of Riddle's past erratic performance and financial standing.

On February 7, 1962, Riddle filed an application to temporarily suspend service to Chicago, Detroit, Cleveland, Indianapolis, Boston, Tampa-St. Petersburg, Atlanta, Philadelphia, and Orlando, citing common carriage losses of $1,669,000 in 1961, then noting a classic statement, that **"the scheduled air freight business was not profitable."**[8] During its history, it was stated, Riddle had lost over $9 million in operations primarily devoted to the development of scheduled air freight. Subsequently, by CAB order, on April 5, 1962, Riddle was permitted to suspend scheduled operations to all points that it had requested on Route 120, except for Orlando, Florida, which service the CAB deemed necessary.

The Board was particularly concerned about Riddle's financial condition, understanding that it had invested heavily in the purchase of the modern Argosy cargo aircraft, which was capable of nose-loading and tail-unloading simultaneously. Because of the heavy financial drain and marginal income from all accounts, Riddle sold back some of their aircraft in a re-organizing effort. For the twelve months ending June 30, 1961, Riddle had a loss of $1¼ million from its common-carriage operations, and as of that date, the airline had a negative net worth as a result of an accumulated deficit of $9,862,240 since 1956. However, Riddle maintained a strong position in charter operations, receiving substantial awards in MATS and Air Force Logair contracts.

In a somewhat surprising move, the CAB re-certificated Slick's transcontinental Route 101 on a permanent basis serving San Francisco/Oakland, Los Angeles, Dallas/Forth-Worth, St. Louis, Chicago, Indianapolis, New York/Newark, Hartford/Springfield, and Boston, despite the fact that Slick had suspended domestic scheduled operations since 1958. The airline had operated primarily military charters as the major facet of its revenue base. Slick's six "demand points" and six truck-air points were deleted from the certification. FTL and Slick remained to be duplicative at San Francisco/Oakland, Los Angeles/Burbank, Chicago, New York/Newark, Hartford/Springfield, and Boston. Effective July 2, 1962, Slick was allowed 90 days to resume scheduled operations under an amendment enacted under the Board's Economic Regulations.

In sincere respect, the CAB noted Slick's achievements in the ongoing development of the air cargo industry since its incipience, and, without government subsidy to "cushion" its losses. Despite the heavy financial drain, Slick devoted a high proportion of its efforts to develop their scheduled domestic services, as opposed to

Tiger's emphasis on charters. "From 1949 through 1958, Tiger devoted an average of 29% of its operations to domestic scheduled service whereas an average of 54.7% of Slick's operations from 1949 to the time of its suspension in 1958 were in scheduled service."[9]

The CAB was very appreciative of Slick's efforts, and in conjuncture with its historical development of the industry, its upcoming acquisition of modern turbine-powered CL-44Ds, its continual contribution to military charters and defense fleet, and reasonable financial status, decided to be supportive of Slick Airways' opportunities. At the time, Slick employed about three hundred persons, and, on March 31, 1961, reportedly had a net worth of in excess of $3.7 million, with current assets exceeding current liabilities. Profits from contracts and charters for fiscal year 1959-60 were over $1 million.

While the three all-cargo carriers struggled for survival, in a sense, Tigers remained competitive in the common-carriage marketplace. As the undisputed leader of the all-cargo carriers, Flying Tiger Line received permanent certification of U.S. transcontinental Route 100, amended to authorize scheduled service between Los Angeles/Burbank, San Francisco/Oakland, Portland, Seattle/Tacoma, Milwaukee, Chicago, Detroit, Cleveland, Buffalo, Binghamton, Philadelphia, New York/Newark, Hartford/Springfield, and Boston. Service to Minneapolis-St. Paul was discontinued because of the declining air cargo market, as were eight previous truck-air points, and four "demand" points, which did not develop sufficient air cargo volumes to justify regularly scheduled cargo service at the time. Tiger's net worth had increased from $1.2 million in 1949 to over $16 million in 1959, at which time it was the second largest volume cargo carrier of all the airlines, behind American Airlines.

That year, American, United, TWA and Flying Tigers carried a record 293,117,000 ton-miles of scheduled domestic airfreight, with all these carriers providing all-cargo east-west transcontinental services. Flying Tiger Line carried 76,173,375 ton miles in 1959, or over one-fourth of the volume generated among the group, and increased their contribution to 8,314,409 ton miles the following year. Tigers operated four transcontinental ground trips daily for six days of the week, deploying Super-Connies. But mid-1962, Tigers began using the CL-44Ds for transcontinental service.

With the advent of jetliners with significant capacity cargo "belly" holds, the combination carriers experienced considerable increase in cargo volumes after the mid-1960s. During 1965 to 1969, American, United, TWA, and Flying Tigers accounted for approximately 83-90% of freighter revenue ton-miles and over 70% of the total scheduled freight ton-miles, being, unquestionably, the leaders in domestic air cargo.[10]

FLYING TIGER LINE'S AUTHORIZED AIR SERVICE POINTS

CAB Domestic Cargo-Mail Service Case Docket 10067

(as awarded May 3, 1962)

Boston
Springfield/
Hartford
New York
Newark
Philadelphia
Buffalo
Binghamton
Cleveland
Milwaukee
Chicago
Seattle/Tacoma
San Francisco/
Oakland
Los Angeles/
Burbank

*Tigers continued to operate truck-air points though not certificated

Flying Tiger Line, however, continued to use CL-44Ds in their service, but, with prospects of acquiring a pure jet fleet. And during the 1960s, the carrier changed its marketing strategy to focus on longer hauls and prime points. During the rapid growth, from 1962 to 1968, Flying Tiger, as with American Airlines, adopted freighter strategies which had the capability of providing low operating costs, at the expense of serving many cities not included in their market, for the long-range aircraft that were most efficient when flying long-stage lengths.

In employing their selective market strategy, Flying Tiger Line used non-competitive non-prime time departures in longer routes. Los Angeles (Burbank)-Detroit, Los Angeles-Newark (New York area), and San Francisco-Chicago routes became Tiger's high-traffic lanes. Tigers served less cities and less flights, concentrating on certain prime cities on longer routes, lowering their operating costs, as compared with American, TWA, and United Airlines.

During that period, Flying Tigers and American essentially served the same cities, while United and TWA increased their cities coverage, concentrating on expanding their depth and breadth route system. Flying Tiger, on the other hand, refused to allocate substantial amounts of freighter capacity to domestic service, but did maintain significantly lower prices during the latter 1960s. Lower prices combined with low operating expenses and high load factors, averaging about 70%, enabled Tigers to move into the number two profit position of all the cargo-handling carriers in 1969. Unfortunately, its yields per revenue ton-mile were lower than its operating costs, considering its high investment capital layout in facilities and ground handling equipment, with resulting deficits in 1967 to 1969. United Airlines and Flying Tigers suffered cumulative deficits in domestic scheduled freighter service in the $4 million to the $7 million range in the period 1965 to 1969.[11]

Tigers followed a policy of minimal increase in capacity, or freight volume, during 1967 and 1968, preferring to utilize its equipment in trans-Pacific military charter service. During 1965-69, the carrier's strategy resulted in its share of capacity plummeting from almost 19% in 1965 to 11% in 1969, among the top four cargo-carrying airlines. The company's policy of diverting its capacity from scheduled to charter operations meant that its share of scheduled traffic was relatively low. However, in 1969, Tigers began operating its DC-8-63Fs in domestic service, and its capacity increased 18% that year.[12] But, in essence, the Pacific airlift subsidized the costly domestic scheduled freight system for Tigers.

Meanwhile, after 19 years at Burbank, FTL moved back to Los Angeles International airport, and by February, 1966, the company moved into its $4.5 million new maintenance and general office headquarters at that airport. By early 1968, the company completed its first fully automated terminal at the headquarters. Twice the size of the original facility, it also served as a training center. That year, automated facilities were also completed in San Francisco, Chicago, and Newark. The new Tiger terminal facilities was part of a concerted effort to accommodate the introduction of the DC-8-63Fs in to Tiger service beginning June of 1968.

In anticipation of the possibility that Tigers would experience considerable growth on its domestic system, in 1967, the company completed an application with the CAB for major domestic points, including sixteen new points. They included Denver, Milwaukee, Phoenix, Omaha, Kansas City, St. Louis, Oklahoma City, Atlantic, Nashville, Charlotte, Williamsburg, Norfolk, Columbus, Baltimore, Indianapolis, and Syracuse. Some of these points had been served on Tiger's previous truck-air and "demand" point route system.[13] Tiger's request was denied, and upheld for another ten years with the coming of domestic air crago de-regulation.

Tigers Acquires a DC-8-63F Fleet

Through FTL's arrangement, the carrier took delivery of the DC-8-63F, which we often called the **Silver Baloney**, commencing June, 1968, with the total cost estimated to be approximately $100 million. Within a year, the company increased its order to seventeen of such aircraft, with most of the latter seven planes on optional lease agreements.

The DC-8-63F (Stretch), or longer version of the DC-8, was actually placed in the commercial market about ten years after the introduction of the first Boeing 707, but offered eighteen standard positions top-side on the main cargo deck for containers or pallets, rather than thirteen on the Boeing aircraft. While the latter had a load capacity of 70,000 lbs. or so, the DC-8 Stretch had over 100,000 lbs. payload capacity. The DC-8-63F also had a proportionately larger belly capacity.

Although the maximum load capacity of the Stretch was some 25 to 30 thousand pounds more than the B-707, theoretically, it required only an additional twelve minutes in "turn-around" time. The "turn-around" time for the B-707-320C required about one hour for a complement full load, while the time required for the DC-8-63F, based on two minutes per position, was calculated to be approximately 72 minutes for the same complement full load.

The general office complex and maintenance hangar at LAX.

The Circle T design was introduced in 1960 and was first displayed on new signs at the airline's Detroit facilities. The markings were derived from freight symbols, and stencil designed lettering for the company name was also adopted at that time.

The T replaced the airline's original shark insignia, which appeared on Flying Tigers aircraft from 1947, with the C-54, through 1967 when the airline stopped flying the Lockheed Super H Constellations. The T appeared on an aircraft for the first time in 1961 when the Canadair CL-44 "swingtails" were introduced into the fleet.

The Tigerface was established as an airline symbol after regular scheduled service was initiated between the U.S. and Asia in 1969.

LAX hangar may accommodate three DC-8s simultaneously.

Flying Tigers DC-8-73 Jetfreighter, a later version of the popular DC "stretched" 8 series.

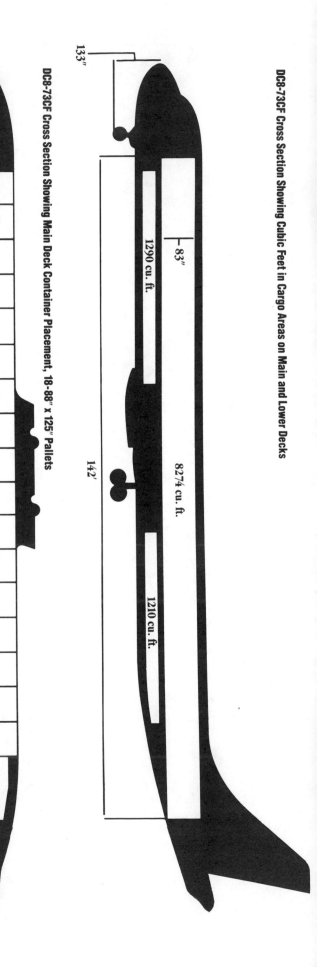

133"

83"

1290 cu. ft.

142'

8274 cu. ft.

1210 cu. ft.

DC8-73CF Cross Section Showing Main Deck Container Placement, 18-88" x 125" Pallets

| P1 | P2 | P3 | P4 | P5 | P6 | P7 | P8 | P9 | P10 | P11 | P12 | P13 | P14 | P15 | P16 | P17 | P18 |

Main Cargo Door

140"

DC8-73CF
Main Cargo Door Dimensions

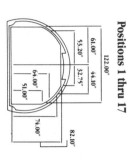

90.5"
100"
1.06"
Deck

Interior Dimensions

Positions 1 thru 17

View Looking Forward

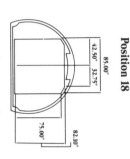

122.00"
61.00"
53.20"
44.10"
32.75"
64.00"
51.00"
74.00"
82.10"

Cargo Clearance: 1.0 inch
Pallet: 88 x 125 inch
Volume: 458 cubic feet
Loading Profile: 88 x 125 inch pallet

Position 18

View Looking Forward

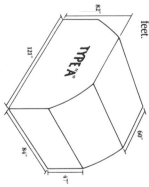

85.00"
42.50"
32.75"
75.00"
82.10"

Cargo Clearance: 1.0 inch
Pallet: 88 x 125 inch
Volume: 487.8 cubic feet
Loading Profile: 88 x 125 inch pallet

Igloo Specifications

Maximum Cube: 445 cubic feet.

Maximum Gross Weight: 13,300 pounds, subject to maximum floor bearing weight of 300 pounds per square foot.

TYPE "A"

82"
121"
60"
84"
47"

FLYING TIGERS

The cargo aircraft design of the DC-8-63F was similar to the Boeing 707-320C with reinforced top-side flooring and a roller system to facilitate the movement of freight positions. By this time, modern air cargo containers contoured to fit the main cargo deck, and featuring a "hard shell" covering had been introduced to the contain the freight. Each position of freight was provided with a set of locks to hold the position in place, while the belly compartments were bulk loaded. A scissors-type elevator mechanism with an automated roller system was joined with modern transporting vehicles with drive wheels which transported each position to the warehouse or aircraft or staging area as needed. With a conveyor belt loader used in the belly section, they formed the core of Tigers' upgraded ground handling equipment.

SEA-AIR program

In 1962, Tigers started its **Sea-Air program**, contributing to the geographic and financial growth of the company's internodal business. As a member of the Pacific Steamship Conference, the airline derived revenue from transloading ocean freight at the west coast terminals for domestic distribution via Flying Tiger aircraft, moving on a "space available" basis. Most of the freight traffic was high value cargo shipped by steamship from Asia ports to the U.S. west coast terminals.

In another internodal arrangement, the carrier instituted an air-truck system known as **Skyroad** which purportedly serviced up to 1500 U.S. cities systemwide. It also involved contract trucking which became a permanent feature of the Tiger system.

The company introduced a new dimension to the **Sea-Air program** in 1964, which was termed the "Official Export Tariff." The program was designed to attract shipments arriving in New York from Europe as ocean freight with west coast destinations. It also included freight shipments originating in the New York area, then transiting through the U.S. to Asia via the west coast.

In 1966, FTL expanded the program to cover points in Europe through interline connections at New York with Trans-Atlantic Airlines. Under this program, freight from Asia was moved by steamship to the west coast, then flown by Tigers' air freighters to domestic and European cities, and vice-versa on the routing. The ocean-air freight program was furthur developed by the carrier after the company acquired the larger capacity aircraft, the DC-8-63F, after 1968.

Re-organization

In 1967 and 1968, FTL assumed an impending re-organizational and equipment posture that was to re-shape the airline for years to come. Fred Benninger, the financial wizard of the company since the very early days, left the airline for another firm. Without a secure revenue base, Benninger had juggled the books to keep the carrier in business thriving on commercial air freight comprising only about 30%, charter and service contract about 21%, and the remaining 49% from military and government contracts.[14]

After twenty-two years, Bob Prescott, while retaining his position as president of the airline, gave up his position as the chairman and relinquished half his CEO position to Wayne M. Hoffman, an experienced executive with the New York Central Railroad whom he hired. A business acquaintance, Prescott met Hoffman in 1959 when the latter, an executive assistant to the president of the railroad firm, negotiated and arranged the Central's purchase of a $5 million Flying Tiger convertible bond issue. The business move placed FTL in a better financial position prior to the acquisition of the CL-44D turbojets, but the relationship was the subject of a CAB investigation that subsequently withered.

Four months after Hoffman joined Tigers, he, in turn, hired Thomas F. Grojean from Southern Airways to the position as FTL's VP-finance. And in mid-May, Hoffman shifted Tiger VP-planning Joseph J. Healy, into a new position as VP and general manager-terminals to implement the "profit center program," an idea used in the trucking industry. Healy was an administrator who had come up "through the ranks" starting as a ramp handler at Teterboro (EWR) airport in 1946 during the early Skyway Freight days.

The new terminal concept of decentralization placed each of the 22 general terminal managers in budgetary and operational control of their major terminal with "in-built" profit incentives. The new concept, the terminal upgrading, and the emphasis on commercial air freight growth, and departure from the dependency on military revenues, were re-organizations formulated in anticipation of two major factors. The first was the introduction of the straight DC-8-63F jetfreighter fleet, and the second factor was the prospect of acquiring the highly lucrative Asia-U.S. air cargo route which had already been CAB recommended in favor of FTL. Needing only President Nixon's approval, the Transpacific case would provide the turn-around for FTL in commercial air cargo.

Notes

1. William Green, Gordon Swanborough, John Mowinski, **Modern Commercial Aircraft** (New York: Portland House, 1987) p. 182.

2. **Jane's All the World's Aircraft, 1958**, and, Frank J. Cameron, **Hungry Tiger: The Story of the Flying Tiger Line** (New York: McGraw-Hill, 1962) p. 264.

3. Ibid.

4. Lewis M. Schneider, **The Future of the U.S. Domestic-Air Freight Industry** (Boston: Harvard U., 1973) pp. 66-67.

5. Stanley H. Brewer, **Military Airlift and Its Relationship to the Commercial Air Cargo Industry** (Seattle: U. of Washington, 1967) p. 29.

6. "The Flying Tiger Line Inc.-Mercury General American Corporation Acquisition," **CAB Report Docket 16387, dated Dec. 30, 1965**, pp. 467-471.

7. **Moody's Transportation Manual, 1965-1970.**

8. "Domestic Cargo-Mail Service Case," **CAB Docket 10067, Vol. 36, Apr-Sept, 1962** (June 29, 1962) p. 384.

9. Ibid.

10. Op. cit., Lewis M. Schneider, p. 55.

11. bid., pp. 74 & 107.

12. Ibid., p. 61.

13. **Moody's Transportation Manual, 1968.**

14. Joseph S. Murphy, "New Terminal Plan, Profit Orientation, Shape Flying Tigers For Jets," **Air Transport World**, July, 1968, pp. 19 & 20.

5

Impact of the Emergency Vietnam Airlift

Flying Tiger Line profited considerably from the Pacific airlift during the Vietnam crisis which, formally, lasted from late 1964 to 1975, the time frame of the U.S. military active participation. Proportionately high revenues were generated by the cargo, mail, and passenger airlift through lucrative contracts. Secondly, Tigers strengthened its position and its commitment in the Military Air Command (MAC) program and the Civil Reserve Air Fleet (CRAF) as compared to other U.S.-based cargo and combination carriers. Thirdly, the carrier furthered its experience in providing continuous long-range cargo airlift, establishing a strong presence in another geographic domicile, the Asian-Pacific air lanes.

In its hour of need, the carrier progressed to a new level in the developing air cargo industry. The military and U.S. Postal Service provided the opportunities set forth by the changing events in the Asian theatre. However , after 1970, the relative contribution of the scheduled commercial service bostered by the Asian imports, became significantly greater as compared to the military-related service income. For FTL, it represented a timely transition.

A financial analysis of comparative income sources for the period vividly illustrates the impact on Flying Tiger Line's revenue base:

Income Accounts

Year	Scheduled freight operation	MATS (MAC)	Charter, sales & services
June 30, 1961	$11,711,088	$16,174,403	--------
Dec 31, 1961*	5,268,126	13,305,366	--------
*(Effective Dec 31, 1961, Company changed fiscal year ending June 30 to year ending Dec 31)			
Dec 31, 1962	10,259,168	38,394,750	$ 3,609,143
Dec 31, 1963	10,918,792	27,465,723	3,825,347
Dec 31, 1964	13,707,443	23,151,385	8,609,557
Dec 31, 1965	17,086,910	30,237,475	8,831,494
Dec 31, 1966	23,483,188	48,074,385	14,461,338
Dec 31, 1967	21,689,211	53,413,028	11,929,255
Dec 31, 1968	21,430,134	43,255,211	12,013,327
Dec 31, 1969	22,467,000	49,386,000	11,938,000
Dec 31, 1970	30,497,000	30,629,000	7,071,000
Dec 31, 1971	39,228,000	34,091,000	9,671,000
Dec 31, 1972	48,802,000	32,862,000	11,455,000
Dec 31, 1973	71,998,000	15,579,000	12,383,000
Dec 31, 1974	73,772,000	15,148,000	16,038,000
Dec 31, 1975	73,191,000	22,590,000	24,783,000

Source: Moody's Transportation statistical data compilation.

Note: Revenue figures for Asia international operations starting 1969, and Corporation equipment leasing starting in 1971 will be provided in the following chapter.

Since the Korean conflict, the CRAF has represented the formal relationship between the military and civilian carriers in consideration of airlift augmentation in time of crisis.   Under a formal contract arrangement, commercial carriers may designate specific aircraft to military utilization in time of crisis. Thus, Flying Tigers had a basic annual contract with MAC (MATS was renamed MAC on Jan. 1, 1966) during the Vietnam crisis to provide air transportation services for personnel and cargo, and military dependents, from the west coast of the U.S. to various military bases throughout the Pacific area. The basic contract was subject to expansion by MAC as the need arose on a day-to-day basis, and military mail, of a seasonal nature, constituted a significant revenue base. While MAC orientation was outside of continental U.S., Tigers also negotiated a Navy QUICKTRANS contract in 1965 to transport freight between Naval installations across the country.

In evaluating proposals and awarding contracts, MAC considered reasonableness of price (effectively the CAB minimum rates at the time), the contribution of carriers to the three stages of the CRAF which involved (1) past performance, (2) relationship of carrier's proposed service to his authorized area of operation, (3) and the carrier's success in developing his business toward a long-run goal of 60% commercial and 40% military. The Department of Defense set a limit for the ratio for fiscal year 1966. The ratio was to be reversed gradually over a period of several years, but because of the Southeast Asia crisis and the need for a significant increase in the commercial augmentation airlift, the implementation of the criterion was delayed, if ever instituted.[1]

For the large combination carriers, MAC augmentation awards represented a small proportion of total transport revenue. The all-cargo carriers, on the other hand, obtained a significant proportion of the total MAC spending, and this source of income also represented a large proportion of each carrier's total transport revenue. Since 1962, the military portion of these carriers' business decreased significantly, probably reflecting the Department of Defense policy requiring progressively larger portions of commercial business for MAC contractors. As indicated in the 1965 figures, however, the percentage of total MAC business to total transport revenue had increased substantially because of the emergency situation in Southeast Asia, including up to 80% in the case of Slick Airways. Slick did not resume its scheduled common-carriage business. And for supplemental carriers, the dependence on military traffic was even more pronounced.[2] In summation, it was readily apparent that a number of U.S.-based all-cargo and supplemental air carriers, some relatively new to the business, enjoyed substantial revenues and other opportunities afforded by the Vietnam crisis.

Fiscal Year 1965

	Total Transport Revenue	Total MATS Augmentation Awards	Percent MATS/TTR	% Carrier Total MATS Award
Combination Carriers				
Pan American	605,150	34,383	6.4	14.7
TWA	615,293	10,703	2	4.6
Northwest	232,237	16,990	7	7.3
Continental	99,396	13,274	3	5.7
United	712,453	---	---	---
Smaller Comb. Carriers				
Trans-Caribbean	25,948	7,765	30	3.3
Alaska	10,564	2,247	21	.9
Northern Consolidated	3,349	504	15	.2
Reeve Aleutian	4,357	603	14	.2
Wien Alaska	4,469	314	7	.1
All-Cargo Carriers				
Flying Tiger	53,476	29,830	56	12.8
Slick	24,430	19,574	80	8.4
Seaboard	30,421	17,448	56	7.5
Riddle (Airlift)	17,492	9,787	56	4.2
Aerovias (7/64 to 12/64)	916	---	---	---
Supplemental Carriers				
AAXICO	9,196	9,265	100.7	3.9
Capitol Airways	17,882	9,573	54	4.1
Southern Air Trans.	6,335	5,031	79	2.1
United States Overseas	540	---	---	---
World Airways	28,607	24,273	85	10.4
Zantop Air Trans.	22,897	11,841	52	5.0
Trans-International	14,976	9,236	62	3.9
Overseas National	---	---	---	---

Source: "Total Transport Revenue"-**CAB Air Carrier Analytical Charts and Summaries** and **CAB Air Carrier Financial Statistics** for the fiscal years ending June 30, 1962; June 30, 1963; June 30, 1964; and June 30, 1965.

From another perspective, Flying Tigers sustained a high percentage of proportionate military revenues in over-all charter operations, apart from the carrier's core business of common-carriage, as indicated from a 1962-68 study:

Impact of Military Procurement for FTL
(data in millions)

Year	Military PAX Cargo Rev. fiscal yr.	Total PAX/Cargo Charter Rev.	Total Operating Rev.	Military % of: Total Chtr.Rev.	Total Ops.Rev
1962	$30.7	$41.8	$52.3	75%	60%
1963	32.1	31.3	42.2	90%	67%
1964	24.5	31.6	45.5	86%	60%
1965	29.8	38.3	56.2	89%	61%
1966	38.3	58.4	86.0	89%	60%
1967	65.1	61.4	87.0	92%	65%
1968	48.0	53.4	76.7	92%	70%

Source: Lewis M. Schneider, **The Future of the U.S. Domestic Air Freight Industry** (Boston: Harvard U., 1973).

MATS (MAC) contracts were placed by competitive negotiation in 1961 and limited to CRAF participants, to Tiger's advantage. One-year firm contracts were used, with two successive options to renew, thus covering a total of three years. CRAF participants were told that new carriers would not be solicited during the three-year term unless the exercise of options in the existing contracts failed to give adequate coverage of the requirements. Preferences were given to carriers offering turbine-powered equipment and to carriers offering expanded capacity during emergencies.[3]

Since the incipience of the CRAF, Flying Tiger Line had always committed its entire cargo fleet, and, in 1964, during the formal outbreak of the Vietnam crisis with U.S. involvement, the carrier's composite fleet included ten newly acquired CL-44Ds, augmenting the six Super-Connies. The company acquired two more CL-44D Swing-tails the following year to meet their domestic and military airlift needs. Being attuned to the opportunities provided by military contracts, Tigers well understood the advantages of maintaining a modern cargo fleet.

In 1963, CRAF noted a deficiency in its proportion of cargo aircraft within its composite fleet. MATS was also noticeably deficient in its cargo airlift capability. The situation was tenuous.

Civil Reserve Air Fleet Allocation by Aircraft and Carriers
October 1, 1965

Aircraft	Aaxico	Airlift Intl.	Alaska	American	Braniff	Capitol	Continental	Delta	Eastern	Flying Tiger	National	NWA	Pan Am	Seaboard	Slick	Southern Air	Trans Caribbean	Trans Intl	Trans World	United	World	Zantop
Intl Cargo Aircraft																						
DC-6A					1								2			4						
DC-7F				4																		
DC-7CF	1	10				8				6		3	1					3				
L-1049H			2												8							
L-1649F			2																			
CL-44		2								12				7	4		4	2		4		
DC-8F				7		1						7	13	1					7		3	
707-300C							4															
TOTAL	1	12	4	11	1	9	4			18		10	16	8	12	4	4	5	7	11	3	
Intl Passenger Aircraft																						
B-707					4	15	2					5	47						20			
DC-8								2	2		2		18					1		16		
CV-880			1																			
TOTAL			1		4	15	2	2	2		2	5	65					1	20	16		
INTL TOTAL	1	12	5	11	5	24	6	2	2	18	2	15	81	8	12	4	4	6	27	27	3	
Domestic Aircraft																						
C-46	2	5																				20
AW-650																						7
DC-7BF																					7	7
DC-6A	11									2												7
L-1049H																						
TOTAL	13	5								2											7	41
GRAND TOTAL	14	17	5	11	5	24	6	2	2	20	2	15	81	8	12	4	4	6	27	27	10	41

Source: Military Airlift, Report of Special Subcommittee on Military Airlift, House of Representatives, 89th Congress, 2nd Session, May 16, 1966.

Combination carriers were reluctant to participate in CRAF and risk their competitive position in the market place. Consequently, commercial combination carriers committed proportionately more passenger only aircraft to CRAF. The result was only about 16% of the aircraft committed to the CRAF program had cargo capability in 1963. These included only twenty-one C44-Ds and twenty-five jetliners that had the convertible configuration which was capable of transporting either passengers or cargo.[4] By 1965, the situation began to improve with FTL's recent contribution, including its commitment of twelve CL-44Ds entered into CRAF. The commitment represented over half of that modern type cargo aircraft enlisted into CRAF at the time (see CRAF Allocation graph on previous page).

On July 1, 1966, FTL formally began its Pacific Airlift Operation in support of the Vietnam crisis. Military cargo and personnel were transported from Travis and Norton AFB to Asia via the North Pacific Polar Route through Cold Bay. The carrier deployed seven CL-44Ds and four Super H Constellations.

Flying Tigers played a very colorful and encompassing role in the Vietnam airlift, providing strategic flights from the west coast of the U.S. to numerous military bases throughout the Pacific and east/southeast Asia geographic region. The commitment included not only cargo flights, but passenger flights for military personnel and their dependents.

The carrier operated ongoing "R & R (rest & recuperation)" flights to numerous popular points from the active Vietnam military front. These MAC charter flights served such points as Hong Kong, Bangkok, Hawaii, Taiwan, Singapore, the Philippines, Australia, New Zealand, Japan, and other places in the Pacific peripheral. In one of its more dramatic moves, Tigers evacuated a number of Vietnamese "political refugees" and Vietnamese company employees and their families aboard departing aircraft during the "final hours" of U.S. troop withdrawal, and impending Communist takeover in South Vietnam in 1975.

Tiger's CRAF commitments through MAC contracts entailed an extensive geographic network extending primarily from the west coast U.S. Air Force bases of Norton AFB and Travis AFB in California, and McChord AFB in Washington. The common Central Pacific route used Hickam AFB in Hawaii and territorial Guam Island as stop-over points, while the North Pacific route incorporated Cold Bay, Elmendorf AFB, or Anchorage in Alaska as stop-over points. More of the cargo flights tended to use Cold Bay, while more of the passenger flights opted to use Anchorage with more appropriate facilities. Along the Pacific peripheral area, some of the more prominent military points on Tiger's airlift system included Kadena AFB (Okinawa), Osan AFB

PRIMARY SOUTH-VIETNAMESE AIR BASES USED BY FTL

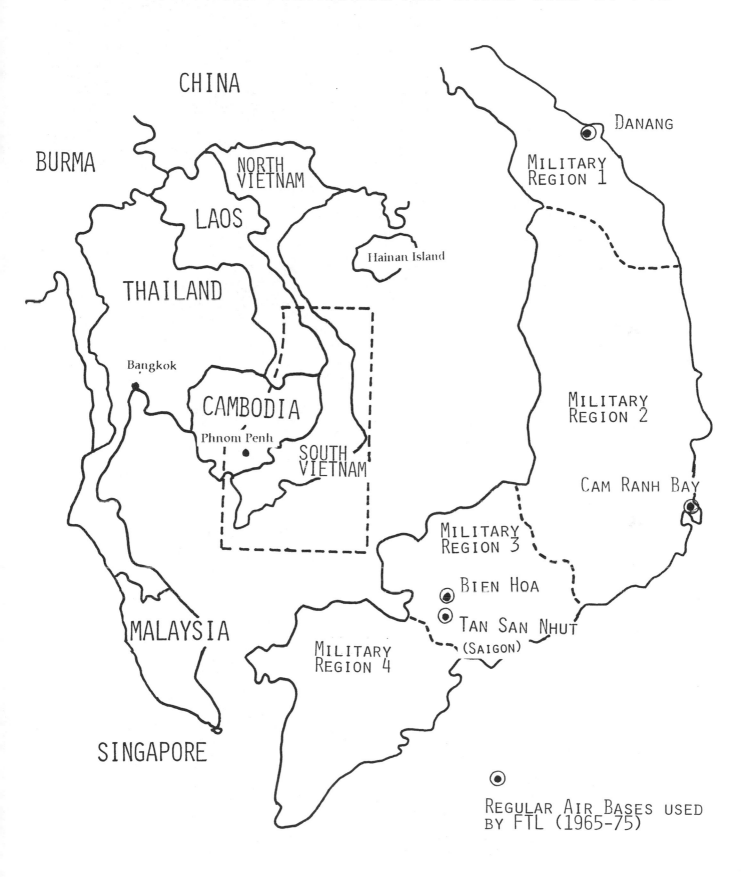

CHINA

BURMA

NORTH VIETNAM

LAOS

THAILAND

Bangkok

CAMBODIA

Phnom Penh

SOUTH VIETNAM

MALAYSIA

SINGAPORE

Hainan Island

MILITARY REGION 1

DANANG

MILITARY REGION 2

CAM RANH BAY

MILITARY REGION 3

BIEN HOA

TAN SAN NHUT (SAIGON)

MILITARY REGION 4

⊙ REGULAR AIR BASES USED BY FTL (1965-75)

For 25 years, give or take months here and there, FTL has flown not only cargo but thousands of passengers. Tigers pioneered low-cost tourist charters. Tiger planes have flown millions of military passengers. On every PAX flight were FTL flight attendants — It is to those lady Tigers, unsung heroines of past and present, this feature is dedicated.

Flying Tigers continued to fly military troops and cargo into Vietnam during the war years.

(South Korea), Tachikawa AFB and Yokota AFB (Japan), Udon and Khorat AFB (Thailand), Clark AFB (Philippines), and four primary air bases in South Vietnam. In regard to the latter, Da Nang air base served the designated Military Region 1, Cam Ranh Bay served Military Region 2, while Tan Son Nhut (Saigon) and Bien Hoa, nearby to the north, both served Military Regions 3 and 4.

Flying Tiger staffed each Vietnam air base with minimal operations and maintenance crews, while Vietnamese nationals were taught to handle Tiger's ground equipment in off-loading and loading each flight. In July, 1969, the carrier deployed its first newly-acquired DC-8-63F on the Pacific airlift route, and also the next two succeeding jetfreighters acquired on delivery. The operation and ground handling of the new jetfreighters effected quick "turn-arounds."

U.S. military personnel handled the build-up and break-down or cargo, and baggage unloaded from passenger flights. Tigers was also contracted to service a number of other commercial carrier flights. And when Tigers began operating Asian terminals along Asia-U.S. international Route 163 in 1969, they closely coordinated with the paralleling MAC movements. And, understandably, many of the FTL personnel associated with the MAC program helped set up and support the new FTL Asian stations:

> "Da Nang was the end of the line, where Flight 0043 became Flight 0044 (commercial route 163). Here Tigers provided a liftline of communication between GI's in Vietnam and their families back in the 'world.' The mail moves off the aircraft to the large mail terminal.providing service for the entire First Corp area. We handle mail for the Army, Air Force and Marine Corps, and give assistance to the Australians and Koreans as well.Nobody brings in mail like those Tiger birds."[5]

It was not uncommon to find a sack of mail strapped in an empty seat on some of the military passenger flights. Keeping the mail moving was a high priority.

Yokota AFB, the biggest USAF facility in Japan during the Vietnam era, served as Flying Tiger's hub operations within the military contract airlift system. Formally known as Tiger's Flight Planning Center, it also served as the crew change base for Tiger's MAC flights, and was a major Asian maintenance center. Yokota was conveniently located thirty miles from Tokyo's Haneda airport, and was Tiger's temporary planning center for the upstart of Route 163 commercial flights through Japan, which increased the center's activities:

"Yokota is a buzzing beehive of activity. From its $85,000 structure housing operations, administrative and maintenance staff and functions, FTL handles not only its own flights but similarly supports under contract a number of other carriers flying for MAC. There are days when we handle a dozen or more aircraft and months when the 30-day figure goes as high as 350.

The FTL people at Yokota meet all incoming charter aircraft on a strict first-come, first-served basis. And a fleet of half a dozen radio-controlled station wagons and micro-buses keeps busy shuttling Tiger and other airline crews back and forth, from aircraft to Japanese Customs and Immigration to hotels in the surrounding area. In addition, Tiger male crews are moved regularly between Yokota and Tokyo International Airport (Haneda) to comply with the daily flight schedules prepared and sent out by headquarters. Add to these the flight personnel from other airlines and the ground total can amount to as many as 250 crew members, often spread out from Yokota to Tokyo to Yokohama. The hotel woes were made even greater throughout the summer of 1970 by thousands of tourists flocking to Expo '70 (Osaka)."[6]

Flight crew change

98

Role of Flying Tiger Air Services

During a portion of the period in which Flying Tigers was involved in the Vietnam airlift, the carrier operated a subsidiary called **Flying Tiger Air Services** which operated independently under U.S. government contract, perhaps the Department of Defense. Apart from MAC operations, Tiger Air was staffed by its own assigned mechanics and operations personnel, and flown by volunteer crew members including some junior pilots contracted from the regular Flying Tiger staff. The personnel involved spent their duty in the Asia military arena.

Flying Tiger Air Services, as a support organization, operated only within the Asia-Pacific sphere serving major U.S. Air Force bases from Kadena AFB, Okinawa, to Clark AFB, in the Philippines. Much of the Tiger Air activities were associated with the Vietnam crisis, and involved military logistical support, and, for a time, were involved in servicing small overseas carriers.

Tachikawa AFB in Japan served as the primary base of operations, which also served MAC flights prior to the relocation to Yokota AFB in 1968 to accommodate Tigers' new DC-8-63F aircraft fleet. Tachikawa air base was restricted in that, at the time, it did not have jet-length required runways necessary for the "stretch DC-8s."

The intra-Asian airlift operations of Tiger Air Services was concluded in the early 1970s, it appears, and re-organized into another mission in the United States as a commercial charter subsidiary. Many of the volunteer crew members contracted with Tiger Air subsequently became regularly Flying Tiger operation pilots.

Cambodian Rice Lift, 1975

Everyday hazards confronted Tiger crews and ground staff involved in the Southeastern Asia military crisis but have never been adequately chronicled. And the closing operations and final flight drew to a very dramatic finish, specifically the Saigon evacuation effort and the Cambodian Rice Life, both occurring about the same period.

During the Rice Life to Phnom Penh, 1975, Tigers landed 176 times at Phnom Penh's Pochentong Airport amidst exploring rockets and artillery, bringing 16,687,265 pounds of rice to the people of war-weakened Cambodia. The operation lasted six weeks, until the fall of Saigon on April 12, 1975. In a **Tiger Track** article, the Flying Tigers ALPA publication, Captains Rick Kingston, Arch Hall and John Franzone recall those events:

Special Mission: Rice to Phnom Penh, Cambodia in 1975.

"The Cambodian Rice Lift was an operation custom made for Flying Tigers. In March of 1975, the Khmer Rough, under the leadership of Pol Pot, had cut off all means of surface supply to the country of Cambodia. The communists had overrun many of the outlying provincial cities and refugees by the thousands were streaming into the capitol city of Phnom Penh. There massive shortages of food and ammunition. The Cambodian people feared that the Americans would abandon them if they did not put up a valiant fight for their country. The U.S. Congress had placed limitations on direct U.S. military involvement in Southeast Asia, so a plan was devised to use 'CRAF.' In April of 1975, Flying Tigers answered the call.

Flight and ground crews volunteered to fly rice to Phnom Penh. The crews were based and the flights staged out of Saigon, South Vietnam, which had been a Tiger freight terminal for most of the Vietnam War. Those were the last days for Saigon itself as several divisions of the North Vietnamese Army had surrounded the city. The mission was straight-forward; depart Saigon, fly the 45 minutes to Phnom Penh, land and unload 18 pallet positions of rice. Depart Phnom Penh empty for the return to Saigon to pick up another load. The trip sequence seems innocuous enough, but set against the backdrop of conflict in the region, it would take all of the 'can do' spirit the Tigers could muster.

The flight departed Saigon, often taking enemy fire

shortly after takeoff. Enroute to Phnom Penh, the crew would don flack jackets and steel pot helmets as the Khmer Rough had truck mounted quad 12.7mm guns and rockets placed in the vicinity of the airport. The approach to Phnom Penh was often hampered by cloud cover and a lack of navigational aids. Just about the time the airplane flared, rockets would be launched from enemy positions toward the airport. Several would usually explode on or near the runway, scattering shrapnell in all directions.

Old Cambodians would crawl out of fox holes and push their wheelbarrows along the runway, filling the rocket holes with stones. Old women, their hands tied with rags, would gather up the hot pieces of shrapnel to protect the tires. The number 3 and 4 engines were left running during the entire offload which usually took less than 20 minutes.

The operation lasted about six weeks, much longer than the three days that some of the military advisors had figured initially. Quite frankly, the Air Force supervisors of the CRAF program were not sure that Tigers would be able to operate so 'close to the edge,' far removed from the type of flying we engaged in normally. The 17 million pounds of rice that Tigers hauled was proof positive that CRAF worked and we helped set a new standard for what could be expected of companies like Flying Tigers during times of military need. Each of the crew members who participated in the operation was issued a Certificate of Recognition and Appreciation by the U.S. Air Force Military Airlift Command.

All of the 'can do' spirit in the world couldn't help the Cambodians. On April 12, 1975, the Khmer Rough overran Phnom Penh. The result was the beginning of an ugly four year period of genocide which has been chronicled in films such as **The Killing Fields**. By some estimates, almost 30 million Cambodians were murdered. It struck home for many of the Flying Tiger crews when they learned that the ground support people who had done such a fine job at the Phnom Penh airport were all beheaded shortly after the city was invaded.

Our crews continued to fly out of Saigon for another couple of weeks until that fateful day at the end of April when Saigon itself was invaded by the communists. This time, the 'final alert' for the Tiger crews was not given by telephone. Instead, the final alert was Bing Crosby's rendition of **White Christmas** blaring out over every radio in Saigon.   The song **White Christmas** had been pre-arranged by the U.S. Command as the signal to commence '**Operation Eagle Pull**,' the code name for the evacuation of Saigon.

Viewed from our present day vantage point, the Rice Lift stands out as a significant event in the history of our Company.   In the proud tradition of General Claire Chennault's AVG and under the watchful eye of founder Bob Prescott, the Flying Tigers had once again set the standard as the world's leading airfreight airline.   As we look toward the future, we can all be justifiably proud of our heritage as Flying Tigers."[7]

Notes

1. Stanley H. Brewer, **Military Airlift and Its Relationship to the Commercial Air Cargo Industry** (Seattle: UW Grad School of usiness Administration, 1967) p. x.

2. Ibid., p. 48.

3. Ibid., p. 34, citing testimony of Robert H. Charles, Asst. Sec. of the Air Force at Military Airlift hearings.

4. bid., p. 25.

5. **Tigereview**, "The Wide Wide World of Operations Services," Vol. 24, No. 6, Dec.-Jan., 1970-71, and **Tigereview**, "Tiger Country - Tigers in Da Nang," Vol. 25, No. 1, Feb., 1971, p. 14.

6. **Tigereview**, Vol. 25, No. 1, Feb., 1971, p. 14.

7. Captain Rick Kingston, "People, Planes & Phnom Penh," **Tiger Tracks** (Los Angeles, FTL MEC) March, 1989, pp. 3, 9-11.

6

Catalyst for International Expansion:
Pacific Rim Route 163

Meaningful insight into the aviation history of Flying Tiger Line should incorporate a study of the geographic expansion of the carrier into a broader scope and greater depth in both domestic and international air freight markets, and, as a supportive adjunct, the role of upgrading cargo aircraft fleet, which has necessarily been instrumental in the airline's general growth pattern. As such, measured in those terms, the significance of developments which occurred in 1969 may be perceived as **highlight benchmarks** in establishing Flying Tigers as a successful air cargo enterprise.

The company received CAB certification, on a temporary basis, for Asia-U.S. Route 163, allowing the carrier to capitalize upon and dominate the increasingly lucrative Pacific Rim import business in air cargo. In an unofficial capacity, Tigers became the U.S. all-cargo flag carrier in the Pacific, as the counter-part to Seaboard serving as the U.S. all-cargo flag carrier in the north Atlantic. Consequently, since the inception of Tigers in the air freight core business, common-carriage finally became exceptionally profitably because of the Asia-North American air cargo markets.

As a corollary, by the end of 1969, the company had placed in operation primarily a single-type aircraft fleet consisting of seventeen DC-8-63F jetfreighters, the most efficient cargo jet of medium-to-long range routes in commercial use at the time.

Furthermore, the company invested heavily in the upgrade of its domestic facilities and equipment, and, subsequently, embarked on an ambitious program to open new terminal services on its Asia route, and establish plans to invest in other corporate interests.

Flying Tigers has long held an interest in servicing the Pacific rim region. It was a logical extension relating to its continuous service in the military Pacific airlift. In January 8, 1959, the company filed with the CAB to be certified for trans-Pacific route as an end-on-end junction with the airline's domestic and transcontinental route. Once again in 1965, Tigers sought CAB authority to operate between the U.S., Hawaii, Wake Island, Guam, Okinawa, Japan, Taiwan, Hong Kong, Phillipines, Thailand, and Vietnam. The central Pacific routing following the traffic lanes set forth during the WWII and Korean conflict periods, as well as consideration for the north Pacific routing. Flying Tigers **spreading its wings** across the Pacific and Asia would be, at the time of the Vietnam crisis, a logical complement to its MATS (MAC) commitment in the Pacific airlift by providing substantial backhaul opportunities.

U.S. imports from the Pacific rim countries grew at an average rate of 58% per year from 1962 through 1966; at 40% per year from 1966 to 1971; and at 16% per year from 1971 to 1976. However, unlike the transatlantic market, the transpacific market had an imbalance in favor of eastbound direction due to a higher demand for U.S. imports, with a trade imbalance ratio beginning to reverse in trend only during the most recent times. In 1962, the U.S. transpacific market for scheduled airfreight traffic represented 2% of the world total, increasing to 13% by 1977.[1] Understanding the potential for all-cargo service in the Pacific rim, historical roots and geographic inertia would bring Flying Tigers to its international geographic domain of Asia.

U.S. Transpacific Airfreight History

| Year | U.S. Exports | | U.S. Imports | |
	Tons	% Growth	Tons	% Growth
1966	13,034		17,102	
1967	18,806	44.3	23,693	38.5
1968	22,969	22.1	34,946	47.5
1969	33,303	45.0	48,772	39.6
1970	41,758	25.4	56,201	15.2
1971	48,153	15.3	92,329	64.3
1972	60,926	26.5	106,334	15.2
1973	92,032	51.1	107,488	1.1
1974	98,687	7.2	109,019	1.4
1975	77,973	(21.0)	155,200	42.3
1976	84,586	8.5	197,240	27.1

Source: U.S. Dept. of Commerce, Bureau of the Census, "U.S. Exports /World and U.S. General Imports/World Area by Commodity Groupings," **Reports FT 455 and FT 155** (1978).

Besides Tigers, in 1969, two other U.S.-based all-cargo carriers demonstrated a strong interest in the trans-Pacific route, namely Seaboard World Airlines and Airlift International. Airlift, who had changed its name from Riddle in 1963, acquired Slick's assets and routes in 1968, continuing the southern transcontinental system. All three cargo lines had invested heavily in military contracts during the 1960s, and, thus, entertained the prospect of enjoying a profitable backhaul in an Asian-U.S. network. And, rightly so, as Flying Tigers Asia has always proven to be profitable.

Individual carrier projections for the future of Pacific airfreight were noted:

(tons)

Carrier	1965 base	1970 forecast	% increase
Airlift - high	24,527	290,914	1,086
Airlift - low	20,118	156,726	539
Northwest	18,686	80,000	328
Pan American	21,499	157,169	631
Seaboard	24,058	122,149	324
Trans World	19,095	206,000	978
Western	22,347	246,857	1,004
Flying Tigers	22,230	425,684	1,814

Source: CAB, "Transpacific Route Investigation," Vol. 51, June- July, 1969, **Docket 16242, adopted July 21, 1969**, pp. 480-481.

Acquiring cargo flight rights into the various Asian countries using the shorter Great Circle Route was quite an accomplishment for the Flying Tiger Line. The process required lengthy and difficult negotiations between the U.S. Department of State, the CAB, Flying Tiger officials, and international delegations, on a country-to-country basis. The Flying Tiger entourage was led by Madame Anna Chennault, the widow of General Chennault, the company's VP of International Affairs, who demonstrated her high degree of influence and negotiating skills. Rather than pursuing the island-hopping central Pacific route, which some CAB members felt was already adequately served, FTL eagerly sought the shorter Great Circle arc route with Japan and the Pacific Northwest as the prime pivotal points of that system. For a measurable length of time, Northwest Airlines had become the only competitive air carrier on that scheduled route, as, historically, it was their domain.

Subsequently, Flying Tiger Line was awarded a temporary five-year certificate for Route 163, authorizing the air transportation of property and nonsubsidy mail between the co-terminal points of Boston, Newark/New York, Philadelphia, Cleveland, Detroit, Chicago, Seattle/Tacoma, Portland, Oregon, San Francisco/Oakland/San Jose, and Los Angeles/Ontario/Long Beach, and intermediate points within the Asian countries of Japan, Korea, Okinawa, Taiwan, Hong Kong, the Philippines, Vietnam, and Thailand. The effective date of the certificate was May 28, 1969.

Of significance, Tigers was not authorized Anchorage as a common-carriage point on its route, and resorted to use Cold Bay, Alaska, as a regular fuel stop point. Northwest retained its position as the only scheduled U.S.-based carrier with commercial rights into Anchorage on the Great Circle route. Pan Am served Fairbanks from the California gateways on its route to Asia at the time.

It is also interesting to note that although Tigers did not actively solicit authorization for an additional central Pacific all-cargo route, the CAB did consider the need of all-cargo service via Hawaii, with Tigers being the prime candidate carrier. However, the decision was made that projected volumes of airfreight traffic for the region did not warrant the initiation o;f all-cargo service by a U.S.-flag all- cargo carrier at the time, but would be reconsidered during the future renewal hearings for Route 163. In their proposal, at the time, Tigers did offer to run a single weekly flight via Hawaii and Guam, "on which it expected to lose money but proposed to operate for public service reasons," which, for economic reasons, the CAB denied.[2]

Northwest Orient Airlines had operated the north Pacific air route since 1946, being the "select instrument" by the CAB for that domain, while Pan American Airlines was the "select instrument" for the central and south Pacific air routes, as well as other

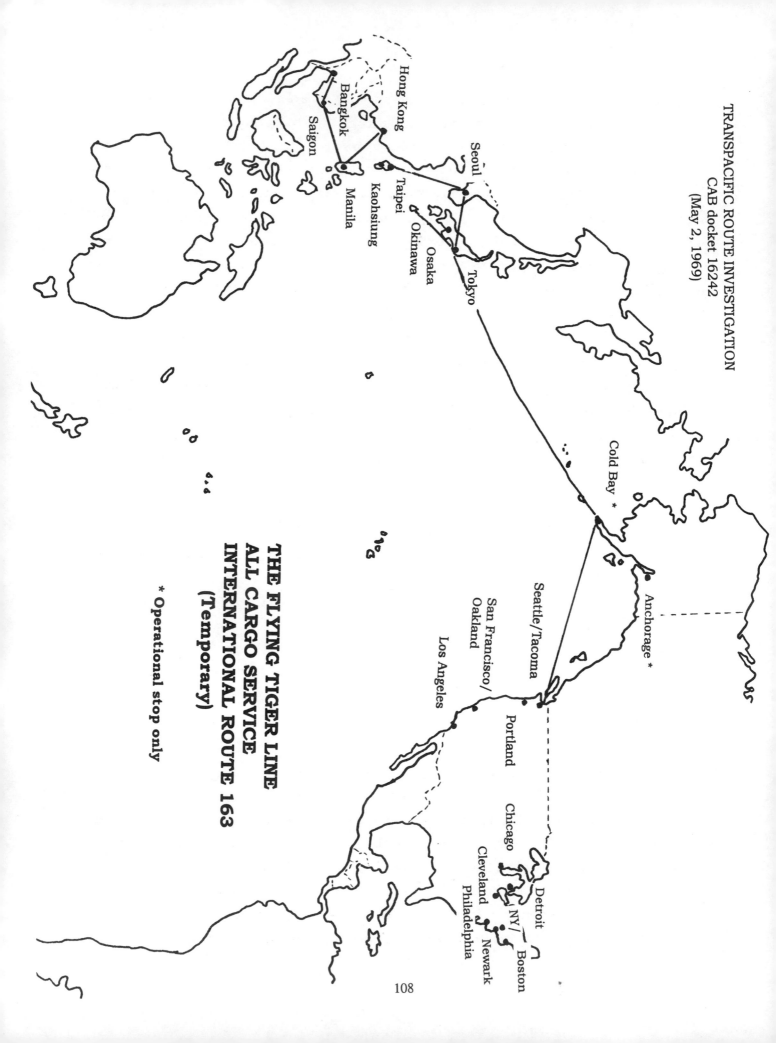

TRANSPACIFIC ROUTE INVESTIGATION
CAB docket 16242
(May 2, 1969)

THE FLYING TIGER LINE
ALL CARGO SERVICE
INTERNATIONAL ROUTE 163
(Temporary)

* Operational stop only

Hong Kong
Bangkok
Saigon
Manila
Kaohsiung
Taipei
Okinawa
Osaka
Seoul
Tokyo
Cold Bay *
Anchorage *
Seattle/Tacoma
San Francisco/
Oakland
Los Angeles
Portland
Chicago
Cleveland
Philadelphia
Detroit
NY/
Newark
Boston

108

numerous international air routes established throughout many parts of the world. However, Northwest provided what the CAB perceived as nominal and inadequate all-cargo service for the Asia-U.S. segment since it was instituted in 1967, which, consequently, prompted the CAB to select a U.S.-based all-cargo carrier for projected Route 163. Northwest Airlines, it may be suggested, did not meet the growing needs of Asian imports air cargo and protect U.S. aviation interests. In the contesting milieu, Flying Tigers was selected over Seaboard and Airlift by virtue of (1) its better financial position, (2) being the largest of the all-cargo carriers with a new fleet of jetfreighters, (3) being based on the west coast, (4) having acceptable proposed rates, (5) having a more compatible U.S. Route 100 linking with ten major cities, including a "satellite" feeder line into California, and (6) having in its proposal an emphasis on a Northwest gateway orientation along the Great Circle route.

In addressing the inequity in air service for the Pacific Northwest where a definite need was projected, a highly acclaimed regional study provided to the CAB noted the dominance of the California gateways in access to and from the Pacific regions. At that time, Seattle/Tacoma airport, the hub of the Pacific Northwest, was served by only two transcontinental air carriers as compared with six for San Francisco and seven for Los Angeles, as transcontinental co-terminal points.

Internationally, the inbalance in air service and authorization between the California and Pacific Northwest air gateways was even more dramatic. Seattle/Tacoma was served by only two U.S.-flag international air carriers, Northwest and Pan Am, but those carriers provided little trans-Pacific service in comparison with foreign-flag and U.S. international operators serving the major California gateways. By contrast, the principal air carriers of Japan, the United Kingdom, India, Australia, New Zealand, the Philippine Republic, France, Thailand, Brazil, and the Republic of China were operating or were authorized to provide air services between San Francisco and/or Los Angeles and the Pacific area countries on a scheduled basis.[3]

Furthermore, even foreign air carriers did not show a strong interest to serve Seattle/Tacoma on their Pacific routes. In 1958, Korean (National) Airlines was the only foreign air carrier authorized to operate between Seattle/Tacoma and Pacific points, yet that carrier did not exercise its rights. On March 30, 1959, a foreign air carrier permit of Japan Airlines was amended to allow a Japan-Seattle route. However, the Seattle route was operated only briefly soon after the award.

From a larger perspective, during 1960 and 1961, in the first round of the decade-long trans-Pacific cases, the CAB recommendations reflected concern over U.S. "open policy" which created a multiplication of foreign carrier rights to U.S. gateways from the Pacific area. International route approval involving U.S. territory required the final approval of the President, besides CAB recommendations. In 1961, he disapproved the majority of the Board's recommendation in the Pacific case, thus retaining Pan Am and Northwest as the only "select instruments" of the U.S. in the Pacific region under an area rather point-to-point authority. No U.S.-flag carrier all-cargo service was offered, although the CAB recommended a possible Flying Tiger central Pacific all-cargo route. At the time, of special concern to the President was our diplomatic view toward Japan, whose international airline was just receiving the opportunity to come into its own with the introduction of long-range jet aircraft. Duplication of U.S. flag-service over routes which they too operated would certainly threaten their newly found profits, especially with the U.S.-Orient market being a relatively unpredictable entity.[4]

By 1969, the sentiments had shifted and economic insights justified instituting a U.S.-flag all-cargo carrier service on a regular scheduled basis. Newly inaugurated President Nixon gave final approval of Route 163 to Flying Tigers. Being awarded the international route, it may be speculated that Tigers had a commitment to the CAB to provide regular air cargo service through Seattle/Tacoma on the Asia-U.S. route. The company responded by providing scheduled service up the west coast, as it had proposed, co-ordinating with the Chicago hub flight carrying an assemblage of transload freight and mail, then flying the Great Circle route to Tokyo and other Asian points via Alaska. Anchorage and Cold Bay, which was situated on the peninsula 650 miles southwest of Anchorage, were used by Tigers as optional refueling points, depending on the need of any particular flight. Thus, flights with heavier loads, whether westbound or eastbound, were allowed to make a double stop for extra refueling between Seattle and Tokyo. Considering the new extensive Tiger network, loading the aircraft for "down line" convenience became exceptionally important.

The inaugural flight for Route 163 took place in September, 1969, originating in Los Angeles, then proceeding through San Francisco and Seattle, and reaching the Asia points via Anchorage. Route 163's Asian pivotal point or hub was Haneda airport in Tokyo, and it was shortly thereafter that the Japanese government adopted airport "slot times," to accommodate the newly instituted curfew hours at Haneda to address the "jet noise" problem. The other Asia points on the early route included Naha (Okinawa), Taipei (Taiwan), Hong Kong, and Seoul (Korea). At the time, the company also had plans to begin service to Osaka (Japan), and, subsequently, to Manila (Philippines), and Bangkok (Thailand). Tigers had also applied for permission to add service to Singapore, Malaysia, and Anchorage as part of International Route 163, and to add

Loading DC-8 in Tokyo

Miami and Puerto Rico to domestic Route 100, as new co-terminals.

The complexities in the implementation of Route 163 was expressed by George Zettler, Tigers' VP of Asian Operations after the first four years of Asia service:

> "At the beginning of this adventure, all of us who made up the initial work force in Asia went through intensive and somewhat painful learning period. Everything happened very fast. We began service in six countries virtually simultaneously. In each country, we had to become acquainted with government regulations and the mechanics of getting freight moved between countries.
>
> Our operations were handicapped by lack of facilities. We were working with airport limitations and a group of new personnel -many of whom never had worked in the field of air cargo before.
>
> In addition, we were faced with the communications problem. While virtually all of our personnel here in Asia speak English, most of us from the States knew only English. The burden of communication, therefore, fell on our indigenous personnel, who had to cope not only with the considerable problems of technical matters and complex tariff and customs regulations, but with translation. And in stressful situations, communications can be a problem.
>
> Gradually, however, things settled down as our scheduling of flights and our ability to handle documentation evolved."[5]

As Flying Tigers "spread its wings" to Asia, leased, new or improved facilities were acquired for the start-up of scheduled international operations. Local temporary arrangements were improvised as needed. Eventually, new ground facilities and equipment were opened at Tokyo, Osaka, Hong Kong, Seoul, and Taipei during 1971. Ground breaking ceremonies at the Haneda terminal facilities took place on November 18, 1970, and construction was completed by May 4, 1971, to accommodate the first Tiger flight worked on Route 163 at the new terminal. Before that time, Tokyo Tigers had worked in JAL leased quarters, and Tiger's flight planning center was located at Yokota AFB thirty miles away, which also served as the crew change base for the company's MAC flights. The new Haneda facilities comprised of a two-story structure including a 4250 sq. ft. warehouse, and a 940 sq. ft. mezzanine area serving as the new flight dispatch operations office which moved from Yokota to handle the commercial flights. At Haneda, All Nippon Airline personnel performed the loading and unloading of the Tiger aircraft at that time.

Tiger service began to Osaka, Japan, in March of 1970 with one flight a week, increasing to three flights a week the following year. Asia common-carriage volumes and revenues skyrocketed with a year of operation on Route 163, the impact was immediate. In 1972, Flying Tigers began service to Bangkok and Manila on its scheduled international route. The same year, the company also applied to the CAB for permanent certification of international Route 163, with added service proposed to Singapore, Malaysia, Jakarta (Indonesia), and Anchorage, to link with domestic Route 100.

When Tigers started flying Route 163 in 1969, it scheduled two flights weekly in to Taipei, and increased its market share so that by 1973, the company scheduled eleven flights weekly to that export region. The carrier also began scheduled service to Kaohsiung, Taiwan, on August 3, 1973, offering the only air cargo service to that area for its growing export trade products. The industrial port city of Kaohsiung is located in the southwestern part of the island, being a free trade zone characterized by no customs duties, and no commodity or sales taxes.

When Okinawa reverted to Japanese control on May 14, 1972, Flying Tigers was the first commercial aircraft to land at the new Japanese prefecture, the Naha airport. According to the CAB, Okinawa was offered on Route 163 to provide regularly scheduled service to the U.S. military installations, as the Pacific airlift was inter-twined with Route 163. Kadena AFB was Naha's alternate airport. It may also be noted that Tiger charter representatives and those based at Asia military charter points were very much instrumental in helping set up the new FTL air cargo operations at the various Asian terminals.

Tigers operated two flights a week to Manila during their early international operations, and operated a Seoul flight on a once-a-week basis in 1969, increasing to five times a week by 1972. The Republic of South Korea, devastated from the Korean conflict, and, historically, over-shadowed by the Japanese, re-oriented its economic base from primarily agriculture to a stronger emphasis on international trade with support and orientation towards the U.S.

The industrial crown colony of Hong Kong, a historical trade center, developed a strong export economic base, especially after 1949 when the Communists controlled mainland China. At that time, many entrepreneurs fled to Hong Kong, as they did Taiwan, and strengthened the existing import-export base, still recovering from the ravages of WWII. Hong Kong became an important integral part of Tiger's Route 163, servicing daily flights of textiles, clothes, toys, electronic goods, plastic goods, and other popular "expendables" destined for North American markets, and, to a lesser extent, European markets via Tiger Interline traffic systems.

Flying Tigers' stretched DC-8-63F on approach to Hong Kong.

Opening Route 163 increased Tigers' revenue base multi-fold:

Flying Tiger Income Accounts
(data in millions)

Year	Dom. common Carriage income	Intl common carriage	MAC	Equipment leasing	Other
	(000)	(000)	(000)	(000)	(000)
1969	$22,467	$13,102	$49,386	-----	$11,938
1970	30,497	57,314	30,629	-----	7,071
1971	39,228	66,467	34,091	$60,093	9,671
1972	48,802	77,610	32,862	86,482	11,455
1973	71,998	84,711	15,579	107,571	12,383
1974	73,772	95,811	15,148	137,184	16,038
1975	73,191	119,368	22,590	150,013	24,783
1976	87,323	141,131	19,753	157,646	24,767

Source: Compilation from Company Annual Reports

Tigers also started scheduled commercial flights into Saigon on August 9, 1973. The flight rights may have been tentative during this period of U.S. troop withdrawal. It may be noted that in 1966, the South Vietnam government canceled Pan Am's landing rights in to Saigon without prior notice in support of demands for a bilateral agreement with the United States which would permit Air Vietnam to operate trans-Pacific service to the U.S.[6] Eventually, Flying Tigers discontinued service to Saigon and Bangkok in 1975, when the U.S. military role in Vietnam ended. In 1973, the carrier also provided service to Singapore and Malaysia through an interline agreement with Singapore Airlines.

The interline agreement was a logical outgrowth of Tiger's expansion plan developed earlier. In 1969, the company expanded its **Skyroad, Sea-Air**, and interline shipping programs to provide service to and from virtually any of the air freight markets world-wide. In the domestic marketplace, Tigers' Skyroad provided combination air-truck service, with through rates and single carrier responsibility, to areas distant from airport terminal cities. Sea-Air, under special tariff approved by the CAB, combined ocean with air service, giving international shipper an alternate means of transport between Asia and the U.S., Europe, and Africa. In addition, the company had interline agreements with some ninety airlines throughout the world.

The enormous increase in flight activity and common-carriage traffic during 1969 and the early 1970s served as an impetus to modernize terminal facilities and ground handling, and to increase staffing in the domestic route system as well. In 1970, in conjuncture with scheduled Asia service, Flying Tigers provided daily scheduled airfreight service between Los Angeles, San Francisco, Portland, Seattle, Milwaukee, Chicago, Detroit, Cleveland, Buffalo, Syracuse, Binghamton, Hartford, Boston, New York, Newark, and Philadelphia. On a selective basis, the needs of terminal upgrading depended upon individual station flight activity, freight volumes, and services provided, and, of course, property investment opportunities.

During 1969, as part of the expansion program, the Los Angeles and San Francisco freight terminals doubled their available space. San Francisco's facilities comprised of a double-sided Pan Am hangar, probably built during the WWII period. One side housed the maintenance and crew supply section, and was large enough to accommodate a DC-8-63F loading operation under cover. In Detroit, a $2.25 million facility was constructed. In New York, a $1.2 million freight distribution and processing center for international air cargo was designed and built off-airport on 150th Street to alleviate Tiger's problem of operating at JFK's limited-space facilities. The new building included a 60,000 sq. ft. warehouse. Space was trebled at Boston, and

FTL San Francisco back ramp

substantially increased at Newark. JFK Tigers had established their separate facilities and flights, apart from Newark, since November, 1964, and had become an east coast international gateway.

In September, 1972, the company announced plans to construct a new $6.4 million air cargo terminal at JFK, encompassing a 90,250 sq. ft. warehouse and office space on a 10-acre site. In April of that year, the company started to build a new $2.5 million, 104,000 sq. ft. building at Los Angeles, adjacent to the then existing headquarters. The ten-story structure was completed about a year later, serving as the new World Headquarters (7401 World Way West), and as headquarters for its subsidiary, Flying Tiger Line, Inc. The building was known as **Hi Tiger**, as opposed to the older and lower adjoining structure.

Initiation of Flying Tiger Corporation

For a decade or better, the business investments of the newly-formed Corporation proved to be extremely profitable, especially equipment leasing which, according to its proportionate financial contribution, over-shadowed even the growing international air cargo revenues.

Drawing on his railroad experience, Corporation Chairman Wayne Hoffman embarked on a program to improve the tax posture and diversify the financial base of the company by acquiring business interests that would provide steady revenue to offset the cyclic (seasonal) nature of the air freight business. The vehicle of plan began with a rail car leasing firm, whose stock price in a depressed stock market was extremely attractive.

In July, 1970, in anticipation of a "take-over," Flying Tiger Line acquired 520,000 common shares, which was equivalent to about 15% of North American Car Corporation of Chicago Ridge. NAC was purportedly engaged in the business of leasing modern, highly specialized railroad equipment in the U.S. and Canada. The firm owned 25,000 rail cars. Situated on a 128-acre tract outside Chicago proper, NAC's assembly and repair facility occupied about sixty-six acres. At the time of NAC's merger in to Flying Tiger Corporation in January, 1971, the former enjoyed revenues of about $50 million annually, with assets of about $300 million, and, over a period of more than sixty years, had never experienced a single year in the "red." Like Flying Tigers, it was a leader in its field.

In sequence, on October 8, 1971, Flying Tiger Corporation acquired National Equipment Rental, Ltd., through the subsidiary, the NAC. National Equipment was

"Hi-Tiger" headquarters building at L.A. International Airport. Original lower building at left and maintenance hangar in rear.

118

engaged in leasing office equipment, computers and aircraft, including two Boeing 737s and two Lockheed L-100-20s leased to Pacific Western Airlines of Canada. The flirtation of acquiring transportation-related investments bolstered the business financial portfolio in the early years. NAC's annual income (revenue) climbed from $60 million in 1971 to $150 million in 1975; then $201 million in 1977, and $308 million in 1980. Low capital investment and low labor costs as compared to the airline characterized the attractive features of NAC during the early years of acquisition. But the good cash flow from the Pacific and MAC business afforded Flying Tiger Line the enviable position as having the sixth best debt/equity ratio (1.72/1) among the U.S. trunks.[7]

In another related Corporation acquisition, on June 21, 1971, the CAB tentatively approved the Flying Tiger Corporation control of Flying Tiger Line, the certificated all-cargo carrier, and Tiger Leasing Corporation, which proposed to engage in aircraft leasing transactions. The general move was a part of the Flying Tiger Corporation re-organization seeking CAB approval. Tiger Leasing was a wholly owned subsidiary of FTC, organized on July 30, 1970, for the primary purpose of leasing real and personal property. In addition, the subsidiary indicated that it would engage in the ownership and leasing of air and surface shipment containers, railroad cars, and other transportation-related equipment. Categorically, Tiger Leasing's operation involved aeronautics, therefore, required CAB approval in the re-organization effort.

The CAB order tentatively approved the transfer of a DC-8-63F aircraft to Tiger Leasing from Flying Tiger Air Services, Inc., which, in turn, would transfer the same aircraft to Flying Tiger Line. However, the CAB stated qualifying restrictions to prevent the development of a monopolistic transportation conglomerate in its order: "Flying Tiger Corporation, Tiger Investment, Flying Tiger Air Services, Inc., or any other company within the existing FTC system of affiliates and subsidiaries shall not in any calendar year, and without Board approval, either individually or jointly enter into any intercompany transactions with or affecting New Tiger which will have an aggregate value of $100,000 or more."[8] Thus, Flying Tiger's overture to incorporate a viable network of transportation modes to support the cargo airline was formally restricted. However, the carrier developed tremendous growth opportunities within itself.

Notes

1. Nawal Taneja, **The U.S. Airfreight Industry** (Lexington: D.C. Heath, 1976) pp. 90-91.

2. CAB, "Transpacific Route Investigation," **Docket 16242, Vol. 51, June-July, 1969** (adopted July 21, 1969) pp. 307-8.

3. The Washington Parties, "Building the Seattle-Tacoma Air Gateway," under the direction of Prof. Stanley H. Brewer (Seattle: University of Washington) July, 1968. This study was submitted to CAB during "Transpacific Route Investigation" hearings.

4. John Vernon Woolley, **Development of Aviation in the Pacific** (Seattle: unpublished M.A. thesis, 1969) p. 52.

5. **Tigereview**, June, 1972, p. 21.

6. Marylin Bender and Selig Altschul, **The Chosen Instrument: The Rise and Fall of an American Entrepreneur** (New York: Simon and Schuster, 1982).

7. James P. Woolsey, "Flying Tiger Line Gains Financial Stability After Years of Struggle as Pioneer All-Cargo Airline," **Air Transport World**, June, 1972, pp. 18-21.

8. CAB Reports, Vol. 57, June-August, 1971, pp. 668-672.

7

Flying Tiger B747F Freightmasters
and the Great Leap Forward

During the mid-1970s, the introduction of the wide-body 38-position Boeing 747F Freightmaster into the Flying Tiger fleet, coupled with the abrupt end of the Vietnam airlift requirement led to the re-deployment of some DC-8-63Fs to the domestic and commercial charter service assignments. However, the deployment of B747Fs supplemented by the DC-8 jetfreighters provided a formidable combination on the Asia-U.S. route, bringing a new dimension to the Tiger network, increasing capacity and frequency of long range flights. As a positive by-product, the increase in capacity relative to other CRAF participants, led to Tigers' increase share in MAC contracts.

On the other hand, the airline faced a serious dilemma in regard to expanding its domestic system. With the increase in aircraft equipment combination available for scheduled common-carriage, there was perceived an urgent need to expand the domestic network and provide more and better services to accommodate the newly-found capacity and meet changing customer needs, especially the carrier's best domestic customers, the air freight forwarders. Yet, Tigers was "saddled" by CAB constraints in route development.

The 1973-74 worldwide oil embargo, or semblance thereof, had a significant adverse effect on Flying Tigers, as it did to all the airlines. As an item of negotiation, the availability of aviation fuel became "spotty" while the prices skyrocketed. The existing high capital investments on terminal costs, jetfreighter acquisition, ground equipment upgrading, and increased staffing expenses came to the forefront. Understandably, after a re-assessment, the problems led to an immediate "belt tightening" systemwide. In fact, with the fuel crisis and ensuing recession which followed, Tigers curtailed some domestic services, and explored alternate trucking supplements until business, economic and operational controls were restored. Fortunately, the economic problems forced upon Tigers was partially absorbed by the continuous increase in common carriage revenues on the Asia route and, for the duration, dependable MAC contract profits. From 1969 to 1976, for example, Tigers' domestic revenues increased four-fold while its international revenues more than doubled.

In light of such circumstances, Flying Tigers had made a prior commitment with American Airlines and the Boeing Company for the passenger to cargo conversion and delivery of two B747-100F **Freightmasters** in late 1974 and early 1975. On July 22, 1975, Tigers took delivery of a third B747-100F converted,[1] and acquired three more in 1977, finally ordering two new B747-200F series for 1979.

For the Flying Tiger Line, the acquisition upgrade to the B747 cargo aircraft proved, in short time, a "great leap forward" in fleet capacity and route schedule flexibility so badly needed with the upsurge of Asian imports. The wide-bodies were quickly deployed in the extended routing encircling Asia and the major U.S. markets including New York, Chicago, Seattle, and adjoining the California points.

It may cause one to wonder if such a large cargo aircraft was even imaginable in the mind of Prescott and his group a decade earlier in time. The B747 was developed from the Boeing C5A project during the mid-1960s, and supported by an agreement between Pan Am and the Boeing Aircraft Company.

Accepting FTL's first B747 Freightmaster, with
Chairman Wayne Hoffman and engineering
personnel in Wichita, Kansas, in 1974.

The first acceptance of the B747 as a freighter was acknowledged by a foreign carrier on its New York-Frankfurt route, with considerable foresight:

> "In the face of almost unanimous industry skepticism, Lufthansa German Airlines took delivery of the first wide body freighter and placed it in service April 19, 1972. For more than two years, 'The Red Baron' shuttled across the Atlantic carrying unprecedented payloads and attracting significant quantities of 'oversize' load units that could not previously go by air. As early as 1973, the first eight-foot by eight-foot, forty-foot long Sea-Land containers was airlifted across the Atlantic."[2]

Orders for B747 Freightmasters were slow because of perceived economic feasibility, financial limitations, airport restrictions and various other reasons. By 1974, Boeing had received firms orders for additional all-freight superjets from only World Airways and Air France, and tentative orders from Japan Air Lines (JAL).
Supplemental carriers were ordering wide-body models with a convertible passenger and/or cargo configuration as an effort to increase aircraft flexibility.[3] Of direct consequence to Flying Tigers, in 1976, Northwest Airlines operated one daily round trip to Tokyo with the B747 combination aircraft and deployed an additional two westbound flights a week with B747 freighters. At that time, JAL operated 23 flights per

week between Anchorage and Tokyo employing a variety of freighter and combination equipment.[4] Flying Tigers acquired converted B747-100s on their first orders, purchasing five and leasing one of the Freightmasters.

Subsequently, the B747 Freightmasters became Tigers' international route "work horse," while the DC-8-63Fs became the carrier's domestic system "work horse," supplementing one another on long hauls. Assuming complementary roles, the DC-8-63F was a $12 million capital investment, not including $1.5 million in additional spare parts. In comparison, the B747-100F cargo aircraft reportedly had a lift capacity of over 200,000 lbs., traveled at a cruise speed of 575 mph, and had a maximum range of 3744 nautical miles with a full containerized load of freight. However, originally designed as passenger aircraft, the B747-100 Freightmaster conversion series did not have "nose load" capability.

Based on the direct operating cost of the B747 Freightmaster, the total cost per cargo ton-mile was 5.00, which, in effect, was more than 166% cost efficient than the DC-8-63F. The cost reductions had come as a direct result of the interaction of lift capability and flying costs. Based on a comparative cost analysis by a business transportation authority, moving cargo in the turbo prop-powered CL-44D cost 6.71 cent per available ton-mile, while DC-8-63F and B707-320C costs were estimated to be 3.66 cents per available ton-mile. A potential of 2.75 cents per ton-mile was projected for the B747 Freightmaster.[5]

The following table compares the specifications of turbo-prop, and jetfreighters commonly employed by Flying Tigers since the 1960s:

Type of Plan	Best Cruise Cargo Capacity	Speed (mph)	Maximum Range
CL-44D	65,000 lbs.	386	3450 miles
B727 freighter	46,000	523	3500
B707-320C	96,800	532	7440
DC-8F	195,124	544	8720
DC-8-63F	106,400	555	7000
B747-200F	257,858	625	7475

Source: Aviation Week and Space Technology, March 10, 1969.

The Plane Truth About Our Growth

From Conestoga To 747

Back in '45, when Flying Tigers started, we knew the business world would be looking to the skies for faster, more reliable freight service. We also knew that this kind of service could not be achieved without the right people and the right equipment.

Our people were experts with years of military airfreight experience. We needed to support them with equipment designed to insure our goal – reliable airfreight service.

The Budd Conestoga was our first aircraft. It looked like a flying boxcar, carried 7,000 lbs. of freight at 150 m.p.h. and had a range of about 500 miles.

Next came the C-47, followed by the C-54, C-46, DC-6A and Super-Constellation. Our Canadair CL-44 was the first turbine-powered freighter aircraft ever placed into commercial service. Its "swingtail"

design and 65,000 lb. capacity moved Flying Tigers into the No. 1 spot as an all-cargo airline.

The jet age came to Flying Tigers with our purchase of 707-349C freighters. Today we fly the largest all freighter fleet in the world, comprising "stretch" DC-8-63F's, with a capacity of over 100,000 lbs. and speeds better than 550 m.p.h., and giant B747 freighters moving 200,000 lbs. plus at 575 m.p.h. between major cities in the United States and Asia.

As the world's largest scheduled all cargo airline, Flying Tigers continues to meet the goal we established 30 years ago. We combine the experience and expertise of our people with the finest aircraft and ground equipment to provide business and industry with reliable airfreight service.

And that's the plane truth.

FLYING TIGERS

125

In domestic service, the B747F had the capability of providing 2.8 times the available ton-miles as the DC-8-63F, but the investment cost was double. In the earlier years of production, Boeing's literature emphasized that whereas B707s required approximately a 50% load factor to break even (on costs), the B747F would break even at about a 33% load factor. Using the same guidelines, in comparison, one may surmise that the DC-8-63F required a 40-42% load factor to break even on medium range routes. It had been indicated that in the analysis of direct operating expenses including such factors as crew expenses, maintenance cost, fuel costs, and depreciation of equipment, a significant spread was found between rail, truck, and the B707 jetfreighter costs. But, interestingly enough, when the stretched DC-8s or B747 freighters were substituted for B707 freighters, the gap between air and truck closed or vanished.[6]

The B747-200F series, which Tigers acquired in the late 1970s, had the optional nose-load capability, larger maximum payload potential, longer range capability, and enjoyed greater fuel efficiency than the side-load only B747-100Fs. For example, the B747F converted freighters could carry about 223,000 lbs. on the 3500-mile segment between Tokyo and Anchorage, while the B747-200F with original freighter configuration, could carry about 257,000 lbs. maximum payload on that same leg. Even more pronounced, on the 5200-mile route from San Francisco to Tokyo, the B747-100F is capable of carrying up to 127,000 lbs., while the B747-200F could carry up to 168,000 lbs. for that segment.

A fellow employee related to me one time about an incident at our LCK (Columbus) hub in which, during an aircraft "swap" of freight loads between two B747Fs, however, one being of the 100 series while the other being the 200 series aircraft. It caused considerable alarm and embarrassment when discovered!

The basic design of the Boeing 747-200F took cargo into consideration from its inception. Placing the flight deck above the level of the main deck, providing a "hump" appearance, permitted installation of a large swing-up hinged nose section for efficient straight-in loading of long cargo pieces and positions, including common twenty-foot maritime containers. The almost entire operation of off-loading and loading is automated, requiring the same amount of manpower working the aircraft as for the B707 or DC-8 freighters, but more than doubling the maximum payload. The "nose-load" operation requires an estimated hour-and-a-half "turn-around time," with the proper ground handling equipment and advanced staging of freight loads.

For Flying Tiger Freightmasters, another development in design helped maximize the usable space in the main cargo section, namely the addition of a very large side cargo door situated on the left-hand side of the fuselage aft of the wing. The

B-747-100 Flying Tigers was the first airline to operate Boeing 747 passenger aircraft converted into efficient air freighters. Each of the awesome giants flies more than 200,000 pounds of cargo at 575 miles per hour over a 3,500-mile range. (1974-present)

B-747-200 --Flying Tigers operates a fleet of B-747-200 jetfreighters on its international and domestic routes. These all-cargo giants, with nose-loading capability, carry a payload of 249,000 pounds at 575 mph over a 3,600-mile range. (1979 to present)

THE HUGE MAIN CABIN of a Flying Tigers B747 jetfreighter is 188 feet long, 19½ feet wide and 11 feet 2 inches high. Available cargo capacity exceeds 200,000 pounds.

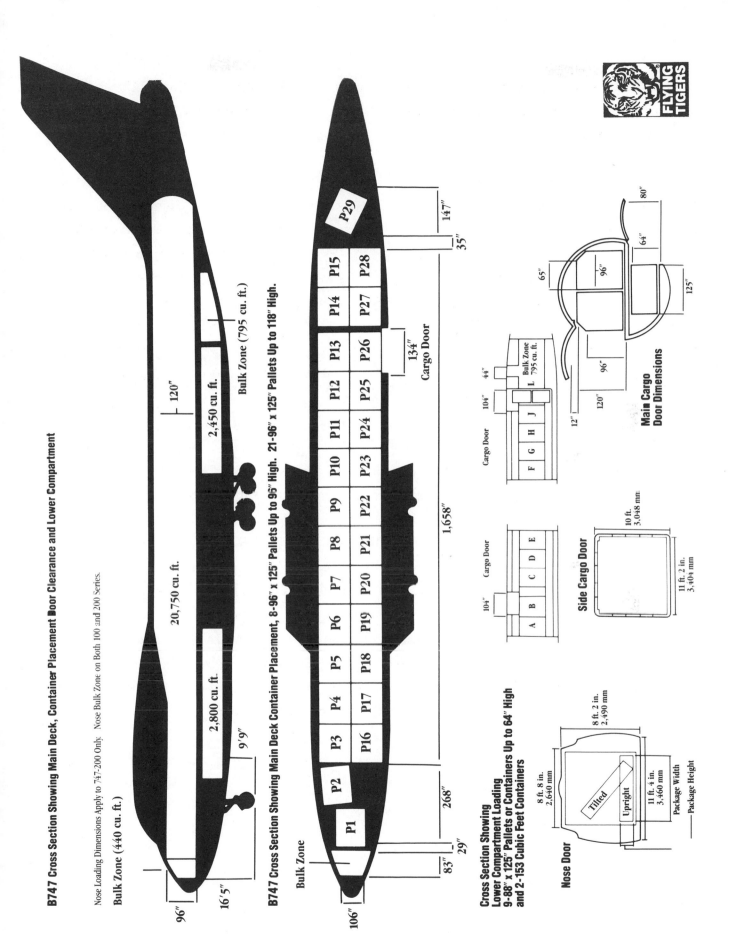

B747 Cross Section Showing Main Deck, Container Placement Door Clearance and Lower Compartment

Nose Loading Dimensions Apply to 747-200 Only.   Nose Bulk Zone on Both 100 and 200 Series.

Bulk Zone (440 cu. ft.)

120"

2,450 cu. ft.

Bulk Zone (795 cu. ft.)

20,750 cu. ft.

9'9"

2,800 cu. ft.

96"

16'5"

B747 Cross Section Showing Main Deck Container Placement, 8-96" x 125" Pallets Up to 96" High.   21-96" x 125" Pallets Up to 118" High.

Bulk Zone

| P2 | P3 | P4 | P5 | P6 | P7 | P8 | P9 | P10 | P11 | P12 | P13 | P14 | P15 |
| P1 | P16 | P17 | P18 | P19 | P20 | P21 | P22 | P23 | P24 | P25 | P26 | P27 | P28 |

P29

147"
35"
134"
Cargo Door
1,658"
268"
83"
29"
106"

Cross Section Showing Lower Compartment Loading
9-88" x 125" Pallets or Containers Up to 64" High and 2-153 Cubic Feet Containers

Cargo Door
104"

A | B | C | D | E

Cargo Door
104"   44"

F | G | H | J | L

Bulk Zone
795 cu. ft.

12"   120"   96"

Main Cargo Door Dimensions

65"   96"   64"   80"   125"

Side Cargo Door

10 ft.
3,048 mm

11 ft. 2 in.
3,404 mm

Nose Door

8 ft. 8 in.
2,640 mm

8 ft. 2 in.
2,490 mm

Tilted

Upright

11 ft. 4 in.
3,460 mm

Package Width
Package Height

FLYING TIGERS

131

design feature was presented by Boeing as an optional feature for the B747 "combi" aircraft. Under this arrangement, appealing to some commercial combo carriers, passengers are seated in front, with use of the upper deck, while the rear cargo door serviced cargo positions.

The rear cargo door is higher than the swing-up nose door, which featured a height of about 98 inches. Freight positions up to ten feet high and twenty feet long could be maneuvered through the side cargo door, although the few positions within the vicinity of the aircraft nose were kept to eight foot or less to accommodate the lowered height. In the translation of freight utilization, side loading made better use of the space in the aircraft which is the strategy of the game. In the loading process, as cargo reaches the nose (or side) door sill area, it is steered by the Load Master from a master control station adjacent to the door. Then the loads are propelled by the drive wheels under control from a series of local control stations, along roller tracks to their assigned position where they are locked in place.[7]

A modification center located at the Boeing Wichita, Kansas, plant, installed the side door, strengthened the cabin floor and main cargo deck, and made modifications to permit the use of a powered loading system on Tigers' B747-100F series. The carrier purchased their first three B747-100s from American Airlines in the passenger configuration, then sent them to Wichita for the conversion and flight testing. Various aluminum design containers and "shelf pallet" structures, collapsible and light in tare weight, were also designed to accommodate the B747 Freightmaster configuration, providing up to twenty-nine main cargo deck positions. The lower section of the aircraft comprises of two power-loading compartments, one forward and one aft of the wing, accommodating up to nine positions allowing 64" in height, and a spacious bulk load section located aft of the rear-powered lower section. Extraordinary over-size freight or containers could also be center-loaded in the B747F main deck and secured to the floor employing "creative tie-downs." This adaptation was a trade-mark Tiger specialty.

The freight loads of the B747 Freightmaster obviously had an astounding impact on Tigers' Asia international network that fed into the U.S. domestic system, or proceeded to Canada or Europe. Supplemented by DC-8-63F service, Tigers was able to better control traffic flow, especially seasonal volumes customary at Tigers.

In January, 1975, the new 438,068 sq. ft. automated warehouse at Seattle/Tacoma airport, costing an estimated $3 million, welcomed the newly instituted B747 Freightmaster service to Asia. From 1969 to 1976, Seattle/Tacoma was a major Route

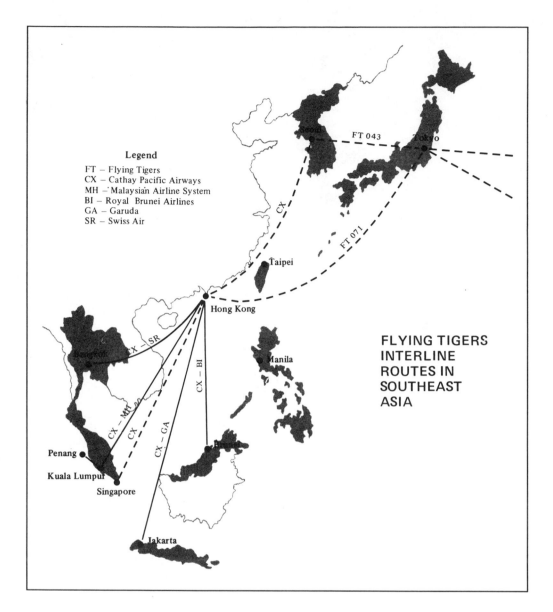

Legend

FT – Flying Tigers
CX – Cathay Pacific Airways
MH – Malaysian Airline System
BI – Royal Brunei Airlines
GA – Garuda
SR – Swiss Air

FLYING TIGERS
INTERLINE
ROUTES IN
SOUTHEAST
ASIA

Source: **Tigereview**, Aug/Sept 1976, p. 4.

The significance of the Singapore-Malaysia markets was brought to light in early 1976 when a marketing services consultant conducting research in preparation for Tigers' new westbound international campaign, found that Singapore, with only 225 square miles of territory shared by 2.5 million mostly Chinese, was, at the time, the second largest importer of U.S. goods by airfreight in Asia after Japan.[9] Singapore was rapidly becoming a serious rival of Hong Kong as the focal point of Southeast Asia's trade, finance, and services.   It was also an important and growing manufacturing center, particularly of high technology and high-value items.   In 1974, the United States ranked third among Singapore's trading partners. Along with Singapore, the airfreight market potential of Malaysia and Indonesia were also noted.[10]

Malaysia's export-oriented industries were textile, wood and rubber products, and electronic components. The United States was both a major importer of Malaysia's products and a main supplier of Malaysia's imports. Meanwhile, Indonesia specialized in textile exports, and the United States was Indonesia's second largest trading partner. However, in 1975, the total airborne freight traffic volumes for Singapore was higher than that of every Asian country then currently served by Flying Tigers except for Japan, and was more than the combined total for Taiwan, Philippines, Korea, Thailand, and South Vietnam.

The project airborne traffic for the forecast year 1977, Flying Tiger employed for the Southeast Asia points the same general methodology it used to predict the traffic for its existing services. The technique involved the utilization of econometric models and stepwise regression analysis. Results were adjusted to those deemed reasonable in light of Flying Tiger's knowledge of particular circumstances in a market and the carrier's experience. Owing to the small airborne volumes to and from individual nations, the forecast was done on a regional basis for Southeast Asia, including Thailand, Singapore, Malaysia, and Indonesia. Data from 1968 through 1975 were used in developing the equations.

Renewal of Route 163

Flying Tigers' certificate for Route 163 expired on May 28l, 1974, but remained in effect until a disposition could be made on the carrier's renewal filing which included additional points. In addition to the renewal of its existing authority, Flying Tiger sought new authority to serve Indonesia, Singapore, Malaysia, and Anchorage, Alaska. Petitions for discretionary review were filed on December 15, 1976, by Flying Tiger, Pan American World Airways, the Bureau of Operating Rights, Trans International (TIA) and World Airways.

Northwest Airlines took no position with respect to the renewal of Tiger's existing authority or the addition of Indonesia, Singapore, and Malaysia. However, the airline did oppose granting Flying Tigers authority at Anchorage which, traditionally, was Northwest's domain for U.S.-based carriers. Likewise, Pan American opposed Tiger's intrusion into the Southeast Asian region. TIA and World Airways, two Oakland-based carriers, in a joint presentation, asked that any renewed or newly awarded authority granted to Flying Tiger be subject to a condition prohibiting the operation of charter flights, both on-route and off-route, in the transpacific area. With the termination of hostilities in Vietnam in mid-1975, TIA and World Airways, among the largest U.S. supplemental carriers, experienced with futility the swindling of their major revenue base. In fact, they could hear the "echoes of the death drum."

On the other hand, the renewal of Flying Tiger's existing authority on Route 163 was unopposed, and Tiger's efficiency was amply demonstrated on record. From 1969 to 1975, the volume of freight carried by air between the U.S. and the major Asian markets served by Flying Tigers increased by more than 2½ times:

	Airborne transpacific freight (000 - lbs.)	
	1969	1975
United States and -		
Japan	84,121	190,713
Hong Kong	47,050	94,984
Taiwan	13,712	71,176
Korea	10,125	57,404
Philippines	5,293	18,973
Total	160,301	433,250

Source: CAB Report, "Flying Tiger Transpacific Renewal Case, "Decided April 6, 1977 (Wash., D.C., July-Sept., 1977) p. 189.

Throughout the period 1970 to 1975, Tigers maintained a weight-load factor in scheduled transpacific service well over 60%, employing the DC-8-63F and a B747F in 1975. The load factors ranged from a low of 64.1% in 1975 to a high of 68.9% in 1972. For the six years, the average weight-load factor was 65.8%, including the two world recessionary years of 1973 and 1974.

The growth of the carrier in the Asian air cargo markets, in such a short span of time, had been unprecedented. And, likewise, the development of the Asian air cargo market had been equally amazing. Tigers' strong presence in Asia was institutionalized. Flying Tigers' transpacific operation contribution within its sysem could not be ignored:

Net operating profit (loss) for all services (000)

Year	FT system	Transpacific
1970	$ 21,866	$19,159
1971	23,269	20,911
1972	30,063	26,229
1973	29,773	20,628
1974	(2,293)	9,946
1975	4,761	11,845
Total	**$107,439**	**$108,718**

Source: CAB Report, "Flying Tiger Transpacific Renewal Case," p. 190.

In submitting the order to the President, the CAB wrote: "Flying Tigers had demonstrated an ability to develop and promote innovative airfreight services since its original certification to perform transPacific service. There can be no doubt that the presence of the all-cargo carrier in the transPacific has stimulated the growth of U.S.-Asian airfreight and that its efforts have inured to the benefit of other U.S. flag carriers as well as the shipping public."[11]

Subsequently on July 15, 1977, President Carter approved the CAB order granting Flying Tigers new all-cargo rights between the United States and Singapore, Malaysia and Indonesia, and between Anchorage and Asia, effective October 13, 1977, for a seven-year period. Incorporated into the original points served by the 1969 certificate authority, the order read:

> "Between the coterminal points Boston, Mass., New York, N.Y.-Newark, N.J., Philadelphia, Pa., Cleveland, Ohio, Detroit, Mich., Chicago, Ill., Seattle-Tacoma, Wash., Portland, Ore., San Francisco-Oakland-San Jose, Los Angeles-Ontario-Long Beach, Calif., and Anchorage, Alaska, and intermediate points within the following areas: Japan, Korea, Okinawa, Taiwan, Hong Kong, Philippines, Vietnam, Thailand, Malaysia, and Singapore, and beyond Singapore, intermediate points and a terminal point in Indonesia."[12]

On January 7, 1978, Tigers introduced scheduled service between U.S. and Singapore, offering three-times weekly service with intermediate stops in other Asian countries. At the same time, the airline continued its interline program to Southeast Asia with Cathay Pacific and Malaysian Airlines to selected points.

Tigers' experienced minimal success in developing its domestic route structure in the years prior to domestic air cargo deregulation. With the introduction of the DC-8-63F into its domestic network in 1969, the airline's capacity and marketing opportunities expanded multi-fold. By 1974, the carrier reportedly had in operation twenty DC-8-63Fs, eleven which were owned and nine leased.

Meanwhile, Flying Tigers' earlier request for additional authority to serve twenty-seven cargo-generating communities lacking service in the late 1960s was finally decided in the CAB's "Additional Points Case," on December, 1971. With the exception of authority to serve Syracuse, the requests were denied, rationalizing that the points in question were already adequately served by the combination carriers and/or did not justify scheduled all-cargo service at the time. Approval would have increased the Flying Tiger system by incorporating southeast and southwest air cargo markets, and strengthened mid-west hubs considerably.

Seeking another form of strategy to open marketing opportunities in the east-west aligned southern markets, and north-south oriented markets east of the Mississippi, and complement Asia-U.S. single-carrier service, Tigers reportedly considered a merger with Airlift International in late 1973. Airlift acquired an attractive east-west system encompassing southern markets in 1968 with the transfer of Slick's certificate and assets to the former. There had been an agreement in principle at that time for a merger between the two all-cargo carriers. However, with Airlift experiencing exceptional financial difficulties, the deal was dropped in early 1974.[13] In 1973, Airlift International reported $2.2 million in the red, while Seaboard World netted $2.4 million, and Flying Tigers profited by $20.2 million. Another indicator of their respective financial portfolio may be surmised by their debt/equity ratio for the period:

| Airline | Long-Term Debt ($) | | Ratio Debt to Equity | |
	1973	1972	1973	1972
Airlift Int'l	4,976(000)	8,486(000)	56:44	66:34
Flying Tiger	43,212	49,746	34:66	54:46
Seaboard World	67,378	78,153	63:37	73:27

Source: Aviation Daily's Airline Statistical Annual, 1974 (Wash.,D.C.: The Ziff-Davis Publishing Co.) p. 62.

In 1973, Airlift reportedly had 672 employees, while Seaboard had 1,690 and

Tigers had 3,550, shortly before the oil shortage fiasco and ensuing company lay-off's.

Despite geographic restrictions requiring a significant proportion of interlining, Tigers experienced a four-fold increase in domestic air freight volumes from 1969 to 1978, at the time of de-regulation. In fact, the increase may be considered dramatic in that the combination carriers significantly increased their market share using expanded capacity of narrow and wide-body jets. Tigers also handled increasing volumes of Asian imports funneled into its domestic network or interlined to Europe via Chicago or New York.

In 1973, the Air Transport Association (ATA) annual report revealed that Tigers flew 681,878(000) scheduled ton miles, second only to Pan American with 866,854(000).[14] Much of the credit may be attributed to the fact that Tigers acquired, up to that time, twenty of the sixty-two DC-8-63F jetfreighters in operation within the entire air freight market.

In 1972, Tigers added daily service to Springfield and Hartford via truck/air routing. And in 1975, the carrier filed an application again with the CAB to add scheduled service to San Juan, San Diego, Dallas-Ft. Worth, Houston, Atlanta, Baltimore, Washington, D.C., and Miami, in an aggressive program to incorporate southern air freight markets. Then, in December, 1976, Tigers also applied for Cincinnati, Charlotte, and Anchorage to be added to domestic Route 100.

Flying Tigers' domestic expansion program was, in part, a response to shipper and freight forwarder requests for increased domestic lift in air freight capacity. It was noted that the top thirty-five domestic airfreight cities had experienced a 57% decline in all-cargo service from 1969 to 1976. To address commitments to forceful customers, Tigers took the initiative, and in 1977, announced plans to dramatically expand and improve its domestic services, more than doubling prime time service (overnight service with an early morning arrival) and substantially increasing capacity.

Thus, on August 15, overnight airfreight service was instituted for Chicago, Cleveland, Detroit, Los Angeles, San Francisco, Philadelphia, Boston, New York, and Syracuse. As projected, in prime time service, 27 new origins and destinations were added to the existing 26 for a total of 53 prime time flights, while daylight flights were increased by 21. To meet service levels, three DC-8-63Fs were added to the existing nine "stretches" in domestic service, including two deployed from the charter division, and one from international service.

Flying Tiger Line

Revenue Ton-Mile Statistics

Fiscal year	Domestic (000)	International (000)
1951	28,125	
1952	31,789	
1953	51,324	
1954	45,152	
1955	36,890	
1956	49,649	
1957	53,520	
1958	54,748	
1959	76,174	
1960	85,314	

*Effective Dec. 31, 1961, Company changed fiscal year ending June 30 to Dec. 31
Company began operating CL-44D's

1962	74,197	
1963	78,306	
1964	99,489	
1965	127,611	
1966	169,811	
1967	163,250	
1968	166,041	
1969	252,983	78,630 (mid-Sept. to Dec)

Company used DC-8-63F's international and domestic
Boosted employment to 2241 system-wide.

1970	213,062	290,126

Employment to 3845 total.

1971	247,254	323,454
1972	289,343	411,858
1973	427,121	407,550
1974	410,172	385,607
1975	361,624	449,359
1976	367,624	446,359

Employment to 4493.

1977	393,288	525,628

1978   February, FTL acquired 600,000 shared (99.9%) of Seaboard World Airways

A 1976 study indicated that Flying Tiger was the only air carrier of the top five which operated only all-cargo aircraft in the domestic market. By comparison with its competitors, the carrier was authorized to serve far fewer city-pair segments. Nevertheless, the carrier did compete quite effectively for air cargo in the most dense cargo markets. With its ten leading volume city-pairs in the industry-wide top twenty ranked volume city-pairs, and nine of its top ten ranked ton-mile city pairs in the industry-wide top twenty ranked ton-mile city-pairs, Flying Tiger has attracted from between 25 to 40% of most of the markets. In the Chicago-Seattle market, Tigers flew almost 50% of the air cargo.[15]

FLYING TIGER'S
LEADING U.S DOMESTIC CITY-PAIRS in 1976
Ranked in Order of Air Cargo Tons and Ton-Miles

Rank	City-Pair	Tons	Market
1.	Chicago-New York	50,470	29.0
2.	Chicago-Seattle	48,162	48.4
3.	Chicago-L.A.	29,360	25.9
4.	L.A.-New York	25,560	26.5
5.	Chicago-San Francisco	23,602	23.1
6.	Boston-Chicago	19,107	37.9
7.	New York-San Francisco	14,994	34.8
8.	L.A.-San Francisco	13,871	14.6
9.	Chicago-Cleveland	10,208	31.3
10.	Boston-New York	10,541	29.3

Rank	City-Pair	Ton-Miles (000)	% of Market
1.	Chicago-Seattle	82,839	48.4
2.	L.A.-New York	63,048	26.5
3.	Chicago-L.A.	51,203	25.9
4.	Chicago-San Francisco	43,568	23.1
5.	New York-San Francisco	38,632	34.8
6.	Chicago-New York	37,125	29.0
7.	Boston-Chicago	16,565	37.9
8.	Chicago-Philadelphia	5,204	29.7
9.	L.A.-San Francisco	4,674	14.6
10.	New York-Seattle	4,625	14.5

Source: Jody Hamako Matsubu Yamanaka, **The Geography of the U.S. Air Cargo Industry** (unpublished M.A. thesis, UW, Geography, 1979) p. 104, citing: CAB Service Segment Data (12 months ending Dec., 1976).

Flying Tigers' creditable performance in 1976 placed the carrier third among the leading domestic air cargo carrying airlines:

LEADING U.S. AIR CARGO CARRYING AIRLINES

Airline	Ton-Miles (000)	Operated Cargo Aircraft On International Routes
United	730,969	
American	544,553	Mexico/Canada/Caribbean
Flying Tigers	367,262	Asia
TWA	366,229	World-wide
Northwest	334,573	Asia
Delta	263,490	
Continental	238,241	
Eastern	163,426	
Western	129,022	
Braniff	91,896	Latin America
Pan American	91,409	World-wide
Airlift	78,006	San Juan

Source: CAB, U.S. Air Carrier Traffic Statistics (Dec., 1976).

It is interesting to note that three of the top eight air cargo carrying carriers did not operate all-cargo aircraft at the time, but, employing another strategy, elected to utilize jet aircraft belly capacity or combination aircraft. The wide-body superjets allow up to 60,000 lbs. of belly cargo in the B747 aircraft, and somewhat less in the DC-10 aircraft, the two popular wide-body models. The belly operation is automated, however, the superjets serviced selected prime points, while the narrow jets with bulk load operations was quite common.

Consequently, Continental, ranked 7th in 1976, discontinued scheduled all-cargo service in 1973, while Eastern, ranked 8th, discontinued in December, 1973, and Delta, ranked 6th, discontinued in September, 1973. Four of the other carriers, American, Braniff, Northwest, and United, continued to offer freighter service, although with less frequency and limited routes. United decreased its night freighter service, and service to secondary cities, as did other combination carriers after 1973.

On the eve of domestic deregulation, Tigers was operating five B747-100Fs and sixteen DC-8-63Fs. And, in a symbolic change, the carrier systematically re-painted its aircraft fleet tail to read **Flying Tigers**, beginning with a DC-8 in early 1977.

Flying Tigers' DC-8-63F #797
The first plane in the fleet to carry the new "Flying Tigers" tail design

And, of great significance, the carrier began approaching Pan American as the world's largest air cargo carrier system-wide.

1977

Airline	Revenue Ton Mile (000)
Pan American	946,483
Flying Tiger	837,198
American	589,337
United	579,105
Northwest	455,627
Trans World	445,972
Seaboard World	339,305
Continental	252,765
Eastern	206,391
Delta	198,206
Airlift	141,159
Western	127,291
Braniff	92,655
National	69,552

Source: Air Transport Association of America,
    Air Transport 1978 (Wash., D.C., 1978).

In summary, the trunk combination carriers had a total revenue ton mile of nearly four billion (3,963,384,000) in 1977, while the three all-cargo carriers totaled a third of that amount (1,317,662,000). Tigers contributed over 64% toward the all-cargo total.

U.S. Scheduled Airlines - All-Cargo Aircraft Fleet, June, 1977

	B707 320C	B707 323CF	B707 300CF	B727 QC	B737 QC	DC-9	DC-8 33	DC-8 63	DC-8 50	DC-8 54	DC-8 55	B747 F	Total
Airlift Intl.	2			1			3	3		2			11
American		10										2	12
Braniff				5									5
Flying Tigerr								16				3	19
Hawaiian						2							2
Northwest	2											3	5
Pan Am	9											4	13
Seaboard								7		4	1	2	14
TWA			12										12
United									15				15
Wien					7								7

Source: ATA, U.S. Scheduled Airlines Total Industry Air Cargo Statistics, 1976.

During the early and mid-1970s, Tigers also focused on the development of its local as well as long-haul truck systems to accommodate the domestic feeder pattern, and expand its service area, within CAB constraints. Numerous trucking contracts were effected. The carrier transported large volumes of Asia imports to Canadian markets via regular trucking shuttle service between Seattle and Vancouver (Canada), Detroit and Toronto, and Boston and Montreal, respectively.

In the mid-1970s, Tigers established the **International Skyroad Service** which was a combination truck/air cargo transportation system which directly linked twenty key cities throughout the United States with Asia. The unique service opened new markets for U.S. manufacturers and exporters who wanted to sell their products in Asia, and, vice versa. In 1976, ten major U.S. cities were linked in the International Skyroad expedited truck/air transport system including Rochester, Providence, South Bend, Columbus, Dayton, Pittsburgh, Baltimore, Cincinnati, and Washington, D.C. Local trucking firms in each city were set up to immediately carry the cargo to one of

Tigers' nearby major gateway terminals for movement on the Asia-bound flight. Eventually, other cities were added to the International Skyroad system including Nashville, Memphis, Louisville, St. Louis, Harrisburg, Cedar Rapids, Indianapolis, Kansas City, Minneapolis/St. Paul, Phoenix, and San Diego.[16]

Flying Tigers' ocean freight-air shipment intermodal program had a significant impact on the west coast stations of San Francisco, Seattle, and Los Angeles. The service was offered at a lower or discounted freight rate, and, consequently, moved primarily on a lower priority "space available" basis, varying with each individual account. Commonly known at the time as the Overland Common Point (OCP) program, it offered shippers appreciable time savings at reasonably competitive costs. In operation, the ocean freight was quickly processed and trucked to the respective Tiger west coast terminal, still under U.S. Customs control, then airfreighted to feeder points as designated for final clearance, distribution, or pick-up. In fact, significant volumes were also airfreighted by Tigers to European markets via Tigers' Chicago and New York (JFK) terminals through interlining. Shippers enjoyed the time savings segment of airfreighting through the U.S. rather than moving the traffic via the Panama Canal to Europe requiring another month for delivery.

As an indication of volumes handled by Tigers in their OCP program, in 1965, the carrier handled eleven-and-a-half million tons of sea-air traffic. At the height of the program in Seattle during the mid-1970s, the terminal was generating approximately one million tons monthly, yet were required to move a portion through freight-forwarding interlining with Northwest and Continental Airlines.

In 1977, Tigers initiated a new European Interline Service providing confirmed space on Flying Tigers domestic and Asian flights for cargo shipped on European carriers to New York and Chicago. The carrier inaugurated the service initially with flights from the United Kingdom, France, Germany, Italy and the Netherlands. Under the program, shippers could take advantage of prime late-in-the-day departures of airlines out of their (European) countries, connecting with Flying Tigers all-cargo jetfreighters for next morning arrival to all major markets on the U.S. west coast. "Space" bookings were also available for through traffic to Asia.

On Flying Tigers domestic airfreight system as a whole, freight forwarder traffic constituted almost 50% of the volume and about 45% of the revenue by the mid-1970s. The largest freight forwarder customers such Emery Air Freight, Airborne, Burlington Northern, CF (Consolidated Freightways), and UPS (United Parcel Service) often booked whole positions of freight on Flying Tiger aircraft, especially on the heavier segment prime time flights. The "blocked space" enabled the all-cargo carrier to offer special rates, or discounts, to volume shippers who contracted for specified amounts of space on regular basis. Containerization, an integral part of the program, allowed for UPS to began a "block space" arrangement with Tigers on March 1, 1970, shipping 83,900 lbs. of air courier freight in twenty-five special (shelled) containers. It was part of a program to carry about 35% of the total UPS traffic into New York, Chicago, Los Angeles, San Francisco, and Seattle, as United Parcel expanded its air service in major U.S. markets.

Freight forwarders consistently booked as much or more traffic on the Tiger domestic system as compared to UPS. And as an indication of their respective volumes, each of those freight forwarders subsequently began their own airfreighter cargo service a short period after air cargo deregulation went into effect in late 1977, each relying primarily on their own respective established accounts.

Notes

1. **Tigereview**, "Behind the Scenes," Vol. 29, No. 7, Aug., 1975, pp. 4-5.

2. "747's Impact Upon Global Air Cargo," **International Business**, Seattle, Nov.-Dec., 1976, p. 30.

3. John Philip King, **The Global Pattern of Wide-Body Jet Routes: A Study of Network Determinants** (Seattle, unpublished M.A. thesis, UW, 1974).

4. CAB Reports, **Flying Tiger Transpacific Renewal Case, Docket 28656, decided April 6, 1977** (July-Sept., 1977) p. 171.

5. Stanley H. Brewer, **The Nature of Air Cargo Costs** (Seattle: UW Graduate School of Business Administration, 1967) p. vi.

6. Ibid.

7. **Jane's All the World's Aircraft, 1974-75,** edited by J.W.R. Taylor (London) pp. 285-88.

8. **Tigereview**, "Look What's Happening in HKG (and SIN...and KUL...and...)," Vol. 30, No. 5, Jul/Aug, 1976, pp. 3-4, and **Tigereview**, "Big in HKG, FT's 747's Serve Crown Colony," Vol.29, No. 7, Aug., 1975, p. 3.

9. Ibid.

10. Op. Cit., **Flying Tiger Transpacific Renewal Case**, pp. 190-91.

11. Ibid., p. 171.

12. Ibid., pp. 180-81.

13. **Aviation Daily's Airline Statistical Annual, 1974** (Wash., D.C.: The Ziff-Davis Publishing Co.) p. 61.

14. **Tigereview**, Vol. 28, No. 6, July, 1974, p. 15.

15. Judy Hamaka Matsubu Yamanaka, **The Geography of the U.S. Air Cargo Industry** (Seattle: Unpublished M.A. thesis, UW, Geography, 1979) p. 99.

16. **Tigereview**, Vol. 30, No. 8, Nov., 1976, p. 1.

8

Ambitious Expansion Plan
with Domestic Deregulation

Throughout Tigers' history, Bob Prescott had continuously struggled with the Civil Aeronautics Board on a host of issues ranging from routings and tariffs to passenger carrier favoritism. And, in a very colorful, if not humorous way, in 1965, he sent "lobsters" to Congress saying "you can ship lobsters cheaper than mail." His point was that government air mail subsidies to combination commercial carriers were extremely and unjustly costly to the public. Legislators needed to bare pressure on the CAB to be more responsible to the public.

However, Prescott's most significant and final struggle with legislators and the CAB took place in 1977 during the hearings of the proposed airline deregulation. Suffering from a chronic illness, cancer of the throat, he stepped forward for the last time to protect the interest of Flying Tigers in the "melee" involving air industry opportunists and conservatists, and the possible dismantling of his long-time adversary, the CAB. The result of the hearings would set the tone and direction of the U.S. airline industry for years to come, reaping a surprising number of casualties of what once were considered strong carriers.

While United Airlines carried the banner for the combination carriers, Flying Tigers was a leading supporter in the airfreight industry which exerted strong pressure for the domestic deregulation of the airline industry. Federal Express, the new and upcoming air express courier, was also a very vocal leader, convincingly protecting its interest. The movement was fostered during the mid-1970s by politicians, economists, consumer groups, and academians well versed in the industry seeking greater efficiency in cost and service industry-wide. The instrument of change was produced with the enactment of the Domestic Airline Deregulation Act of 1978, which removed virtually all CAB authority over the U.S. air cargo and combination airfreight operations, beginning November, 1977, with President Carter's approval. According to the time table, entry controls and price regulation disappeared from the law in 1982-83, and the CAB, as a regulatory agency itself disappeared in 1985. Management of the transition was delegated by Congress to the CAB.[1]

On November 9, 1977, the domestic all-cargo deregulation statue, Public Law 95-163, was enacted in the first phase of airline deregulation. Deregulation of the airfreight industry opened competition in the domestic market by eliminating the CAB's control over all-cargo market entry and exit and curtailed sharply its jurisdiction of airfreight rates.

Under part 418 of the act, the CAB created a new class of air carriers-domestic operators of all-cargo equipment. Initially the grant of 418 authority was limited to the carriers that had provided continuous all-cargo service in the twelve months just before the enactment of the new law, and had satisfied the requirement of transporting at least "20 million interstate freight revenue ton-miles" during that same period. However, as of November 9, 1978, entry was open to any U.S. citizen who, according to the CAB, was fit, willing, and able to offer domestic all-cargo service. Thus, the doors were open to traditional freight forwarders in the coming years. Carriers were also permitted to use aircraft of any size. In addition, the CAB issued its final rules implementing P.L. 95-163, eliminating the necessity to file tariffs. And, finally, as a ruling, 418 carriers did not have to obtain prior CAB approval for mergers and acquisitions.[2]

Flying Tigers had petitioned the CAB repeatedly since the mid-1960s for authority to expand its domestic routes. Tiger contended that customers needed widespread geographic coverage, overnight delivery, size and weight flexibility, door-to-door service, and single-carrier responsibility. In addition to route and rate flexibility, Tiger supported deregulation, hoping that it would allow the formation of multimodal corporations, resulting in improved surface transportation for door-to-door shipments.[3] From Tigers' perspective, domestic air cargo deregulation offered an opportunistic viable alternative to address chronic problem areas and issues that had developed in the air cargo industry, especially those affecting the carrier.

Domestic deregulation opened up a new spectrum for Flying Tigers, culminating in unprecedented geographic expansion highlighted by new service products, and supplemented by an expanded trucking system. Beginning in 1978, with considerable pre-planning, Tigers was able to offer freighter service under the air/truck system to all fifty states, Puerto Rico, and the Virgin Islands. That year, the carrier almost doubled its domestic route system and domestic air freight volume.

In prior years, Tigers had experienced consistently marginal profits, if not losses, in domestic operations, partly because of inefficient aircraft and ground handling systems in earlier years, chronic low domestic airfreight rates, and route constraints. In 1970 and 1971, the carrier attempted to address the low rate-route constraint problems through CAB hearings known as the "Flying Tiger Additional Points Case" and the "Domestic Air Freight Rate Investigation," but to no avail.

Testifying before the U.S. Senate Subcommittee on Aviation on March 24, 1977, Flying Tigers **"tongue-lashed"** the CAB for strongly and consistently supporting combination carriers at the expense of all-cargo carriers, even though the latter attempted to develop the domestic air freight industry at high cost, effort, and time. Suggesting ineptness, the carrier noted that "the intimate knowledge of production costs and marketing requirements for the wide and changing variety of products which normally move in commerce, which is an essential part of freight pricing, is apparently beyond the ability of the government agencies to acquire the necessary expertise." And, further, the carrier was adamant that, in order for the air freight industry to be profitable, there needed to be a greater reliance on the open market forces or mechanisms rather than on government regulatory controls on domestic routes and rates, among other matters.[4]

Tigers was convinced that the CAB deprived numerous communities of jet freighter service by denying its applications, a strong point also voiced by the freight forwarders. For example, the carrier applied three times for service to Atlanta and Charlotte. Each time the application was turned down, alleges Tiger, to protect the freight operations of the combination carriers. These carriers, however, could not fulfill the shipper needs because the passenger aircraft belly restricted the cargo it could carry and because passenger flights were operated during the day. To highlight it all, a number of combo carriers finally ceased all-cargo aircraft service, and others decreased their level of operations during and after the 1973-74 fuel crisis and its accompanying recession. The inability of the air cargo industry to generate reasonable profit on its freighter operation had resulted in a substantial deterioration in the quantity and quality of service offered.[5] In fact, in 1978, Airlift International discontinued its domestic operation altogether. Delta pulled out of the all-cargo freighter business in 1973 after twenty-seven years. Continental dropped its service in 1973, having operated fourteen B707Cs for MAC during the Vietnam War. Eastern Airlines ceased the service in 1975, followed by TWA in 1978. The potentially growing Southeast airfreight market was severely handicapped.

Similar to the Atlanta and Charlotte cases, Tigers had made numerous requests to the CAB to serve Anchorage, a refueling stop on its Asia route from the 1960s to 1976. The carrier experienced high load factors on its eastbound flights and low load factors on its westbound flights since the end of the Vietnam airlifts. Given this imbalance in the traffic flow and given the fact that Alaska represented a destination point for goods from the lower forty-eight states, Tigers' application for Anchorage was a logical move.[6]

Prior to deregulation, Tigers felt that unreasonable constraints including airport restrictions and ineffective CAB regulatory practices and judgements, kept the air cargo carrier from experiencing much needed flexibility, growth geographically and servicing, scheduling and pricing in the market place. Air cargo carriers, under the inherent system, had to rely on air freight forwarders and other indirect air carriers. For example, service by direct air carriers was restricted to certain cities plus a twenty-five or fifty mile pick-up and delivery zone. Substitute service by truck was limited to points that were included in the carrier's route certificate. As to the rate structure, it was not economical for air carriers to offer service in the short-and medium-haul markets. Indirect carriers, on the other hand, enjoyed unlimited geographic coverage and substantial tariff flexibility. The CAB's economic regulations had therefore impeded the operations of a carrier such Flying Tigers from offering the full complement of service features to the shipping public.[7]

According to Tigers' viewpoint, all-cargo carriers needed an effective augmenting truck service to complement their air services in order to compete effectively with combination carriers and freight forwarders, and to expand the utility and profitability of the freighter services. Tigers was certificated to service only fourteen domestic points directly by air, and had authority to provide freight services, including air or substitute truck, to only 182 markets, as compared to United Airlines with authority to service about 110 domestic points by air, and potentially 12,000 domestic markets by air or truck.[8]

The air carrier views the shipper as much more service or time sensitive than price sensitive, including detail to prime-time departures, delivery schedule, and door-to-door service. Other service elements views important by shippers include ability to track shipments, a good pickup service, and broad coverage. The all-cargo carriers had repeatedly pointed to the shipper's need for door-to-door, not airport-to-airport service. Handling the ground portion of the transportation through subcontractors was one option, but Tigers did not believe that it was as effective or user responsive as the one where Tigers would own long-distance trucking companies, and send its own trucks beyond the exempt zone limit around the airports. The carrier espoused on the merits of its successful Tiger Skyroad service.

In support of regulatory reform, Flying Tiger summarized key points affecting the cargo carriers during the U.S. Senate Subcommittee hearings on Aviation:

> "To be specific, we support legislation which would authorize the all-cargo common carriers, on a grandfather basis, to engage broadly in domestic all-cargo services without restriction as to linear routes or equipment size; should employ entry procedures for airfreight limited to proof of fitness; should, for a two year transition period, exclude from expedited procedures for entry into domestic all-cargo service combination carriers whose passenger business continues to be protected by public convenience and necessity entry standards. We further believe that rate regulation in the case of domestic air freight services by all-cargo and combination carriers should be limited to review of unjust discrimination, undue preference or prejudice or predatory pricing issues. And we urge that the all-cargo carriers should be authorized to provide expedited freight services by contract with ICC licensed truckers under tariffs filed with the CAB to facilitate the growth of intermodality to both serve our nation's needs for expedited freight service in communities which do not now have the economic base to support direct air services."[9]

Broad coverage, including geographic coverage as well as varying forms of services offered, is much more important in freight than in passenger transportation. Shippers want no weight or size limit, or dealing with numerous carriers; they look for a single carrier responsibility, which includes pickup, delivery, a spectrum of services offerings, and broad geographic coverage.

Prior to deregulation, airfreight rates were low and so was the quality of service provided. Even the CAB's Domestic Air Freight Rate Investigation concluded, after a seven year study starting in 1970, that average prices were almost 40 percent below average costs. The study was prompted by Tiger complaints initiated in September,

1965, petitioning the CAB to reinstate the minimum rates which was discontinued in 1961, leading to the endless process of price cutting. Tiger was convinced, entering deregulation, that shippers would pay for prime-time lift, single-carrier responsibility, and broad geographic coverage. As evidence, shippers had turned to commuter carriers and charter operations, despite the existence of lower rates for freight hauled in the bellies of passenger aircraft. Before deregulation, freight forwarders were chartering entire aircraft to meet their customer needs.[10]

It has been previously noted that the top thirty-five domestic airfreight cities had experienced a 57% decline in all-cargo service, from 1969 to 1976, and severely impacted the secondary cities to a larger degree. Tigers had no major domestic expansion since 1973, and, in fact, had curtailed some domestic services during the 1973-74 fuel crisis. John Emery, Jr., the articulate CEO of the U.S. foremost freight forwarder, Emery Air Freight, noted at the time that:

> "81% of today's domestic all-cargo lift is confined to only four cities. Emery illustrated the 10-year slide during which freighter service dropped from a total of 50 cities to less than half that number. The resulting increased reliance on the cargo bellies of daytime passenger flights has slowed air freight delivery. Even the quick-change 727 aircraft have all but disappeared."[11]

This situation, in mid-1977, he explained, caused his company to turn to what became known as the Emery Air Force concept, developing an airfreight distribution hub and an assorted fleet of air cargo aircraft in Dayton, Ohio. The move was preceded by the utilization of many charter flights to accommodate Emery shipper needs.

The structure of the air cargo industry changed dramatically shortly after deregulation. A number of carriers including some which were supplemental carriers, freight forwarders, or air-taxi operators before deregulation, inaugurated scheduled airfreight service. The most significant change that took place was the increase in the number of airfreight forwarders and the introduction of extensive freighter service by four of these forwarders. In 1976, there were 366 certificated U.S. airfreight forwarders. As of July, 1980, the number increased to 1,284. And four of these forwarders, namely Airborne, Air Express International, Emery, and Profit-by-Air, operated 50 percent more freighters and serviced twice the number of cities served by the scheduled carriers. Most of the aircraft operated by this group were leased from the other 418 operators.[12]

Flying Tigers, itself, responded to the domestic deregulation by instituting an extensive bi-modal air-truck network providing varying service levels throughout the U.S., which served as the root system for its present **door-to-door** program and highlighted by prime-time air and truck service. In 1981, the transportation network was augmented with the LTL (less than truckload) program for long-haul truck traffic.

Best of both Modes - GM Ron Pfefferle, standing, reviews single invoice used in conjunction with FTL's new San Francisco area expedited pickup and delivery system

The acquisition of five DC-8-61F jetfreighters in 1978, and the introduction of the B747F on selected domestic route segments bolstered the carrier's continental feeder system. The airline acquired two DC-8-61F aircraft from Overseas National Airways in December, 1977, and leased five others from Trans International Airlines (TIA), including two aircraft in a "lease back" to TIA, increasing Tigers' fleet to twenty DC-8s and three B747F jetfreighters.[13] The DC-8-61F series aircraft had a load capacity of approximately 90,000 lbs. as compared with a maximum capacity of 106,000 lbs. for the DC-8 "stretch" version, and was more appropriate for selected routes.

On January 9, 1978, Flying Tigers inaugurated service between the lower 48 states and Alaska. Previously, the carrier was restricted to transporting international cargo between Asia and Alaska since 1976, and refueling its aircraft at Anchorage. With domestic deregulation, the CAB awarded Tigers a new domestic certificate, granting authority to serve all fifty states, Puerto Rico, and the Virgin Islands. The airline's scheduled all-cargo service to Atlanta, Georgia, and Charlotte, North Carolina, commenced on March 6, and to Houston and Dallas/Fort Worth, Texas on April 3. San Juan, Puerto Rico service was inaugurated in May, and, subsequently, service was added to Miami, Florida, Cincinnati, Ohio, and the Baltimore/Washington, D.C. area that year.

In the 1978 expansion year, Tigers hired more than a thousand new employees, including over two hundred new pilots. To accommodate its new extensive domestic network, the system was re-organized into four regions with a regional VP administering each area. Tigers increased its domestic route system and traffic volumes 90% from the previous year. And, with the year's statistics compiled, announced that **Flying Tigers had surpassed Pan American as the free world's largest airfreight carrier, based on revenue ton kilometers.** This benchmark served as the basis for Tigers' 1978-79 advertising campaign.

With the domestic sub-regional hubs in order covering all states, Flying Tigers pursued their objective of a "door-to-door" service in early 1979. Without imposing size or weight restrictions, Tigers introduced the new airfreight program with rate reductions up to 25 percent. Theoretically, the reduced rates was implemented to encourage shippers to make greater use of the airline's pick-up and delivery service, saving both money and time. The first year proved a marked success, with domestic revenues increasing about 90 percent.[14]

Flying Tigers attained their domestic objectives of broad geographic coverage and single carrier service including pick-up and delivery under a network of Tigers-controlled truck system. This system included local sub-contracted trucking service involving many trucks painted with the imposing Flying Tiger logo blazoned on a red background. The door-to-door service offered the shipper a diversification of services and price options. The new tariff decreased the cost of door-to-door shipments of packages under 200 pounds; increased the airport-to-airport charges for these shipments; reduced the overall cost of shipping containers that were more densely packed, and canceled 3000-pound bulk general commodity rates. As a general strategy

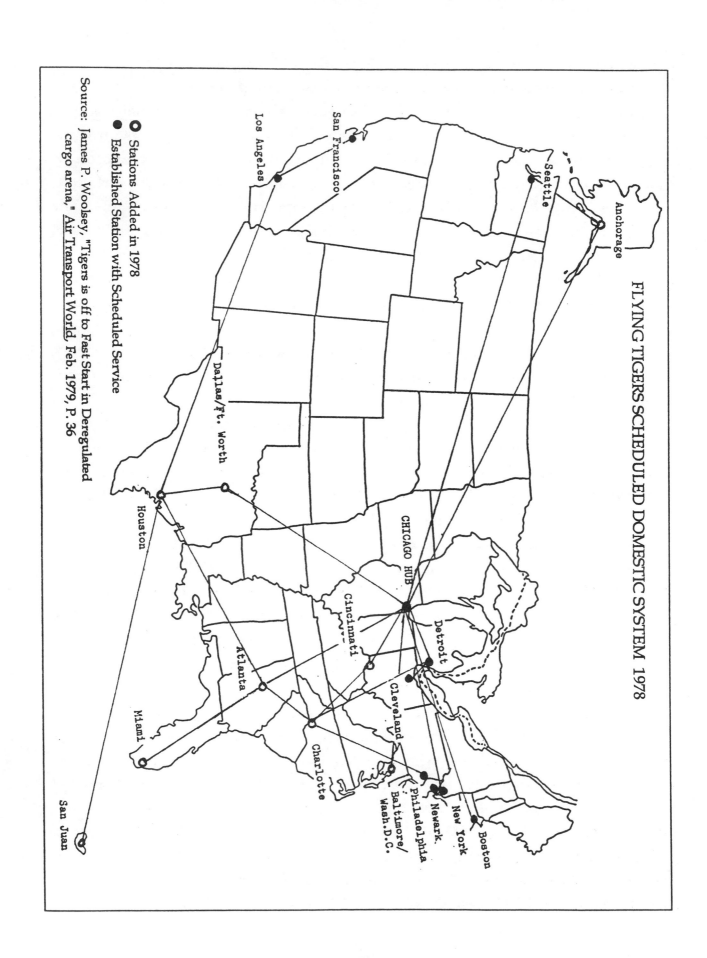

FLYING TIGERS SCHEDULED DOMESTIC SYSTEM 1978

○ Stations Added in 1978
● Established Station with Scheduled Service

Source: James P. Woolsey, "Tigers is off to Fast Start in Deregulated
cargo arena," *Air Transport World,* Feb. 1979, P. 36

Anchorage

Seattle

San Francisco

Los Angeles

Dallas/Ft. Worth

Houston

San Juan

Miami

Atlanta

Charlotte

Cincinnati

CHICAGO HUB

Detroit

Cleveland

Philadelphia

Baltimore/
Wash.D.C.

Newark

New York

Boston

New Ad Campaign Stresses Identity

Identity is a major goal of Flying Tigers' 1978-79 advertising campaign which recently premiered in national business and airfreight trade media with the ad on the back cover of this issue of *Tigereview*. "This program will help us accomplish our marketing objectives and meet the challenges we face in 1979," explained Bill Caldwell, vice president-marketing.

The new campaign, which was developed in conjunction with the airline's new advertising agency, keye/donna/pearlstein, is based on the theme, "Flying Tigers — the world's leading airfreight airline."

According to Advertising Director Deborah Brenner, the campaign is designed to create a leadership position and a positive image for Flying Tigers in the minds of airfreight shippers. "Now," Brenner said, "advertising will provide an environment that is supportive of the personal selling effort. It is the first step to begin solving the awareness problem which has been identified as a deterrent to further growth and sales.

"The print ads are dominated by the bold Tigerface which is really a personification of the company's character," Brenner said. "It is the look of a leader and clearly distinguishes us from our competitors."

In addition to the print ads, direct mail, sales aids, and sales promotion give-aways will all begin to reflect the same theme and feeling in an effort to create a coordinated marketing communications program.

New print ads feature Flying Tigers' Tigerface and brief lines of copy promoting the airline and its service. At top, one of the new ads, complete. At right, another of the copy blocks to be used in conjunction with the Tigerface.

in entering new markets, Tigers matched the major competitors where freighter service existed and established higher rates where its night time freighter service clearly represented a differentiated product.[15]

During 1980-81, Flying Tigers instituted a long haul "filler type" traffic using the Apollo Truck firm. A lower rate was applied so as to compete with surface carriers for the same type of traffic, which included low-prioritized freight. The LTL program, taking advantage of Tigers' increased fleet capacity, included size restrictions, a cube weight built into the tariff charges, and allowed for 3 to 5 working days in-transit, and oriented coast-to-coast directional traffic.

In operation, Apollo handled the pick-up and delivery to the Flying Tiger terminals at Boston, Cleveland, Philadelphia, Newark, New York (JFK), Syracuse, Seattle, Atlanta, and Miami. On a daily basis, in each area during every week day, Apollo would contact the respective Flying Tiger station, and offer the availability of "LTL" freight to the air carrier. Tigers would use their discretion as to whether or not it wanted to handle such freight as "fillers" for their aircraft that particular day on a space available basis. Any significant volumes of LTL freight meant the failure of any given station area to generate meaningful revenue airfreight, and, as such, was never a popular account but reflected, in part, the increased capacity on the Tiger domestic system.

In July, 1978, Tigers leased a B747 jetfreighter from World Airways, and ordered two new B747-200Fs from Boeings in August for an October, 1979 delivery. The cost for the latter was $115 million, including spare parts, with an option for four more; two in 1980 and two in 1981. The leased B747F was also put into domestic service including a transcontinental routing of Boston-New York-Chicago-Los Angeles. Using the DC-8s, non-stop service was inaugurated between San Francisco and New York, and between Los Angeles and Atlanta. Service from Charlotte to San Francisco was instituted via the Chicago hub. Scheduled 747 jetfreighter service was also initiated between New York, Detroit and San Francisco on Tuesday through Saturday, besides the daily DC-8 Detroit-Los Angeles service.

Also to accommodate the domestic deregulation program, Tigers provided an extension of daylight service from Charlotte to San Francisco on a non-stop scheduled basis. Opening marketing opportunities, Carolina shippers could continue to use the daytime flight for overnight delivery to other U.S. cities, and second day service to Asia. To augment the heightened domestic traffic, a Los Angeles-Chicago-Atlanta flight was added boosting prime-time overnight deliveries through the hub.[16]

In 1978-79, Flying Tigers was in an enviable position as an air cargo carrier, employing a large capacity jetfreighter fleet of B747s and DC-8s on its extensive global charter, Asia, and domestic network. One may speculate that had the CAB restricted freight forwarders and other non-direct air carriers from entering the domestic air cargo carrier field during the period of deregulation, Tigers would have been in an unprecedented dominant position.

Tigers implemented the door-to-door domestic overnight service on a continental scale in 1982, along with Federal Express, UPS, Airborne Express, Emery Air Freight, and a number of other cargo carriers.

Federal Express, the air express courier, had established its overnight service employing a hub-and-spoke system a few years earlier, using a fleet of small aircraft. Tigers' Chicago hub changed from a down-line hub to a hub-and-spoke center in the Flying Tiger network with the acquisition of new stations in the south, southwest and southeast.

In offering its domestic door-to-door service, Flying Tigers did not emphasize the express document and small packages of the domestic air freight market, as with Federal Express and UPS, but rather offered freight services to direct shippers of the type previously provided by the traditional freight forwarder. In its marketing plan, the carrier emphasized a guaranteed product in 1983, at no cost for service failures. Tigers has displaced its dependency on freight forwarder traffic, for the most part, in its domestic operations. The carrier has developed and has continued to expand its domestic trucking capabilities, which rely on non-affiliated contract trucking services set up at each terminal. Thus, Tigers' domestic door-to-door service is marketed directly to retail customers. The carrier currently offers both first-day and second-day delivery options, and both guaranteed and non-guaranteed delivery times to approximately 60,000 U.S. communities via fifty-five major U.S. points.

Established as the "core" program of the domestic system for Tigers, it merges the air carrier and traditional freight forwarder function including pick-up and delivery, and offers an array of service products and tariffs to meet different customer needs. In 1985, 1986 and 1987, door-to-door service revenues represented 57%, 66% and 66% respectively of all domestic scheduled service revenues.[17]

Flying Tigers door-to-door service.

NEW EXPRESS
SERVICES INSIDE

FLYING TIGERS
DOOR-TO-DOOR

SERVICE GUIDE
APRIL 1984

Notes

1. Nawal K. Taneja, **Airlines in Transition** (Lexington: D.C. Heath, 1981).

2. **The U.S. Airfreight Industry** (Lexington: D.C.Heath, 1976) p. 9.

3. Ibid., p. 8, and Joseph Healy, **Marketplace Should Determine Domestic Rates, Routes, Healy Says**, testimony on Regulatory Reform Hearings, U.S. Senate Subcommittee on Aviation, March 24, 1977, pp. 12-13.

4. Ibid.

5. Op. cit., **The U.S. Airfreight Industry**, pp. 35-36.

6. Op. cit., **Airlines in Transition**, p. 218.

7. Ibid., citing Wayne M. Hoffman, "The Best May Yet Come," **Corporate Planning Under Deregulation: The Case of the Airlines** (Northwestern U., June 11-12, p. 1979) p. 40.

8. Op. cit., **Marketplace Should Determine Domestic Rates, Routes, Healy Says**, p. 12.

9. Ibid.

10. Ibid., and op. cit., **The U.S. Airfreight Industry**, p. 6.

11. "For Emery Another Kind of Tomorrow," **Cargo Airlift**, Vol. 63, No. 2, Feb., 1973, pp. 4-11, and "Emery Air Force, **Air Cargo Magazine**, July, 1977.

12. Op. cit., **Airlines in Transition**, p. 218.

13. **Tigereview**, "Pilots, Planes, Routes," Vol. 32, No. 1, Jan., 1978, pp. 1 and 11.

14. **Tigereview**, Vol. 33, No. 1, June, 1979, p. 1.

15. Op. cit., **The U.S. Airfreight Industry**, p. 11.

16. **Tigereview**, Vol. 32, No. 7, Nov., 1978, p. 1, and **Tigereview**, Vol. 33, No. 1, Jan., 1979, p. 1.

17. **Tiger International, Inc., 1987 Annual Report**, p. 4.

9

(We'll Fly)
Anything, Anytime, Anywhere

Bob Prescott, Flying Tigers' visionary, leader and achiever, often noted that "We're unique, so let's not imitate, as imitation let's you catch up to the guy ahead, but never lets you pass." Pursuing such a policy, by the early 1960s, Tigers became America's foremost all-cargo carrier, through all the trials and tribulations. Innovative and unwavering in an explosive air cargo industry, by 1979, FTL by-passed Pan Am to become the free world's number one air cargo carrier for that year, according to IATA statistics.

By the early 1980s, Flying Tigers acquired a formidable fleet of B747 and DC-8 jetfreighters. The capabilities of such a fleet of the most modern commercial cargo aircraft type strongly complemented Prescott's familiar slogan throughout the years, **"Anything, anytime, anywhere."** The policy opened the doors for a large array of unusual "air freight anomalies" collectively at a scale not experienced by any other airline.

Tiger memories are abound with challenging and incredible "things we've carried and how we moved them." And, in many cases, there is no need for exaggeration. It brings to mind an interesting story that Laura (Fish) Greimes, a former Tigereview (employee publication) editor, related to me:

"I first heard of the airline (FT) when I was writing a column with my then husband, By Fish, in the Seattle Times (local newspaper). I saw their ad: 'If you can get it through the door, we can ship it!' and saw the possibilities for a series on the relatively new concept of airfreight.

I called the young station manager noting, 'I can get it through the door....ship me to New York (Idlewild).' Whoa!, he said, ' Don't call me, I'll call you.

He apparently called LAX (headquarters) and got the go-ahead. We came up with a publicity gag. My husband made me a large crate and I climbed in to be shipped as a 'Live Animal.' Of course, I traveled in the cockpit, not in the cargo hold. The Seattle Times was enough taken with the series to feature it, with photos on the front page. In New York, I picked up a Pan Am flight to Spain and spent a couple weeks doing travel pieces from there.

Bob Prescott and Len Kimball (then Public Relations VP) were taken with the series. And, subsequently, I became the editor for Tigereview for six years (1969-75)."

Thus, from a humorous perspective, the story illustrates the commitment to the slogan, "Anything, anytime, anywhere." That slogan was well understood throughout the air cargo industry, and formulated the basis for the great variation for unusual size, shape and weight combination of air freight that have traveled in the Flying Tiger aircraft. All too often, we heard shippers and truckers bring over-sized or otherwise unusual freight to our terminal facilities and mention the all too-familiar line, "nobody else will take it."

During the very early years of operation, the Budd Conestoga had the experience of transporting a famous **Tucker car**. Eventually, the Tucker auto company purchased a Budd for Skyway Freight Corporation for that very purpose.

Tiger C-47s transported the likes of "Elsie the (Carnation) Cow" when the Borden Company chartered a plane for a one-month tour, and Roy Rogers' famous horse, Trigger, in another instance. And I was fortunate enough, in 1977, to be on the ramp crew at Sea/Tac airport that handled the highly acclaimed race horse, Seattle Slew, a Triple Crown winner. Then an unbeatened three-year-old, Flying Tigers had transported Seattle Slew from New York to Los Angeles to run in Hollywood Park's Sweep Stakes race. The Slew caught a Flying Tigers charter flight to Seattle, making a public appearance at the local Longacres Race Track before returning to New York on board a scheduled FT 747 flight.[1] I happened to capture the off-load and on-load events on my home video camera, and my wife and I enjoyed free tickets to Longacres in appreciation of the ramp work on behalf of the race track owner.

Flying Tigers is well known for its cattle, horse, and pig charters worldwide, and had been a pioneer in the air transport of live animals enmass. Just through Seattle, itself, there have been more than I care to count. In the 1970s, a corral-type staging area was put in place across from the Sea/Tac Tiger ramp area. Tigers set up cattle charters from numerous areas including Moses Lake, Washington, eastern Oregon, the Midwest, Oklahoma, Calgary, New Zealand, and Australia, just to name a few.

I've seen all types of zoo animals shipped through our Sea/Tac terminal. I recall reindeers shipped to Japan to adorn their Christmas activities in the mountain area. I've seen Llamas transported from South America for local breeding purposes. I remember penguins being moved to the local zoo. And, I've seen millions of "baby chicks," transported in and out of the area, chirping their version of "We Are the World."

During spring of 1976, a Flying Tigers DC-8-63F jetfreighter charter transported one hundred and twenty-two wild animals from San Francisco to Fukuoka, Japan, enroute to the new Koizumi African Safari Park in the hot springs resort town of Beppu. Among the park's first inhabitants, the shipment included 33 lions, 37 tigers, 9 bears, 25 Egyptian geese, 6 black swans and 12 mandarin ducks, all collected by International Animal Exchange of Ferndale, Michigan, from zoos and habitats around the United States, consolidated in Oakland, California, then trucked to Tigers' San Francisco terminal for air shipment. A veterinarian, two animal handlers, and a Flying Tigers operations supervisor accompanied the shipment.[2]

The Tigereview articles, as pictured, portray the difficult planning, preparation and ingenuity involved in the transport of live and sensitive creatures.[3] Flying Tigers had been selected as the air carrier to move numerous live creatures into and between the various Sea World Theme Parks.

Among the more challenging air cargo handled through the Seattle Flying Tiger terminal have been the occasional Boeing Aircraft Company "Aircraft on the ground (AOG) shipments of assorted-size assemblage of aircraft parts destined to any point in the aviation world. The difficulties rest, in part, in the build-up preparation of the numerous inordinary and incompatible size and shape shipment pieces associated with the Boeing aircraft. For instance, the elongated wing section or the B747-mounted engine, all needing to fit jig-saw fashion in a limited time on the next available flight ASAP, or on a charter flight involving what may seem like an endless number of distorted AOG parts. Sometimes the skills and calculation seem so enormous that truckers often comment after "backing up" to our docks that , "if Tigers can't move it, nobody can."

With such a reputation for dependability, Seattle Tigers was entrusted with the handling of a weather satellite and bullet-proof limousine (purportedly for the Emperor) to Japan in the mid-1970s. Though the list is endless, I also recall the shipment of lengthy telephone poles and complete bowling alley assemblies to Asia during that time period. And, I remember preparing a partially disassembled helicopter with a Tiger logo towards the tail end, used in a James Bond movie.

Perhaps the most memorable Flying Tiger charter flights out of Seattle were the weekly **Safeway charters** during 1978-79 from Seattle to Doha, Qatar, the wealthy Persian Gulf country. "Once a week, a chartered Flying Tigers 'stretched' DC-8 jetfreighter transported up to 100,000 pounds of fresh and frozen meat, fresh fruits and vegetables, dairy products and dry goods, such as paper products, soaps, spices and other household items to Doha, enroute to the newly built and enormous Doha Center."[5] The cross-shaped center, without the western-style mall within the structure, comprises of four 20,000 square-foot departments, each forming an arm of the cross.

One arm of the center houses an air-conditioned supermarket containing 20% local foodstuff, and 80% flown in every weekend from Sea/Tac airport, satisfying a two-year contract. Regular items included fresh fruit, vegetables, and meat, dairy products, bakery goods, and other common American supermarket goods. The Flying Tiger air freight system allowed the Doha Center supermarket to order and re-order fresh food supplies just as if it were located two miles away from Sea-Tac rather than being several thousands miles away.

I recall, on a regular basis, non-perishables were delivered to our docks on Wednesday and Thursday afternoons, inventoried, and prepared for air shipment on flat pallets. Perishable foods, such as meat and ice cream, were delivered to our docks in refrigerated trucks on Friday mornings, some being in special containers and some we protected by applying special packaging, styrofoam, and dry ice combination during palletizing to endure the long flight. "Because of the sensitivity of the perishable items, four temperature zones were maintained on the aircraft."[6]

Artist's rendering of the new "Doha Centre" shopping complex

Above: *Detail of Centre's planned supermarket section.*
At left above: *Model of the complex shows the building's cross shape.*
Below: *Logo for Jashanmal & Sons at left; logo for "The Centre" at right.*

Below, the Slew is off-loaded in Seattle.

168

FT transports Shamu, the famous performing killer whale, and 30 other marine mammals and fish between Sea World's marine amusement parks in Cleveland, Ohio and San Diego, Calif.

The animals, in their various specially made and selected crates and containers, are off-loaded at Fukuoka, Japan.

Flying Tigers is flying tigers. It's no secret. Not only did the airlines carry 37 of the regal beasts from San Francisco to Fukuoka, Japan, but, it also provided transportation from Los Angeles to Manila for "celebrity" tiger "Gombi", pictured above with trainer-actress Susan Backlinie. Gombi made the 22-hour trip to the Philippines to appear in the Vietnam movie "Apocalypse Now." As with most movie stars, Gombi watches his diet to keep movieland trim, consuming a mere 15 pounds of meat and chicken per day. The tiger was fed five raw chickens before his flight on the DC-8-63F jet freighter. Before Gombi, Flying Tigers also transported camera equipment, explosives and a helicopter for use in making the movie.

And what happened to Oliver, once thought by some in anthropoligical circles to be the "missing link in the human chain?"[4] Among Flying Tiger's more passionate "air cargo celebrities, his story comes to light in a summer, 1976, Tigereview article:

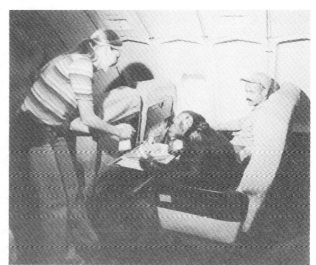

Above left, accompanied by a handler, Oliver steps off the plane in Tokyo. At right, JFK secretary Barbara Berkey serves juice and sandwich to Oliver on board the flight prior to departure from New York.

OLIVER: He's "Cargo" Now, But...

While most of the freight traveling on a recent Flying Tigers' flight 071 from New York to Tokyo was loaded in the usual way, one item of "cargo" sat in the upperdeck lounge area of the 747 munching a roast beef sandwich, sipping orange juice and dealing with members of the news media.

The special shipment was "Oliver," a stocky, humanoid creature theorized by some to be anthropology's long-sought "missing link," on his way to Tokyo to be studied by a panel of scientists and anthropologists.

Oliver stands four feet six inches tall and weighs in at 120 pounds, and at present is generally regarded by informed scientists as a hybrid between an ape and a chimpanzee. However, owner Michael Miller, a New York attorney, believes there may be something more to a number of decidedly man-like characteristics displayed by the creature.

He continually walks upright, Miller says, with posture more like a man than an ape, appears to possess a higher degree of intelligence than the usual primate and has distinct bone structure unlike that of chimps and other primates. Oliver is also inexplicably bald, adding to his mystique.

Miller himself assembled the panel of experts from various scientific and anthropological disciplines to assist in tracing the animal's origin and perhaps answer such questions as to why the ape-like creature is exclusively bi-pedal

(walks only on two legs, never on four) and is able to walk in the lock-knee position characteristic of man and unheard of in apes. The animal also exhibits a physical characteristic — a particular opening in the skull through which the nerves are connected to the brain — generally considered to differen-

Missing link? *Oliver strolls on board the 747, displaying the bi-pedal posture that has the experts baffled.*

tiate man and his forebears from apes.

During his five week stay in the Orient, Oliver took part in a series of experiments, television shows and the filming of a documentary, before climbing back on board a Flying Tigers jet for his return to the United States.

Oliver, now seven years old, came into the public spotlight earlier this year when he was purchased by Miller from a South African explorer who toured amusement parks, carnivals and similar attractions with trained chimpanzee and dog acts.

"I heard that during performances he sometimes would bring out this strange looking creature which he kept as a pet," Miller remarked. Intrigued by the description Miller went to see the man's show and wound up parting with $8000.00 to become the animal's new owner. Miller believes Oliver comes from the Congo River region of Africa.

Oliver's diet includes fruit, vegetables, cheese and lean meats. His roast beef sandwich and orange juice meal, served to him by JFK secretary Barbara Berkey, was only part of the special pre-flight arrangements necessary for the journey. At JFK special accomodations were provided on board the aircraft, and in Tokyo officials pondered over what entry procedures should apply for the celebrity-creature. Both his U.S. departure and TYO arrival brought out the news media, including television, and more than 40 newspapers in Japan carried a photo and story.

By the 1980s, with the introduction of the B747-200F series to the fleet with nose-loading capabilities, Flying Tigers accommodated significantly greater challenging air freight combinations in size, shape and quantity.

FT B747 charter from Basel, Switzerland to Muscat, Oman, loading Heliswiss helicopter.

**Crane-assisted nose load operation of 97,000 pound chemical
compressor reactor from Chicago to Brussels, Belgium.**

Notes

1. "On Tour with Seattle Slew," **Tigereview**, Vol. 31, No. 4, July, 1977.

2. "Here, Kitty, Kitty, Kitty....Kitty," **Tigereview**, Vol. 30, May-June, 1976, pp. 4-5.

3. "ORC-ARK Flies Again," **Tigereview**, Vol. 30, No. 7, Oct., 1976, p. 6.

4. "Oliver:He's 'Cargo' Now, But..." **Tigereview**, Vol. 30, No. 6, Sept., 1976, p. 7.

5. "The Shopping Cart Connection:Weekly Charters to Carry U.S. Foods, Dry Goods to New Middle Eastern Supermarket," **Tigereview**, Vol. 32, No. 1, January, 1978, pp. 12-13.

6. Ibid.

10

The Seasons Change

The rhythm of time marked 1978 as the year that witnessed the end of the original pioneer aviators era of the Flying Tiger Line with the passing of Robert W. Prescott, its founder and President since incipience. Hence forward, the carrier was to take a different course which was to prove to be its "final approach." Developing into a global carrier within the next decade, its attractive niche within the industry was not amiss by other investors and other carriers.

From March 6th through the 10th, 1978, the U.S. flag was flown "half-mast" throughout the Flying Tigers' domestic system to mourn the death of Bob Prescott, the carrier's **guiding light**. Suffering from the debilitating effects of cancer, both the disease and the treatment, Prescott had struggled through the Congressional deregulation hearings, stepping forward for the last time to protect the interest of the carrier which he had brought up as a Tiger cub to the forefront of the industry. Being the empathetic person that he was, Prescott well understood the risks in the industry, and the possible havoc that may occur with disorganized deregulation. He had been immersed in the struggle for over thirty-two years. And, unfortunately, he lost his two-year struggle with cancer on March 3, 1978 at age 64. He had proven to be one of America's greatest aviators, and it was an honor for all those who were fortunate to serve under him.

In retrospect, the undulation during the early years impacted the original investors, some who fell victim to the despairing conditions during the early turbulent years while the select visionaries, with determination and skill, stayed in the ongoing struggles long enough to usher the carrier into the jet age.

The famous Flying Tigers fighter group which performed its exploits from December, 1941, to July, 1942, mainly in the China, Burma and southeast Asia region, comprised of only about seventy pilots on its roster. As previously mentioned, there existed a common thread between the AVG and CNAC crews, and both had a major air base at Kunming, China. The fraternal bond was unmistakable.

After the AVG was disbanded in July 4, 1942, a significant number of its members joined commercial airlines. CNAC, whose crews were staffed by primarily high paid American pilots, enticed eighteen former Flying Tiger crew members. Eight of these AVG aviators subsequently flew for CNAC over the "Hump" route before becoming party to the original dozen aviation investors of the Flying Tiger Line (National Skyway Freight Corp.).

"Red" R.H. Holmes, a former CNAC pilot during WWII, was one of the original aviator investors but withdrew his money shortly thereafter.

Jules Watson, another former CNAC aviator, flew with the Flying Tiger Line for a while, then left the airline to follow other pursuits in housing and real estate development.

Another investor, **Jack Cornelius**, a former AVG crew chief, filed a legal suit to recover his money investment.

Clifford G. Groh from Chicago, Illinois, had been a Flight Leader for the AVG's Third Pursuit Squadron, nick-named the Hell's Angels, originally based in Rangoon. After flying for CNAC, he flew for FTL for quite a few years with top seniority but finally was relieved of duty in 1966 because of an alleged alcoholism problem. Because of his significant contributions, a new Flying Tiger Boeing 747-200F aircraft was named in his honor in 1980, designated N801FT.

C.H. Link Laughlin from Ashland, Missouri, also a former Flight Leader for the Hell's Angels, and "Ace" pilot credited with 5.2 downed or destroyed enemy aircraft (kills). After the CNAC, he flew for FTL in the early years, but his wife refused to live in California, so he quit and moved to Miami where she subsequently divorced him. He remarried and lives in Florida.

Camille Joe Rosbert from Philadelphia, PA., was a Flight Leader for the AVG's First Squadron, the Adam and Eve, along with Bob Prescott.He was credited with 4.5 "kills."After his CNAC experience, Rosbert flew for FTL in the early years, and had served as a FTL Supervisor of Operations. He left on a one year leave-of-absence to fly for Chennault's Civil Air Transport (C.A.T.), which employed a number of former AVG pilots. He is living in North Carolina.

John Dick Rossi from San Francisco, Calif., had been a Flight Leader for the First Pursuit Squadron of the Flying Tigers, achieving "Ace" with 6.25 "kills." He was quick to join CNAC, and originally invested in FTL while he was still in Shanghai, China, and subsequently tallying over 700 Hump flights. Rossi did

They shared dreams.

not return to the United States until its fall in 1948. He also took a "non-schedule" for a year, involving himself in the renting of FTL planes. He started flying for the Flying Tiger Line in May, 1956, but was prevented by the pilots' union from obtaining the seniority promised him at the time of investing. He flew until 1971, went on a leave-of-absence, and did not fly again.

Rossi lives in Fallbrook, California, and, has been previously mentioned, continues to set up the regular Flying Tigers (AVG) reunions, which he originated in 1952.

William (Bill) Bartling from Middletown, Indiana, was a former Flight Leader for the AVG's Adam and Eve Squadron, and a top "Ace" with 7.25 enemy "kills" before joining CNAC. He flew for FTL in the early years, then went into management, starting as a VP in Operations. In 1980, the new Boeing 747-200F cargo plane, designated N808FT, was christened the William E. Bartling, in his memory as a FTL pioneer.

R.J. Catfish Raines from San Francisco was a former Flight Leader for the Hell's Angels, credited with three enemy "kills" with the AVG. He then became a naval aviator in the Pacific theater and was credited with an additional six enemy "kills." Raines flew for FTL in the early years, then left on a one year leave-of-absence to fly for Chennault's C.A.T. He rejoined FTL after China came under Communist control in 1949, and C.A.T. moved its operations to Taiwan, but lost his seniority during the interim. He subsequently retired from FTL in 1976, and now lives in Fallon, Nevada.

Tom C. Haywood from St. Paul, Minnesota, and **R.P. Duke Hedman** from Webster, S. Dakota, were both Flight Leaders of the AVG's Hell's Angels, and were among the first National Skyway pilots. Both were AVG Ace pilots noting Haywood with 5.25 enemy "kills," and Duke with over five.

Haywood worked his first flight for FTL in 1945 as co-pilot to Bob Prescott on board one of the notorious stainless steel Budd Conestogas. He piloted Flying Tigers aircraft around the world for the next fifteen years, until his flying career ended with a major heart attack in 1959. Upon recovery, he directed the airline's flight operations and served as manager of ground training until his retirement in 1973. He passed away in April, 1979. In December of that year, FTL received it's second new Boeing 747-200F aircraft, and designated N807FT in the name of Thomas C. Haywood. (That aircraft was destroyed in a fatal crash approaching Kuala Lumpur, Malaysia, on Feb. 19, 1989.)

Duke Hedman had been an exceptionally close associate of Bob Prescott throughout their careers. They were the two who sought the first fleet of aircraft for the endeavor. Duke had been number one pilot since he joined the airline on June 1, 1945, up until his retirement on December 17, 1976. Throughout his 31-year career, he had served in varying capacities including holding the position as the airline's first vice president. He was the last active pilot to have commercially flown every type of aircraft operated by Flying Tiger Line.

As an AVG pilot, Duke distinguished himself by becoming the first American "Ace" of World War II when he shot down five enemy aircraft over Rangoon on Christmas Day, 1941. He reportedly attacked fifty-three twin-engine Mitsubishi bombers accompanied by a support fighter group of Zeros. Furthermore, as the enemy aircraft turned back toward their Thailand base, Hedman turned with them and flew along in the middle of their formation, to the surprise of everyone. The enemy pilots were afraid of accidentally firing upon their own.

Above left: *Tommy Haywood, heading up flight operations.*
Above right: *Haywood with three fellow Flying Tiger Line founders and pilots, also members of the AVG "Flying Tigers" fighter squadron in China, l-r, Robert "Catfish" Raine; Dick Rossi; Haywood; and Duke Hedman.*
At left: *Young man in China.*

Captain Dick Rossi, in China days.

Like most of the original Flying Tiger Line investor aviators, Duke also flew for the CNAC for two yeaars. Joining that airline after AVG disbandment, he logged 750 flying missions over the Hump, which was more than any other CNAC pilot.

In a less dramatic but memorable flight, Duke piloted one of Flying Tiger Line's first three shipments on the same historical day of August 21, 1945. Duke flew 10,000 lbs. of furniture from New York to Burbank.

During the early years, Duke and other FTL pilots not only flew the aircraft but also helped sell the airline's services and load the cargo. Duke recalls such incidents as dropping 30-lb. bundles of silverware into open fields from 520 feet as a publicity stunt, and gasping across the country at 13,000 feet in an unpressurized C-47 to preserve a shipment of strawberries. It was Duke, along with a team of mechanics, who put the first seven stainless steel Budd Conestogas in flying shape enough to make the trip from Augusta, Georgia, to their new home base in California in 1945.

Upon retirement, Duke relinquished the official spot as number one pilot to Bob Prescott, who was voted number one on the seniority list by Flying Tigers' 485 pilots, at the time.

Of interest to note, Leon Colquette, a former AVG crew chief, was an original FTL member, although not an investor.

Eriksen E. Shilling, a former AVG Wing Man, and Group Photo Officer, flew for FTL a brief period, then became a flight scheduler for medical reasons.

Ernest "Bus" Loane, a former AVG and CNAC pilot, joined the FTL crew from 1950 to 1970.

Greg "Pappy" Boyington, a former Flight Leader of the AVG's First Pursuit Squadron, and distinguishing himself in the Pacific theater as a Marine pilot, served for a while as a FTL executive plane pilot, rather than a line pilot as most others. In the mid-1950s, Boyington used an FTL executive five-passenger plane for charter for which he received commission on portion of charter business which he sold. In return for the privilege of using the aircraft, he piloted for the company officials.

"Bob's No.1," Pilots Say

At the recent Silver Tiger banquet honoring 25 year employees, President Bob Prescott passed out the last plaque, extended thanks and good wishes to all and turned to leave the stage. "Wait a minute, Bob . . . stay right there," he was ordered. For a few minutes, President Prescott was the guest of honor as Flying Tigers' pilot group made its blockbuster announcement that Bob had been assigned the number one spot on the pilots' official seniority roster. "Bob was the airline's first pilot," said Flying Tigers' Captain Parker Goldsmith, Air Line Pilots Association representative, "and it's because of him that we're all flying for this airline today. We just wanted to let him know what we think of him." Following a formal presentation (above) of the revised seniority list with Prescott's name in the number one slot, and a framed certificate (below), a rather informal presentation took place as now-number two Captain R.P. "Duke" Hedman stripped to the waist to "turn over" to Bob his "#1" T-shirt (photos right, top to bottom)

Pictured above, l-r, are Goldsmith; retired veteran Flying Tigers Captain Dick Rossi; First Officer Don McComas, ALPA representative; Hedman; and Prescott.

(The Silver Tiger banquet will be featured in detail in the next issue of *Tigereview*.)

181

Some original Tiger investors: left, Jules Watson, Dick Rossi,
Tom Haywood, Bill Bartling, Cliff Groh, Duke Hedman salute Bob Prescott.

The most celebrated of the group, Robert William Prescott, the visionary and founder, originally from Fort Worth, Texas, had been the airline's president and chief executive officer during his 32 years of service. His spirit and enterprise was manifested in his popular phrases "Anything, anywhere, anytime," and "If you can get it through the airport gate, we can fly it." And, the most memorable to Duke Hedman was, "We're unique, so let's not imitate. Imitation let's you catch up to the guy ahead, but never lets you pass."

Prescott participated in five major campaigns while serving with the AVG, becoming a Flight Leader and "Ace" credited with 5¼ "kills." He was co-pilot of the famous "Mission to Moscow" flight of Ambassador Joseph E. Davies in 1942.

Later that year, he returned to China as a captain with the CNAC, completing over 300 flights on the famous "Hump" route.

He returned to the U.S. in November, 1944, and founded the airline the following summer. Bob had witnessed the original fleet of WWII surplus aircraft develop into a multi-million dollar fleet of Boeing 747 and "stretched" DC-8 jet freighters. His airline became the leader of the air cargo industry.

Prescott Coat-of-arms:
"Make me a Proposition

In 1976, Bob Prescott was honored as a prominent figure in the "Giants of Air

Transportation" display in the Smithsonian Institution's new Air and Space Museum. In addition, there needs to be a biography written of Prescott and his colleagues while memories are still in place.

Piloting a P-40 in 1942

Bob poses by his photo, featured in the Smithsonian Institution Air and Space Museum's Giants of Air transportation display, 1976.

On August 14, 1978, Flying Tigers' ten-story headquarters building at Los Angeles airport, the "Hi-Tiger," was dedicated in the memory of the beloved founder. And, on November 2, 1979, Flying Tigers dedicated its first Boeing 747-200F Freightmaster, designated N806FT, to Robert W. Prescott.

Characteristic of the difficult times after Prescott's death, Flying Tigers experienced a "revolving presidency of the airline" involving a number of administrators in that particular leadership position during the following seven years or so. In retrospect, Bob Prescott left with unfinished business amid a horizon of a myriad changes to come. He was sorely missed.

And, just five days after his death, the story of his accomplishments were incorporated into the Congressional Record of the U.S. as an appropriate and timely tribute to the great aviator and entrepreneur.

FLYING TIGERS

AMERICAN VOLUNTEER GROUP • CHINESE AIR FORCE

1st SQUADRON

Adams and Eves

2nd SQUADRON

Panda Bears.

3rd SQUADRON

Hell's Angels.

Insignia of the AVG and the three pursuit squadrons:

ROBERT W. PRESCOTT: A TRANSPORTATION PIONEER

HON. CHARLES H. WILSON
OF CALIFORNIA
IN THE HOUSE OF REPRESENTATIVES
Wednesday, March 8, 1978

● Mr. CHARLES H. WILSON of California. Mr. Speaker, "We'll fly anything, anytime, anywhere." That slogan typified the attitude of the man and the successful company he founded over 30 years ago. Robert W. Prescott, who died Friday from cancer at his home in Palm Beach, Calif., pioneered the air cargo industry in the United States when he founded the Flying Tigers as the first airfreight carrier in 1945.

As a personal friend of Bob Prescott's, I was constantly amazed at his determination and courage. With little else, he built what has become one of the most successful companies in the business. Today, Flying Tigers is the world's largest all-cargo airline linking key cities throughout the United States and Asia and covering some 17,500 miles.

Bob Prescott is definitely a model example of the American dream. Starting out with only an idea and heavy competition from hundreds of other war flight veterans who had the same thought, he convinced some of his old flying buddies and a number of businessmen to invest $178,000 in a new kind of airline—designed specifically for cargo transport.

The name Flying Tigers is familiar to many. It is the popular name given to the famous American volunteer group (AVG) led by General Claire Lee Chennault. The volunteer pilots, one of whom was Bob Prescott, painted snarling jaws filled with sharp teeth on the noses of their P–40 fighters and gave free China an air defense against the Japanese during World War II. Bob took part in five major campaigns with the Flying Tigers against the Japanese, shooting down six enemy aircraft and finally becoming a flight leader.

When the Flying Tigers disbanded in 1942, Prescott returned to this country where he began flying with the Intercontinental Division of Trans World Airlines. While employed by Trans World, he served as copilot on the plane that took then Ambassador James E. Davies on his famous Mission to Moscow in 1942.

Later that year, he returned to China as a captain with the China National Aviation Corp., and was assigned to fly military supplies from India to China over the Himalayan mountains. He completed more than 300 of what became known as the famous "Hump" crossings.

For those of us who knew Bob and certainly based on his flight experience in the early 1940's, it is hardly surprising that he would undertake the task to form the Flying Tiger Line. Starting out with only four airplanes and 16 employees, he began flying a transcontinental route across the United States—an idea that he sold to the Los Angeles businessmen who helped him raise the initial capital.

After 4 years of flying, the company finally received official Government certification in 1949 and approval for the Nation's first commercial-all-cargo route —No. 100. Twenty years later, in mid-1969, Bob was able to see his idea receive approval for the first scheduled transpacific all-cargo route that linked its U.S. domestic system with service to eight Asian nations and territories.

In 1970, the airline became a subsidiary of Flying Tiger Corporation, later renamed Tiger International. Prescott was also director of that corporation as well as the airline and Tiger Leasing Group, another subsidiary of Tiger International, which is engaged in transportation and equipment leasing and financing.

Prescott was born to a large, poor family in Fort Worth, Tex., where he tried, for a time, managing prize fighters. Later, he moved to California where he attended Compton Junior College. He then entered Loyola University to study law, but left in 1939 to enlist in the U.S. Navy as an aviation cadet. He was commissioned as an ensign in 1940, and served as flight instructor until he resigned to join General Chennault.

Being the hard-driving chief executive officer for a major company would seem to be enough for anyone. But Bob Prescott was not just anyone. He was also a member of the board of the Transportation Association of America and was a member of the Board of Directors of the Air Transport Association. Because of his outstanding contributions in the transportation field, the National Defense Transportation Association named him "Man of the Year" in 1973.

Bob was also very active in civic affairs. He was trustee of the City of Hope, held regional industrial chairmanships in the United Crusade and was an honorary member of the Air Line Pilots Association and the Wings Club of New York. Last year, Northrop University conferred an honorary Doctor of Science degree on him.

Bob Prescott was a man of personal courage who not only distinguished himself in combat, but in the business world as well. I think his own statement about his accomplishments exemplifies the type of person he was. "It is difficult to express the pride I feel at what has happened to a struggling idea I had so many years ago."●

Congressional Tribute to Prescott

After an interim period following his death, the position as President of Flying Tigers was bestowed to 30-year veteran Joe Healy, who had been the Executive VP-Chief Executive Officer for the carrier since 1974. Wayne Hoffman retained the position as Chairman of Tiger International as well as Chairman of Flying Tigers, a role he held since 1967. And the other elected office as President of Tiger International, the parent company, was filled by Tom Grojean, who had been director of the FTL Corporation since 1971.

Wayne Hoffman and Joe Healy were strong advocates of deregulation intermodalism, and their influence were to impact the strategic planning of the corporation, and the airline segment as well. Healy left his position as President of Flying Tigers after a year and was succeeded by Tom Grojean in August, 1979. Healy emerged in a new position for the corporation with the intent to develop the long range intermodalism.

Grojean was followed by John E. Flynn in 1983, who rose to that position from Sr. VP Administration for the airline, then Lewis H. Jordan in October, 1985.

To place matters into perspective, in 1985, Saul P. Steinberg, Chairman and CEO of Reliance Group Holdings, Inc., became the youngest member of Tiger International's Board of Directors. At age 46, he joined the ten-member group including such notables as former U.S. President Gerald R. Ford (then 72), Charles Luckman (then 76) founder of Luckman Partnership, Inc., and Houston Rehrig, President of Rehrig Industries. Reliance Group Holdings, Inc., had been a significant share-holder of Tiger International since 1979, and with that vested interest offered, by design, an added dimension to that Board never witnessed before.

Robert P. Jensen replaced Hoffman as the Chairman and CEO of the corporation after a stormy "downslide," which, subsequently brought in Stephen M. Wolf in 1986. He eventually became Chairman of the Board, and President and CEO of Tiger International. Then Wolf was succeeded by young 33-year old James A. Cronin, III in September, 1987, who rose from the position as Tigers' VP Marketing, and held the presidency until mid-1989 when he was replaced by an interim President , Jeff Rodek, designated by Federal Express.

As of this writing, Stephen M. Wolf is the Chairman and President of mega-giant United Airline Corporation, and James A. Cronin became an executive administrator with Northwest Airlines for a period of time.

References

Questionnaires to Dick Rossi dated May 7 and August 5, 1991 (exceptionally helpful).

Tigereviews:
Special Issue "Robert W. Prescott...'Bob'" May 5, 1913-March 3, 1978.
"Bob's Number One," October, 1976.
"Remembering Bob," March, 1979.
"In Memorian; Robert W. Prescott," Feb/March 1978.

Nalty,Bernard C. **Tigers Over Asia**. New York: Elsevier-Dutton, 1978.

Toland, John. **The Flying Tigers**. New York: Random House, 1963.

Whelan, Russell. **The Flying Tigers: The Story of the American Volunteer Group**. New York: The Viking Press, 1942.

Hotz, Robert, edit. **Way of a Fighter: The Memoirs of Claire Lee Chennault**. New York: G.P. Putnam's Sons, 1949.

Cornelius, Wanda, and Thayne Short. **Ding Hao: America's Air War in China, 1937-1945**. Gretna: Pelican Publishing Co., 1980.

Hotz, Robert B. with the assistance of George L. Paxton, Robert H. Neale, and Parker S. Dupouy. **With General Chennault: The Story of the Flying Tigers**. New York: Coward-McCann, Inc., 1943.

Charles R. Bond, Jr., and Terry H. Anderson. **A Flying Tiger's Diary**. College Station: Texas A & M University Press, 1985.

Leary, William M., Jr. **The Dragon's Wings**. Athens: University of Georgia Press, 1976.

Young, Arthur N. **China and the Helping Hand, 1937-1945**. Cambridge: Harvard U. Press, 1963.

Boyington, "Pappy." **Baa Baa Black Sheep**. New York: Arno Press, 1972 Reprint.

11

Tiger on its Tail

During 1984, a group of Flying Tiger Airline executives held a series of system-wide employee meetings to expound upon the possibility of implementing an optional "hatchet" plan to liquidate the airline's domestic system save for six or seven international gateway cities in the U.S., which included Los Angeles, San Francisco, Chicago, New York, Miami, Dallas/Ft. Worth, and possibly Seattle or Atlanta. From an objective perspective, the ill-conceived strategy may have been interpreted as a survival method of starving off but ultimately settling serious organizational and financial problems which had developed since 1981, if not before. In fact, the corporate group had even advanced the idea that, as a last resort, the corporation may be forced to dismantle the entire airline. During the entire proceedings, there was no elaboration on any viable optional long range objectives of growth.

Subsequently, efforts to address the problems led to the sale of corporate non-airline subsidiaries in a series of "spin-off's" except for Warren Transport, in a move to focus on and strengthen the financial portfolio of Flying Tigers, the all-cargo airline, itself. In dismal irony, the entire DC-8 fleet was discarded by the end of 1984, substituted by a smaller number of much-lower capacity Boeing 727-100s cargo aircraft for deployment on the domestic system, which was experiencing a spiraling revenue decline. Corporate subsidiary losses became a liability at a time when subsidiary profits would have supported the worsening airline financial condition. Meanwhile, six B747s were acquired between 1981 and 1983 to bolster the still profitable Asia international freight segment.

The basis for Flying Tigers' **alarm** was reflected in simple statistical analysis extracted from the balance sheet. The company had a negative net worth in excess of $520 million in accumulated losses over the four-year period ending in December, 1985. Using a standard profit-and-loss measure, the airline sustained a pretax loss in four of five consecutive years since 1981, including a $22.9 million pretax loss that year; a $72.6 million loss in 1982; a $67.5 loss in 1983; a pretax gain in 1984, primarily due to the sale of aircraft and other assets; and, finally, a $44.2 million pretax loss in 1985. The carrier curbed its pretax loss to $18.6 million in 1986. Part of Tigers' demise was the escalating operating costs of which one significant uncontrollable element, aviation fuel costs, became almost prohibitive until 1983 when the prices dropped substantially.

In 1973, domestic cost of aviation fuel was about 12 cents per gallon, and rose to about 34 cents per gallon during the ensuing fuel crisis. For international operations, the price had increased from an average of 13 cents per gallon to about 34 cents per gallon the following year. From a general perspective, in 1974, the additional cost of aviation fuel amounted to more than $1 billion, which was more than three times the total net profit of all the U.S. scheduled airlines that year. By 1980, the cost of domestic aviation fuel doubled from 1973 prices, and the cost of international aviation fuel jumped about two-and-a half times The average price of aviation fuel was $1.13 per gallon in 1981, but decreased to 84 cents per gallon by 1984.

Burdened by the heavy acquisition costs in the Seaboard transaction (next chapter) in late 1980, Flying Tigers was also adversely affected by commitments to high-interest loans incurred during the early 1980s when interest rates peaked out. Loans negotiated in 1983 carried borrowing and spending restrictions of which the most punitive ones were the equipment capital trust loans involving Tiger aircraft. The exorbitant debt ratio became a key point during the 1987 "turn-around" when the airline was finally placed back on the road to profitability. Meanwhile, for five years or so, capital expenditures for growth almost came to a "standstill."

Fuel conservation poster designed to create company-wide awareness of ever-increasing fuel prices, their impact on our business, and ways employees can help conserve.

Source: Tigereview, August 24, 1981.

In early 1982, Flying Tigers expanded the door-to-door service with guaranteed delivery time directly to retail customers. As a result of door-to-door service increasing its share of the domestic volumes over airport-to-airport service, average domestic yields increased significantly. Consequently, although the 1982 airfreight volumes declined 42% from 1981 levels, the domestic revenues only declined 10% for the same period. The steady decline in domestic volumes was accounted for, in large part, by the impact of competing air cargo carriers established through the liberal policies associated with domestic air cargo deregulation.

Tigers' domestic route system experienced intense competition since the 1978 deregulation, on an increasing scale, when Tigers' former best customers set up their own air hub-and-spoke systems and freighter aircraft operations to complement their well-entrenched truck and courier service. Observing one parameter, for example, from 1978 to 1985, one air/truck courier and four foremost air freight (forwarder) carriers developed their fleet size from a collective total of zero to 177 air freighter aircraft to accommodate their re-structured needs. These opportunists included Airborne Air Freight having twenty-one aircraft with hub location at Wilmington, Ohio; Burlington Express with thirteen aircraft and hub location at Fort Wayne, Indiana; CF Air Freight using sixteen aircraft with hub location at Indianapolis, Indiana; Emery Air Freight employing forty-two aircraft and hub location at Dayton, Ohio; and United Parcel Service (UPS) with eighty-five aircraft and hub location at Louisville, Kentucky.[1] And, since 1973, UPS had regularly tendered high volumes of containerized small-package freight on a "blocked space" basis, having no aircraft of their own. Collectively, these couriers and consolidators were the mainstay of Tigers' domestic traffic constituting regularly 50% or more of the revenue freight on any given Tiger domestic flight.

Prior to domestic air cargo deregulation, the freight forwarders were CAB structured entities that did not actually transport the air freight but instead acted as agents between the shipper and the air carrier, although some charters were utilized. The air freight forwarders were indirect air carriers that conducted business under the exemption authority of the CAB. The air freight forwarder collected individual shipments, consolidated them into a large load, and trucked the shipment to an airline to fly to various destinations per container or bulk (loose freight). The forwarder could not charge rates higher than those available from the airline. Its profits came from the discounts available from the airline for tendering large loads at container or bulk rates. By tacit agreement, Flying Tigers, like other air cargo carriers, did not "chase" air freight forwarder customers, the primary shippers. Thus, understanding the matrix of the business-economic relationship between the air carrier and air freight forwarders, needless to say, Flying Tigers suffered a dramatic uprooting experience when the major air freight forwarders became air carriers on their own. Tigers' adjustment was slowly forthcoming.

The core asset of Flying Tigers' business was its aircraft fleet, and from 1982 to 1986, the carrier reduced the number of aircraft in its fleet by 21%, and its lift capacity even more, since all 26 or the DC-8s were replaced, on a few routes, by B727-100s having considerably less lift capacity and efficiency. Ironically, decreasing marketing opportunities, 21 or the 26 DC-8s were sold to competitors including twelve to UPS, five to Emery Air Freight, and four to German Cargo Service, a subsidiary of Lufthansa. **Tigers was doing a good job of going out of business!**[2]

The Tiger International Corporation, the parent organization of Flying Tigers, entered into a relatively brief and untimely interlude to develop a diversified transportation services portfolio in the early 1980s, involving aviation services and existing railcar services. In fact, the corporation also invested in a mortgage insurance company and other non-transportation related businesses.

North American Car, which was acquired by Tiger International in 1971, was an overwhelming success during the 1970s as an international lessor of railcars, conducting business in the U.S., Canada, Mexico, France and England, with a very large owned and managed fleet of railcars. It also; had a car manufacturing division which produced specialized covered hoppers and was involved in the development of a prototype railcar (RoadRailer) which was purportedly capable of running on railroads or being moved on highways by truck.

In 1976, the corporation acquired Flying Tiger Air Services, a firm engaged in the containerization program in the auto industry. And, in June, 1978, Tiger Air acquired AVIGUIPO, Lyndhurst, New Jersey, an export distributor of aviation parts and equipment.

Hall's Motor Transit Company was acquired on January 24, 1980, engaging in motor common carrier transportation, and was further expanded by the acquisition of Dohrn Transfer Company in January, 1981. Hall's as a general commodities carrier, operated primarily in the Central, Mid-Atlantic and Northeastern portion of the U.S., providing LTL and truckload services to those areas.

In February, 1981, the company acquired Colorado Air Center, Englewood, Colorado, which was also known as the Denver Jetcenter. It was operated by Tiger Air, Inc.

Warren Transport was acquired on June 1, 1981, operating as a specialized truckload hauler of heavy machinery and other specialized equipment for both the farm and construction industries. During 1982, Warren also expanded its operations into hauling truck-load shipments of general commodities, in particular, glass, packing materials and textiles.

In May, 1981, the corporation acquired Texas Railway Car Corporation, and numerous transportation-related businesses, for the most part, under the Tiger Leasing Group. NAC had merged with Tiger Leasing Group in March, 1977. Some of the firms included:

> California Tank Car Line, Inc.
> North American Car (Canada) Ltd.
> North American Hopper Car
> Tiger Rail Car Leasing (U.K.) Ltd.
> P & R Railcar Services Corp.
> Surface Transportation International, Inc.

The relative contributions of the corporate transportation sectors may be noted in the following consolidated income accounts:

Revenues (000)	1978	1979	1980	1981
Air cargo Services	$413,187	$465,152	$713,123	$924,702
Railcar Services	199,621	256,642	308,657	308,385
Aviation Services	53,001	88,803	118,500	148,476
Trucking	-----	-----	187,049	286,567
Other	26,687	36,723	45,548	5,220

	1982	1983	1984	1985
Air cargo	$924,202	1,019,832	1,171,017	1,109,022
Railcar Services	$254,535	-----	-----	-----
Trucking	$259,615	42,932	39,453	38,023
Other	$6,925	(5,896)	(580)	-----
Trucking & intermodal		$236,340		

Source: Moody's Transportation Manual, 1982 & 1986

Unfortunately, while forming the transportation conglomerate, the Tiger International Corporation had not tied all of its acquisitions together into a single operating company in an attempt to financially assist the airline operation, its main business. The Corporation had chosen to keep the newly acquired companies separately managed and operated except for its Seaboard World Airline acquisition in October, 1980. There has been speculation that perhaps it may have been appropriate for Tigers to explore the possibilities of entering the small package courier business during the period from 1976 to 1979 before and during the onset of domestic deregulation. Tigers was in a good financial position and the deregulation laws were liberal had the air carrier desired to acquire or merge with a freight forwarder with an established courier service, or some similar business arrangement.

Prior to domestic deregulation, U.S. antitrust laws and the CAB prevented Tigers from consolidating the individual operating companies which would have made Flying Tigers one of the largest American logistics companies in the world. And, it was doubtful that the CAB would have permitted Flying Tigers' domestic route expansion into additional U.S. cities and/or allowed its corporate involvement in closely aligned freight service companies.[3]

However, the corporation did create a scheduled and charter passenger airline, named Metro Airlines, aside from the air cargo operation. It is interesting to note that Seaboard had entered into the small-package service across the Atlantic during the deregulation period, and had received authority to carry passengers in the upper lounge of its B747 freighters.[4]

Subsequently, the recession of 1980-82 and the competition derived from trucking deregulation had an adverse effect upon the Tiger International Corporation subsidiaries. In effect, the Corporation sold or liquidated the subsidiaries except for Warren Transport, and re-aligned its primary its primary objectives to focus on its main business, Flying Tigers Airline.

In May, 1982, Tiger Air, Inc., announced that Lear Siegler, Inc., had acquired AVIQUIPO, Inc. Then, on December 31, 1982, the Corporation announced its plan for the sale and disposition of its Aviation Services segment, Tiger Air, itself. In 1983 and 1984, Tiger completed the sale of its AVIQUIPO subsidiary, its Aircraft Tank Services subsidiary, its Spare Parts division, and its fixed based operations at Salt Lake City, Utah, Denver, Colorado, and White Plains, New York.

Combined trucking and intermodal operations for 1983 reported a pretax loss of $9.6 million as compared with a pretax loss of $13.1 million in 1982, and 1981 pretax loss $3 million. The economic recession had severely impacted Hall's revenue base and although the economy had recovered to some extent in the latter half of 1983, there was no corresponding increase in volumes compared to 1982. The impact of deregulation also adversely affected Hall's revenues, as competition had intensified during 1983 as evidenced by competitive bidding and rate discounting in the trucking industry.

In consideration of assessed liabilities, the Corporation decided to sell Hall's Motor Transit. By the end of 1984, the Corporation had sold 75% of its equity interest in Hall's to certain members of Hall's management group. And a year later, the Corporation sold its remaining 25% interest in Hall's to Hall's Acquisition Corporation. Hall's was completely spun off in 1985 and subsequently filed Chapter 11 bankruptcy in March, 1986.

North American Car Corporation which merged with Tiger Leasing Group on March 31, 1977, also fell on hard times. Throughout the 1970s, North American Car had been an extremely profitable and separately managed enterprise of Tiger International Corporation. However, revenues for leasing and railcar sales activities experienced a significant decline during 1982 and 1983 as a result of lower fleet utilization and the continuing soft railcar market. Fleet utilization had declined from approximately 91% at the end of 1981, with an owned and leased fleet of about 63,000 cars, to approximately 81% utilization at the end of 1982, to an estimated 75% at the end of 1983 with about 46,000 railcars. Fleet utilization as the standard measure represented the proportion of railcars which were leased for specific trips with rentals based on mileage.

Railcar sales were also adversely affected as a result of the existing excess supply of railcars as well as high interest rates during 1982 and most of 1983. North American realized a pretax income of approximately $17.7 million in sales of tax benefits during 1981, and $13.5 million was realized in 1982. No tax benefit sales were made during 1983.

On September 7, 1983, North American Car entered into a Purchase and Loan Agreement with General Electric Credit Corporation (GECC) for the sale of certain assets. On December 15, 1983, North American Car completed the transfer of the management of, and the sale of certain of its railcar services to GECC. Upon the receipt of certain required consents by North American Car, it would sell some additional assets of its railcar services business and the majority of its railcar repair division facilities to GECC. At this time, Tiger International executed a promissory note in the principal amount of approximately $132 million payable to North American, representing advances previously made to Tiger International by North American. The debt was secured by 47% of Flying Tigers' stock. NAC was spun off, and filed Chapter 11 bankruptcy in 1984, and the debt was finally satisfied in March, 1988, retiring the note through finance restructuring.

In February, 1984, the Corporation announced plans to sell or liquidate all of the Tiger Leasing Group's operations in order to decrease the corporate debt by approximately $850 million. In its final hour, the Tiger Leasing Group made its most significant contribution to Flying Tigers. As planned, after the transaction, the company would have $750 million in restructured debt remaining. On December 5, 1984, Tiger Leasing Group, its direct subsidiary North American, and substantially all of its subsidiaries, and another indirect subsidiary of Tiger Leasing Group, filed voluntary petitions for reorganization under Chapter 11 of Title 11 of the United States Code. It is important to note that Tiger International was not a party to the Chapter 11 proceedings involving its "spun-off" subsidiaries. At the end, the diversification drive into intermodal plane, rail and truck cargo hauling proved to be quite disastrous.

Warren Transport, the other remaining subsidiary, was able to maintain profitability as a result of controlling its variable expenses in relationship to its lower revenues during 1983. That year of operation, it reported a pretax income of $2.3 million, as compared to $3.5 million in 1982, and $3.7 million during the last seven months of 1981. The decline was primarily a result of the severe economic problems of the farming and construction industries during 1983 as Warren was dependent upon those industries for majority of its revenue. Warren reported a pretax income of $2.1 million in 1986, and $2.5 million in 1987.

With the focus on Flying Tigers, itself, by 1983, substantially all of its operating fleet, being the main asset, was encumbered by equipment trust certificates, capital leases or similar obligations. In its financial nose dive, the company eventually sold off its entire fleet of efficient DC-8 jetfreighters, the domestic workhorse, by the end of 1984, and replaced them with B747 flights on selected domestic-gateway segments augmenting B727-100s, clearly a regressive policy. **Indeed, Tiger was on its tail!**

The relative net income losses was highlighted during the October-November, 1986 system-wide conferences as follows:

($ Millions)

	1981	1982	1983	1984	1985	6-30-86
Tiger Int'l	16.6	136.2	222.8	88.9	72.7	57.0
Flying Tigers	10.6	43.8	67.5	60.8*	44.2	44.4

* reflects the sale of assets and the capital gain booked

Source: **Tigereview,** "Chairman's Conference Highlights," Oct.-Nov., 1986.

B-727 Jetfreighter

B727-100 — Cross Section Main Deck

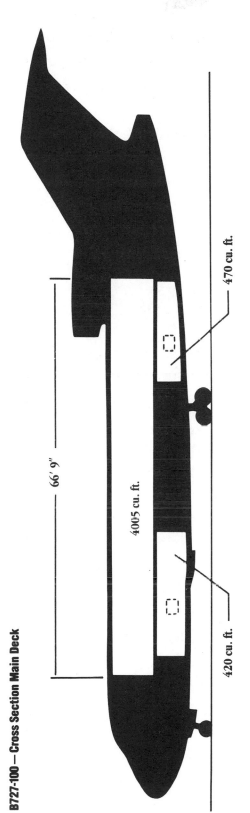

66' 9"

4005 cu. ft.

470 cu. ft.

420 cu. ft.

B727-100 — Cross Section Showing Container Placement

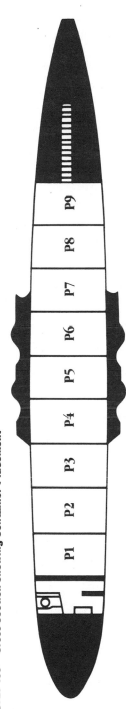

P1 P2 P3 P4 P5 P6 P7 P8 P9

B727-100 — Main Cargo Dimension

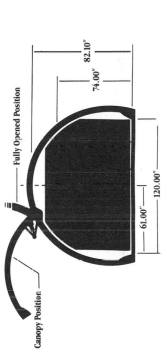

Fully Opened Position

Canopy Position

82.10"

74.00"

61.00"

120.00"

At a point of desperation, the Company sought out and hired, in August of 1986, an industry expert in the form of Stephen M. Wolf with proven "turn-around" experience. He became the Flying Tigers new Chief Executive Officer (CEO) and President, replacing Lewis H. Jordan, who, himself had held that position since October of the previous year.

Wolf's impact was rather immediate and stunning, especially at the company headquarters in Los Angeles airport. He quickly discontinued the employment of a "headquarter's chef" who had been hired to serve preferential personnel at Hi-Tiger's tenth floor service area. He also discontinued the company program of using leased cars for sales and executive staff system-wide. And, among other matters, in a strong symbolic "hatchet move," he instituted the sale of **Sea Tiger**, the company yacht, a pleasure craft harbored at nearby Marina del Ray.

After a short period of assessment and pre-planning, the Company established the three general building blocks to effect a "turn-around" for the carrier, which were categorically (1) reduce operating expenses to competitive level, (2) effect comprehensive financial restructuring while interest rates and terms remained favorable, and, (3) implement the long-term strategic plan in the marketplace while the global economy was growing.

In order for Flying Tigers to survive, it was deemed essential by arbitrary parties to obtain the unions' cooperation in lowering labor costs and institute work rule changes, along with other concessions. Once again, Wolf employed another "stunning" approach. In a pre-Thanksgiving ultimatum, particularly aimed at the Tiger pilot group for obvious reasons, he threatened to "close the airline down" should they not agree to the concessions in general. In fact, on November 19th, the Flying Tigers board of directors had presented its resolution through its system-wide bulletin to obtain offers for the purchase of the Company's assets. In a strong innuendo, the "hour was late," thus, bargaining was not a viable option. Terms were, in general, almost dictated. And, subsequently, the other unions fell in order.

Involved were three unions including (1) 650 pilots under the Air Line Pilots Association (ALPA), which, on November 27th, reached an agreement on a 42-month comprehensive economic cost reduction plan; (2) 2,000 mechanics, ramp service and related employees under the International Association of Machinists and Aerospace Workers (IAM), who reached agreement on December 17th on a three-year plan and (3) 200 flight attendants represented by the Association of Flight Attendants (AFA), altogether constituting almost half the work force of 6200 workers, who finally reached an agreement in January. Included in the wage cuts were most of the 2600 General and

Administrative personnel, and approximately 700 foreign-based employees. The rollback reduced Flying Tigers' labor bill about 22% (fixed) over the following 3½ years. Overall, contract cuts and work rule changes helped pare about $58 million a year from operating costs. The work force was reduced including purportedly 8% from the management group, totaling over 120 from the management and sales segment.

In exchange for the substantial sacrifices extracted from the employees, Tiger established a profit-sharing partnership program that would distribute 15% of company profits after the first $10 million to full-time participating employees. Included in the plan was a newly instituted employee stock option program.

Other moves to rebuild employee pride in the Flying Tiger airline included re-introduction of the "Circle T" tail symbol, used from 1961 to 1976, on jetfreighter fin sections. The movement included the development of an enlarged logo, the Tigerface, all with the intent to rekindle the "Tiger spirit."

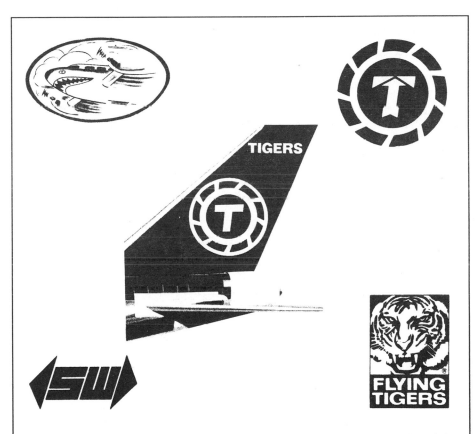

Logos . . . past and present. Flying Tigers original logo, the shark insignia, **above left,** gave way to the Circle T, **above right,** in 1960, but continued to appear on Flying Tigers aircraft through 1967. Seaboard World Airlines, which merged with Flying Tigers in October 1980, used the S and W logo, **bottom left,** from 1960. Flying Tigers logo today, the distinctive Tigerface, **bottom right,** will remain as a service mark along with the reintroduced Circle T, **center.**

Another tactic to get Tigers' finances in order was a restructuring of equipment debt. Lower interest rates and a higher market valuation of the company's B747 jetfreighter fleet helped reduce debt from $327 million at the end of 1984 to $274 million in 1986. These changes are expected to trim Tigers' principal and interest expense by $100 million over a five year period. Satisfying the loans also would free the company from capital expenditure limitation of $10 million a year, enabling the carrier to increase its fleet, and gain an advantage in the marketplace derived therefrom.

By January, 1987, the company was concentrating on restructuring about $300 million of its $525 million long-term debt, removing some very restrictive covenants, and devising a new marketing strategy to strengthen Flying Tigers presence in the global air cargo arena. And while pilot wages had been slashed appreciably at the beginning of 1987, airline expansion had swelled their ranks from 650 to 780 within a year to accommodate the upcoming acquisition of six leased DC-8 jetfreighters to serve the domestic market and international gateways.

In general, the marketing approach appeared to involve building the fleet capability, and offer shippers a wider spectrum of new destinations and routing, more frequent flights on selective segments, together with providing a variation of service offerings to meet customer needs. However, noting the "building blocks" sequence, Tigers' move to lease the additional aircraft couldn't have been accomplished without a debt restructuring completed earlier in 1987, in a period characterized by a more promising economic climate with lower fuel costs and favorable interest rates and terms. The timely reduction of Tigers' interest costs occurred as the air cargo industry experienced a steady period of growth, both domestically and internationally.

However, for Flying Tigers, the seemingly favorable climate was moderated by the new mix of players within a keener field of competition. The carrier needed to meet the challenge and re-establish its position and image in the changing global air cargo industry.

If you want to stay first in this business, you have to earn your stripes every day.

FLYING TIGERS

The world's leading airfreight airline.

A Tiger International Company

Notes

1. **Tigereview**, "Chairman's Conference Highlights," Oct.- Nov., 1986.

2. Ibid.

3. Nawal K. Taneja, **Airlines in Transition** (Lexington: D.C.Heath, 1981).

4. --------,**The U.S. Airfreight Industry** (Lexington: D.C. Heath, 1976) p. 41.

5. Additional source: Much of the material included in this section was acquired from Moody's Transportation Manuals with information provided by the Flying Tiger Airline and its parent, Tiger International Corporation.

12

Seaboard World Airlines Acquisition

Prior to Tigers' global expansion in scheduled service, it was primarily a scheduled U.S. and Asia-oriented air cargo carrier, deploying a limited amount of charters to cover its other geographic and time-selection needs not afforded by its limited scheduled flight structure. Interlining was also an alternate heavily employed. However, commercial charters provided an avenue for air cargo marketing opportunities which were, for the most part, inherently profitable. Understandably, Flying Tigers became the largest all-cargo charter airline in the world before 1970, and, at one time, as has been noted, derived 30 to 40% of its gross revenues from air cargo charters during its early years.

The thoughts of liberalization with the removal of CAB constraints, and the promise of opportunity ushered in by deregulation provided the rationale for the merger of Flying Tigers and Seaboard World Airways, two of the largest scheduled and charter all-cargo carriers based in the U.S., with the former being the surviving company. For Flying Tiger Line, Inc., an obvious benefit of the merger included the immediate authority to offer or continue scheduled air freight services to Seaboard World's international routes in Europe and the Middle East, stretching from London to Bahrain, on the Persian Gulf, a possible "stepping stone" in establishing a round-the-world route. From a long term perspective, Tigers would be able to directly service, if not develop, all the major global air cargo markets in the foreseeable future.

In addition, Tigers would receive authority to transport passengers, with some restrictions, on existing Seaboard international routes, linking with the New York (JFK) gateway. The carrier also would inherit the lucrative MAC commitments serviced by Seaboard in both the Asia and the North Atlantic region, thus, fortifying and strengthening its allocation of MAC contracts.

However, attached to the acquisition was the debt structure of Seaboard which added to the financial woes of Tiger International when the thrust for "intermodal" in the early 1980s proved to be a very untimely decision, though taking advantage of the liberalization of regulatory constraints in the U.S. transportation industry. In 1980, the European air freight market was hammered by a rate war and escalating aviation fuel costs.

Seaboard World Airlines, principally a U.S.-Europe traffic operator, was formally merged into the Flying Tiger operation on October 1, 1980. The strategy was a culmination of efforts by Tigers, who, in February, 1978, acquired 600,000 shares (99.9%) of Seaboard World common stock, which, ultimately, became a $450 million investment for the acquisition. Subsequently, in August, 1979, the companies announced that definite merger agreement had been approved by both boards, and in September 8, 1980, Company shareholders approved the plan of merger. Both airlines were certificated all-cargo carriers but with each's focus of operation in different air freight markets, and employing different strategies of operation. Tigers had a larger fleet mix and capacity, and had a work force of almost 6800, while Seaboard had almost 1700 employees throughout its system.

The Seaboard acquisition enabled Flying Tigers to connect its Asian routes with Seaboard's European routes in New York, allowing the carrier to service approximately 80% of the major air cargo routes in the world, at the time. Thus, Tigers acquired access to selective high traffic European air freight markets, modern cargo facilities at the JFK gateway, route rights beyond Europe to Bahrain, and five key European air cargo points including London (European hub), Frankfurt, Zurich, Milan, and Paris, and retained the Seaboard personnel to handle the operations.

The staff merger Stateside seemed somewhat amicable, especially among unionized employees. Seaboard employees, many holding high seniority, were able to hold their seniority positions in the integration.

Nevertheless, in profiling Seaboard prior to the merger, the carrier was certificated to also serve U.S. domestic markets between Los Angeles, San Francisco,

Seaboard World B747 Containership

Chicago, Detroit, Cleveland, Baltimore, Philadelphia, Washington, D.C., and Boston. However, the carrier was not allowed to operate between any of these cities and New York, which was not only the hub of its operations but an important city and gateway for feeding its transatlantic flights from these other domestic cities. This severe operating restriction forced Seaboard to cease its money-losing domestic operations at one time. However, as a result of deregulation, the carrier had restarted its domestic service on a limited basis to feed its transatlantic operations.[1]

Seaboard maintained offices in eleven U.S. cities, eighteen European points besides four in the United Kingdom, Canada, Japan, and Lebanon, with the executive offices at JFK in New York. The carrier also reportedly had MAC contracts between the U.S. and various points in Europe and Asia, and was authorized to carry U.S. mail between the U.S. and ten foreign countries on a non-subsidy basis, and carry European mail to the U.S. on the same routes.[2]

Prior to the merger, Seaboard reportedly had a composite fleet of five B747-245Fs, one B747-273C (convertible), five DC-8-63Fs, one DC-8-55F, and a DC-10-30CF. The B747-245Fs were equipped with nineteen passenger seats in the upper deck to accommodate the carrier's supplementary passenger service. Except for the DC-10, which was disposed of before the merger, Flying Tigers acquired the complementary fleet in support of its fleet mix which included thirty jetfreighters, namely two B747-200F (with another two on order), seven B747-100Fs, fourteen DC-8-63Fs, and seven DC-8-61Fs.[3] The use of the B747 jetfreighters allowed Seaboard to transport large 8 x 8 x 20 foot containers through a "nose load" operation.

Although the carrier had focused on the transportation of the air-truck intermodal containers, it had also hauled heavier maritime 40-foot containers. Seaboard specialized in transporting heavy containerized shipments; almost half of its freight (in weight) consisted of shipments weighing more than 20,000 lbs. In 1974, Seaboard introduced the 20-foot intermodal containers, a special lightweight design of which they owned 152 units with 100 more on order, at the time, and options for 200 additional units.[4] Seaboard's B747 jetfreighters were referred to an **Containerships**, projecting their image in competition with Lufthansa, but enjoying little success.

Seaboard nose-load operation

Seaboard posted highest revenues in its history in 1979, and a net profit of $12 million, up from $11 million in 1978. However, a careful analysis indicated that $58 million of the $204 million in revenues received in 1979 were derived from maintenance and leasing activities, and substantial portion from MAC revenues. Due to heavy competition and characteristically low tariffs in the North Atlantic air cargo routes, Seaboard continued to operate in "the red" in that segment of its operation, which was its primary business. Beginning to experience an upturn, Seaboard instituted a $11 million program prior to the merger to upgrade its JFK cargo facilities, as well as those at Heathrow and Frankfurt. Unfortunately, Seaboard experienced an unexpectedly poor financial report during the third quarter of 1980, on the eve of the merger, and, consequently, with the executive shuffle which came about, more than two hundred Seaboard middle managers, who had hopes of retaining their jobs, were furloughed.[5]

Despite Seaboard's concentration on the transportation of intermodal containers, the carrier had been active in broadening its service. Seaboard had entered into the small-package service across the Atlantic. In May, 1978, the carrier commenced operations of Speedway, a transatlantic parcel express service between the U.S. and London, Paris, and Frankfurt. Seaboard was also receiving additional revenue exercising its authority to carry passengers in the upper lounge of its B747 freighters. The supplementary passenger operations served as a wedge against the carrier's seasonal variation in freight volumes and revenues, taking advantage of the summer and Christmas tourist seasons when the air freight business on the North Atlantic experienced substantial decreases.

With the Seaboard acquisition, Flying Tigers did not continue the international parcel express service nor the supplementary passenger operation on its B747 freighters in the North Atlantic. In fact, while Seaboard was primarily a container "nose load" B747 operator, Tigers preferred the better capacity yield "side and/or nose load" option for loading purposes on its B747 freighters on all its routes.

Tigers was also hindered by the low tariffs characteristic of the North Atlantic air cargo area of which the carrier sought to address as early as possible. The carrier also inherited a host of discriminatory regulatory policies favoring European national carriers which ultimately caused Seaboard to withdraw its membership from eco-political oriented IATA in 1971. At the time, Seaboard filed its own tariffs independently in the United States and Germany, and these tariffs were approved by the governments, despite the objection of IATA members.[6] Tigers, however, remained an active member of IATA.

To adjust to Flying Tigers' system-wide needs, effective October 1, 1980, the date of the merger, Tigers cut North Atlantic flight capacity by some 30%, to twelve flights a week. In 1981, the carrier established Heathrow (LHR) airport in London as its European hub, and opened up a new cargo terminal at Frankfurt, Germany, which became the other European hub in 1983, serving continental Europe.

Flying Tigers was spreading its wings!

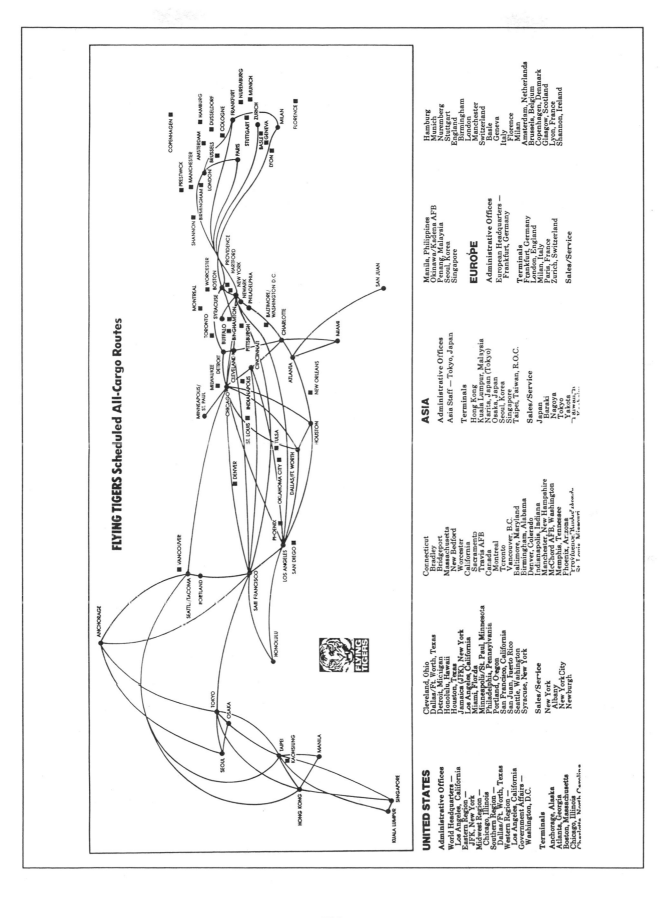

FLYING TIGERS Scheduled All-Cargo Routes

By March 1, 1982, Tigers provided single-carrier scheduled service to fourteen foreign countries, and accelerated its domestic door-to-door service through its Chicago hub. The foreign countries spanned the three most progressive air cargo regions of Asia, Europe, and North America, though not exercising its flight rights in to the Middle East at that time:

Mexico City (Mexico)	Singapore
Tokyo & Osaka (Japan)	Shannon (Ireland)
Seoul (S. Korea)	Paris (France)
Hong Kong	Frankfurt (Germany)
Taipei & Kaohsiung (Taiwan)	Zurich (Switzerland)
Manila (Philippines)	Milan (Italy)
Kuala Lumpur (Malaysia)	London (United Kingdom)

Service to Benelux and Scandinavia was provided via truck service to and from Flying Tiger cities served by its air route. Primarily because of the geographic features of Western Europe and the significant amounts of short and medium-range hauls between Tiger points, the carrier's European system lends itself more efficiently to a well-developed air/truck hub system, despite the matrix of numerous international borders. The region's surface transportation system had been successfully developed since WWII. There, Frankfurt, for example, was suitable as a centralizing air cargo hub for Tigers, as with many of the other air carriers serving western Europe.

In 1983, the transatlantic market for Tigers experienced an 8% decrease in revenue ton miles which, in part, was the result of Flying Tigers revising its marketing approach in that market to adjust to the low yields prevailing at the time. The transatlantic route system continued to be adversely affected during 1983, and excess capacity made implementation of rate increases difficult. Therefore, effective October 8, 1983, the carrier reduced flight frequency across the Atlantic by 50% and established two European hubs, one located at London and one in Frankfurt. Scheduled flights to the Netherlands, France, Switzerland, and Italy were replaced by a trucking system operating out of the hubs. The new approach, though, temporary, reduced fixed costs in Europe, and allowed Flying Tigers to re-deploy aircraft to the Asian market where demand continued to increase. The Tiger transpacific route network remained strong during 1983 with revenues increasing by 45% due primarily to higher volumes,[7] and high yields supported by JAL.

In Europe, Flying Tigers inherited from Seaboard an intensely competitive field of well-established national and consortium European community air carriers, and

U.S.S.R.'s national carrier, Aeroflot. In 1984, Tigers accounted for 182.5 million freight ton kilometers (FTKs) in its European system. Though system-wide statistics are available for carriers serving Europe in 1984, a comparative analysis between the carriers may offer the reader an objective viewpoint of Tigers' competition in that air cargo arena:

Carrier	1984 FTKs (000)
Aeroflot of U.S.S.R.	2,750,000
Air France	2,413,268
Lufthansa of W. Germany	2,274,800
British Airways	1,120,390
KLM of Netherlands	1,423,646
Alitalia of Italy	681,235
Cargolux of Luxembourg	744,000
Swiss Air	634,093
Sabena of Belgium	533,851

Source: Air Transport World 1984 statistics

After a period of re-organization, Tigers renewed service to Brussels, Belgium in 1984, and Zurich, Switzerland in 1985, to strengthen its global commitments by providing more scheduling and routing flexibility within its network. The Zurich facility included the installation of a new low profile warehouse system and the utilization of surplus equipment from other Flying Tigers European stations. Considerable savings was realized and a more efficient cargo-handling system was implemented through the collective "brainstorming" effort of airlines' maintenance and terminal staffs with extensive Tiger and Seaboard experience.

Metro International Airways B-747-200B passenger aircraft.

Metro International

Interestingly enough, in March of 1981, Flying Tigers started a commercial scheduled and charter passenger airline named Metro International. From a historical perspective, it was a relatively short interlude.

Flying Tigers had for three decades or more been a successful military and private passenger charter operator, and during the 1960s and 1970s, with CAB charter authority, had operated many commercial passenger charters between the U.S. and Europe on a seasonal basis. Shortly after the Seaboard merger, Tigers started a commercial scheduled and charter passenger airline, while still maintaining its MAC passenger commitments worldwide, including those contracts acquired through the merger.

As a corollary to the Seaboard acquisition, Tigers acquired passenger authority across the North Atlantic on routes feeding between the U.S. east coast (New York) and certain European and Middle East points. About the same time, it had been noted that the carrier had acquired three former Singapore Airlines B747-200 convertible aircraft, purchased by another Tiger International subsidiary, Tiger Air, but did not have a buyer or lessee immediately at hand.[8] This combination offered an opportunity to bolster the cargo and charter business segment with additional lift, and, for the immediate needs, could be profitable in passenger service.

In a sequence of developments, North Atlantic commercial passenger charter flights took place in December, 1980, using this equipment and a DC-8. Metro International, itself, made its public debut in March, 1981. The name **Metro International** was selected in order to preserve the Flying Tigers' image as a cargo carrier, and concurrently gave the passenger operation its own identity on which to build a reputation. However, the flights were operated by Flying Tigers pilots, flight attendants and support staff. The new paint jobs were done at the LAX main maintenance facility by Tiger personnel.

'Tail'ored by Flying Tigers

Through 1981, Metro operated charters to Israel, Greece, Portugal and other popular points in Europe, and to the Caribbean. Changing market developments caused scheduled New York-Brussels service to be postponed from December until March, 1982, while Metro continued its worldwide passenger charter flights. On the B747 flights, Metro featured three types of passenger service: the Captain's Deck with premier business class seating on the upper deck; Metropolitan Class with conventional business class seating; and Economy Class in the aft section.

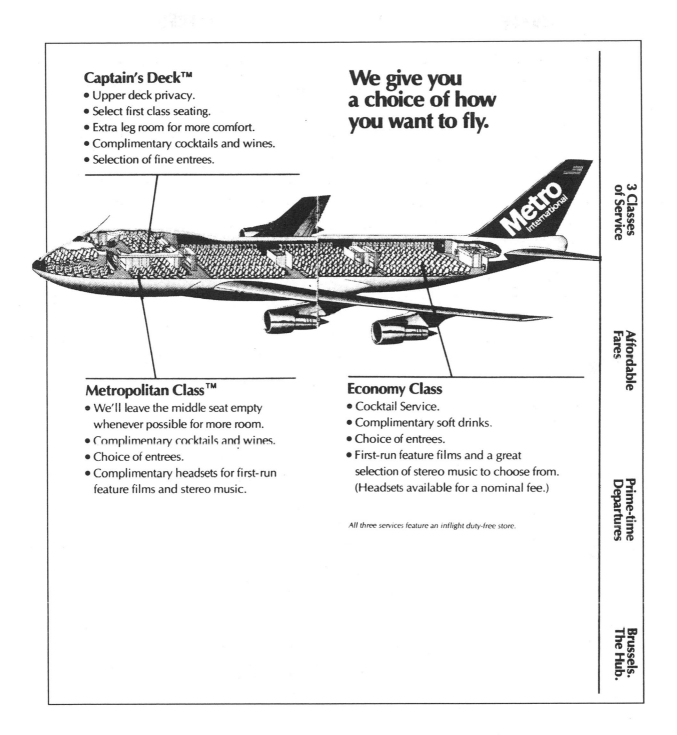

Captain's Deck™
- Upper deck privacy.
- Select first class seating.
- Extra leg room for more comfort.
- Complimentary cocktails and wines.
- Selection of fine entrees.

We give you a choice of how you want to fly.

Metropolitan Class™
- We'll leave the middle seat empty whenever possible for more room.
- Complimentary cocktails and wines.
- Choice of entrees.
- Complimentary headsets for first-run feature films and stereo music.

Economy Class
- Cocktail Service.
- Complimentary soft drinks.
- Choice of entrees.
- First-run feature films and a great selection of stereo music to choose from. (Headsets available for a nominal fee.)

All three services feature an inflight duty-free store.

3 Classes of Service

Affordable Fares

Prime-time Departures

Brussels. The Hub.

Metro suspended DC-8 passenger operations February 23, 1982, as the result of lower expectations in its DC-8 segment. DC-8 MAC passenger trips were suspended in September, 1981. And, unfortunately, changing circumstances resulted in disposing of its three B747 passenger aircraft in early 1983, and, consequently, the termination of Metro operations. Leased aircraft were employed to continue the Tiger military passenger service. And some flight attendants were re-assigned to that service segment of the airline.

Metro had utilized about two hundred and fifty flight attendants, including some new hires, to staff the on-going military and commercial (charter and scheduled) operations for the program, with the personnel serving the North Atlantic operation based at JFK, Metro's base of operation. The carrier continued to retain the military charter personnel based at San Francisco to service the Pacific military charters.

In the final analysis, passenger charter operations had played a significant role in the Tiger worldwide charter system during 1980 and 1983, and is reflected in its relative contribution in generated revenues during that period, as follows:

Commercial Charter operations

Generated Revenues ($000)	1980	1981	1982	1983
Total cargo and passenger	$80,164	$98,981	$93,154	$66,644
Passenger charters (PAX)	25,326	35,087	39,997	16,372
MAC charters (cargo & PAX)	86,035	112,045	112,045	114,984

Source: Moody's Transportation Manual, 1984.

The commercial charter revenues in 1983 represented a decline of 31% from 1982, while the 1982 revenues, in turn, declined 6% from 1981 levels. The substantial decrease in 1983 was primarily a result of the termination of Metro International Airways passenger flights, reverting back to Tiger charter operations only. It appeared as though the problem with Metro's operation was the timing, in that, as an off-shoot of the Flying Tiger system, it came under scrutiny during the period of rising financial and operational crisis, and fleet capacity adjustments. Perceived as a supplement to the air cargo carrier segment, Metro's equipment was measured along the competitive lift requirements of the freight sector in the growing Asia market and European markets, thus falling victim to its parent system. Also, at the time, the carrier's newly developing South American routes required the replacement of DC-8s with B747 freighters.

In early 1983, Flying Tigers and Pan American World Airways exchanged four Pan American World B747-100 freighters for three Flying Tiger B747-200 passenger aircraft involved with the Metro program. In essence, Tigers exchanged three B747-200 PAX airframes and related equipment for four B747-100 freighter airframes, four engines, and related equipment. The swap enabled Flying Tigers to concentrate resources into its air cargo business where its utilization would suggestively produce higher yields than the Metro operation. Thus, the chapter closed on Metro International.

Notes

1. Nawal M. Taneja, **The U.S. Airfreight Industry** (Boston: Lexington Books) 1976, p. 38.

2. **Moody's Transportation Manual**, 1978, 1979, and 1982.

3. **Air Transport World**, May, 1980, Vol. 17, No. 5.

4. Op. cit., **The U.S. Airfreight Industry**, pp. 40-41.

5. Joan M. Feldman, "The Flying Tiger and Seaboard: After 32 onths, Finally A Merger," **Air Transport World** (Cleveland) January, 1981, Vol. 18, No. 1, p. 46.

6. Op. cit., **The U.S. Airfreight Industry**, p. 42.

7. **Moody's Transportation Manual**, 1984.

8. Op. cit., "Flying Tiger and Seaboard: After 32 Months, Finally A Merger," p. 46.

9. **Air Transport World**, October, 1984, Vol. 21, No. 10.

13

Flying Tigers Emerges as America's First
Scheduled Around-the-World Air Cargo Carrier

During the 1980s, Flying Tigers developed into the world's foremost commercial scheduled air cargo carrier with an extensive global network while still promoting its truck/air segment, its commercial charter operations, and its MAC opportunities. Since 1975, after the Vietnam airlift, Tigers has been the largest recipient of MAC awards because of its increase in CRAF fleet contribution and other considerations, while competing participants have proportionately decreased their contribution, if not deceasing service altogether. Tigers' thrust to gain prominence in the international air cargo marketplace has been highlighted with the development of its new air cargo hub near Columbus, Ohio. The facilities feature the latest technological advantages and full-service capability to handle domestic and international shipments in a single integrated system. Through systematic design, the carrier has expanded its geographic network to include five round-the-world scheduled flights, interconnecting with its single-carrier service to all major air cargo markets supporting B747 freighter service.

By 1986, Flying Tigers had expanded its scheduled single-carrier air freight service network extending to all continents except for Africa, which is served through interlining. The carrier's global network provides scheduled service to twenty-five foreign countries through Asia and the Pacific Rim, Europe, the Middle East, Latin

America and the Caribbean, Australia, New Zealand, and North America. According to IATA statistics, Tigers has been the largest scheduled air freight carrier since 1979 when the carrier accounted for 1.7 billion revenue freight ton-kilometers (FTKs). Tigers is also the world's number one air freight carrier by virtue of its extensive geographic network in scheduled service. This significant new dimension places Flying Tigers in a preferred positive posture within the air cargo industry operating in the developing global economy promoting international trade.

In September, 1983, Flying Tigers inaugurated scheduled service to Australia via Honolulu and Los Angeles, taking advantage of the carrier's fleet flexibility. The circular route provided opportunities for the South Pacific-Asia lift, then repositioned the aircraft to the regular Asia-to-U.S. east-bound schedule.

After the Seaboard acquisition, the Asia and Pacific Rim air cargo markets continued to be the most profitable segment of the entire Tiger system. Because of its more dominating posture in Asia, Tigers purportedly handled 20% of the international air cargo in 1982, but declined to 14% market share by mid-1986, in terms of total air cargo volumes.[1]

Akin to the European situation, discriminatory policies and regulatory constraints against Tigers was also prevalent in Asia. For example, the airline could not negotiate the authority through bilateral agreements to carry Hong Kong-origin air freight to any other Asian points which the carrier served, thus, excluding Tigers from a significant market segment. Consequently, the situation resulted in unused or under-used capacity in its aircraft during slow traffic seasons, accentuating chronic cyclic downturns during the first half of each year.

According to 1984 statistics, although system-wide for each carrier, Flying Tigers' major competitors in Asia appeared to be:

Carrier (Asia operators)	System-wide FTKs (000)
JAL of Japan	2,501,619
KAL of S. Korea	1,458,000
Singapore Airlines	961,194
Northwest Orient Airlines	1,410,167
Cathay Pacific of Hong Kong	668,035
China Airlines of Taiwan	478,029
Flying Tigers (Asia only)	479,100

Source: Air Transport World magazine statistics for 1984.

Nippon Air Cargo (NAC), presently a prime competitor, began operations in 1985, but increasing its trans-Pacific market share to 7% by the end of 1986. In May of 1987, **Air Transport World** computations reported NCA still holding 7% trans-Pacific market share, while JAL held 21%, Northwest at 17%, KAL at 14%, and Tigers rose back to 20%.

In 1984, with the Pacific and North Atlantic route system in place, Flying Tigers entered the Middle East and Latin American air freight markets, offering scheduled air freighter service for the first time to some points. In continuing the development of its international market niche as a scheduled global carrier, Tigers inaugurated service through the Mid-East corridor as another "stepping stone" for its soon-to-be east-west round-the-world system using single service. The prime focus was moving Asian air freight traffic to European markets. Extensive studies of the directional growth of international air freight had noted that the high potential for marketing opportunities in the Tiger world-wide system should incorporate an around-the-world route.

As an initiating strategy, on May 1, 1983, Flying Tigers instituted a joint operating agreement with Saudi Arabian Airlines (Saudia), starting a scheduled weekly all-cargo service to Jeddah, reaching the Saudi Arabian markets with direct B747 jetfreighter service from the United States. In addition, the airline allocated 50,000 lbs. of space to Tigers on a weekly service to Dubai, United Arab Emirates, situated at the mouth of the Persian Gulf. Serving U.S. shippers rather than European shippers, as had been the case previously, the routing of the flight proceeded from New York, London, Brussels, then to Dubai. Service for Tiger shippers to other major Middle East markets was provided for in agreements with other national flag carriers of the Middle East. In addition to Mid-East markets, Tigers also served Ankara and Istanbul, Turkey, through an interline agreement with Turkish Airlines, providing the only regularly scheduled all-cargo service between the U.S. and Turkey. The interline freight was transferred at Frankfurt and London, the Flying Tiger hubs, onto Turkish Airlines B707 freighter and DC-10 passenger aircraft lower compartments.

Subsequently, Flying Tigers inaugurated its own single-carrier direct jetfreighter service from the interior U.S. to Saudi Arabia on October 5, 1985, using Dhahran on the Persian Gulf as the gateway terminus. The weekly joint venture with Saudi Airlines allowed Tigers to utilize the entire B747 freighter from San Francisco to Houston, then to New York, where Flying Tigers and Saudia shared space on the aircraft exiting JFK. Cargo destined to Jeddah or Riyadh, among the larger Saudi Arabian markets, were interlined through Saudia Airlines. The Tiger aircraft was routed through Brussels to coordinate with transload and European-origin traffic destined for or through Mid-East areas, then proceeded to Dubai, U.A.E. after departing Dhahran. From Dubai, through an interline agreement with Air India, Tigers provided all-cargo service to Bombay, Delhi, Calcutta and Madras, India.

On October 1 of that year, Tigers entered an interline agreement with Viking Airfreight to promote marketing opportunities to Africa and the Middle East with air shipments to Sudan, Egypt, Nigeria, Pakistan and Somalia. By December 1, the interline involved over 108 destinations throughout Africa, the Middle East, and the Indian Sub-Continent. And, by spring of 1988, this segment of the Flying Tiger global system extended to over 130 off-line destinations, including additions in the Soviet Union and Eastern Europe. Although London continued to be the designated transfer point for the interline, Tigers hoped to establish transfer points in Asia and Latin America, and retaining Viking Airfreight as the single transfer agent.

Systematically, employing interline arrangements, charter agreements, and joint ventures, Flying Tigers extended its world-wide coverage to augment its single-carrier global network. The manner of penetration was unmistakable. In late 1984, the carrier established a bilateral agreement with Air Lanka of Sri Lanka, the island nation situated off southeast India, for interlining air freight to sub-Asia via Asian and European interline points. The connecting gateways were Tigers' London and Frankfurt hubs in Europe, and Hong Kong, Singapore, and Tokyo in Asia, using B747 and L-1011 aircraft. Subsequently, Tigers entered negotiations with Air Lanka to provide scheduled service to Colombo in the form of a joint venture between the two carriers. At the latest, Tigers is seeking a weekly scheduled service to Colombo should the carrier obtain flight rights, adopting the same strategy upon entering the Australian and New Zealand markets, then increasing frequency as needed. Meanwhile, Colombo serves as an important fuel stop on its round-the-world system, circumventing China, and proceeding to Bangkok.

Flying Tigers began charter service to Mexico City in 1981, leading to regular scheduled service the following year using a Houston gateway. Subsequently, the route was discontinued, however, the carrier is presently negotiating for a resumption of scheduled service. And, in 1983, Tigers penetrated the Latin American air freight market with scheduled service once provided by another U.S.-based all-cargo carrier. Airlift International was the last significant U.S.-based all-freight carrier to offer scheduled service to Latin America and the Caribbean before Tigers developed its network. In 1978, Airlift served twelve countries in Latin America and the Caribbean region with the U.S. markets.

Flying Tigers' primary competitors in that global segment were Avianca, Varig, and Aerolineas Argentina, and Pan American:

Carrier	FTKs in 1984(000)	FTKs in 1985(000)
Varig of Brazil	651,571	700,689
Avianca of Chile	221,526	194,259
Aerolineas Argentina	Unk	
175,200		
Flying Tigers		
(Latin America only)	32,339	45,799

*Pan American's statistics for Latin America FTKs appeared to be within the range of those for Avianca and Aerolineas Argentina.

Source: Air Transport World 1984 and 1985 statistics, derived from DOT and IATA.

In the Latin America route system, Flying Tigers used JFK and Miami as the international gateways, with the latter designated as the regional hub for the north-south route operating between the U.S. east coast and industrial-commercial east coast of South America, namely Brazil and Argentina. Scheduled service was also extended to selective intervening Caribbean points. After opening scheduled B747 freighter service to Buenos Aires, Rio de Janeiro, and Sao Paulo in 1983, the carrier commenced service to Port of Spain, Trinidad, on January 23, 1985, an island nation located off the northeast coast of Venezuela. Consequently, Tigers became the only B747 all-cargo carrier connecting Port of Spain with single carrier scheduled service linking North America, Asia, Europe and South America. The additional traffic provided an intervening opportunity to supplement Tigers' freighter in support of B747 wide-body capacity. Prior to this service, Trinidad air cargo service was limited to B707 freighter lift and passenger belly-pit operators. It was noted that Trinidad ranked sixth in size among all U.S. air tonnage export markets in Latin American countries, at the time.

On June 3, 1985, Tigers inaugurated B747 jetfreighter service to Caracas, Venezuela, offering shippers the only all-cargo single-carrier service linking Caracas to North America, Asia, and Europe. The flight frequency was three times weekly, with, reportedly, the highest yield per ton air freight on Tigers' system. In Caracas, the warehouse facilities for imports and exports were owned and operated by Flying Tiger personnel, and provided interline service to other Venezuelan points.

Subsequently, Tigers inaugurated scheduled service to Manaus, Brazil, and

FLYING TIGERS LATIN AMERICAN SYSTEM (1988)

Santo Domingo, Dominion Rep. (SDQ)*

New York (JFK)

Curacao (CUR)

Miami (MIA)

Port-of-Spain, Trinidad (POS)*

Caracas, Venezuela (CCS)*

Manaus (MAO)

BRAZIL

Rio de Janiero (GIG)

São Paulo (VCP)

Buenos Aires (EZE) Argentina

* Scheduled service suspended

Curaco, an island nation located northwest of Caracas. And, in 1987, Tigers shifted the Latin America hub to Sao Paulo as a logical move for better control, being more geographically situated to the area of business.

A comparative analysis of Flying Tigers' area revenue statistics reveal the profound dominance of Asia traffic as a contributor in the entire system:

Scheduled Cargo Operations (000)	1983	1984	1985	1986	1987
Domestic (U.S.)		$214,872	$212,929	$155,601	$142,985
TransPacific	$503,953	653,395	544,177	599,781	689,407
Trans Atlantic	123,721	98,367	105,368	83,848	82,010
Latin America	23,397	41,402	63,988	45,409	50,409

Source: Moody's Transportation Manual, 1987, and Tiger International, Inc., 1987 Annual Report.

In its quest to establish a round-the-world scheduled service, Flying Tigers expanded its geographic base in Asia. On February, 1987, Tigers commenced with a weekly scheduled B747 jetfreighter service to one of the largest gateway cities in Southeast Asia. The event marked the second time that Flying Tigers had offered scheduled service to Bangkok, Thailand, initially serving that point from October, 1970, to December, 1975, shortly after the cessation of hostilities in Vietnam.

On February 2, 1987, the carrier inaugurated charter service to Colombo, Sri Lanka. Being strategically located, as with Dubai, U.A.E., the point served as an intervening opportunity along Tigers' global route, providing the role as an important fuel stop and potential market for scheduled service. Its significance is apparent in Tigers' global routing including New York, Brussels, Zurich, Dubai, Bangkok, Taipei, Tokyo (Narita airport),and return to the U.S. Subsequently, Tigers initiated regular scheduled service to Muscat, Oman, in the Persian Gulf region, from JFK via Europe. The freighter service provided an important outlet for manufacturers and shippers of oil industry-related products.

Tigers expanded its extensive international coverage and service capability in March, 1987, with the commencement of scheduled west-bound B747 Asia-to-Europe jetfreighter flights, and the initiation of DC-8 jetfreighter service to Milan, Italy, with the U.S. The deployment of the DC-8 marked the introduction of six newly acquired DC-8-73CFs during the early part of 1987, providing a balance of medium load capability on both domestic and international routes by augmenting the long-haul B747 aircraft and the shorter range B727 aircraft. The reappearance of the DC-8 to the Tiger fleet, in the form of the DC-8-73CFs, with modified "hush kit" engines, were deployed on domestic route during the week, and operated internationally during the weekends. As planned, one DC-8-73CF was positioned at JFK on weekends, available for charter flights or routine maintenance.

The addition of the six aircraft to Tigers' fleet allowed the carrier to provide more product capability, such as the Milan/JFK service "gateway to gateway," while freeing up B747F lift to take advantage of opportunities elsewhere, especially in the growing Asia-to-Europe direct air route. Deploying DC-8s on weekends, Flying Tigers also established direct Zurich to Charlotte, and Frankfurt to Charlotte service, whose volumes of air traffic may not support direct B747 service.

Flying Tigers' new routes provide considerable flexibility in scheduling and service offerings to the company's global shippers. The addition of the 19th B747 jetfreighter to Tigers' fleet in October, 1987, and the 20th B747 freighter in September, 1988, has produced greater frequency of flight and expediency within the Tiger global system. Improving service leverage, **the carrier's B747 jetfreighter fleet accounts for over one-fourth of the world's entire B747 jetfreighters in operation**. Exercising its capacity, inauguration of Tigers' scheduled Asia-to-Europe flights, with through service to the U.S. and back to Asia, link the major commercial centers of the world via one full-service cargo carrier o;n an around-the-world basis in both east-bound and west-bound directions. The north-south Latin America traffic connects with the east-west traffic along Tigers' U.S. eastern seaboard route.

With added capacity, the carrier established an east-bound around-the-world B747 jetfreighter service in 1987, operating from the U.S. through Europe and the Middle East to Asia, and return to the U.S. Another west-bound flight operated weekly on a Taipei-Bangkok-Dubai-Brussels-London-New York routing. The Asia-to-Europe market is one of the fastest growing air cargo markets in the world, and complements Flying Tigers' existing capability in providing air cargo service from the U.S. back to Asia.

In May, 1988, Flying Tigers initiated a Hong Kong to Europe B747 jetfreighter service via Anchorage, using low competitive rates as a marketing tool to dominate that segment of Tigers' world-wide system, and causing market rates to drop 10%.[2] It was the inauguration of the carrier's fourth scheduled B747 Asia-to-Europe flight. The new east-bound flight operates weekly on a Hong Kong-Taipei-Seoul-Anchorage-London-Brussels routing, exercising Sixth Freedom rights (transport foreign country to foreign

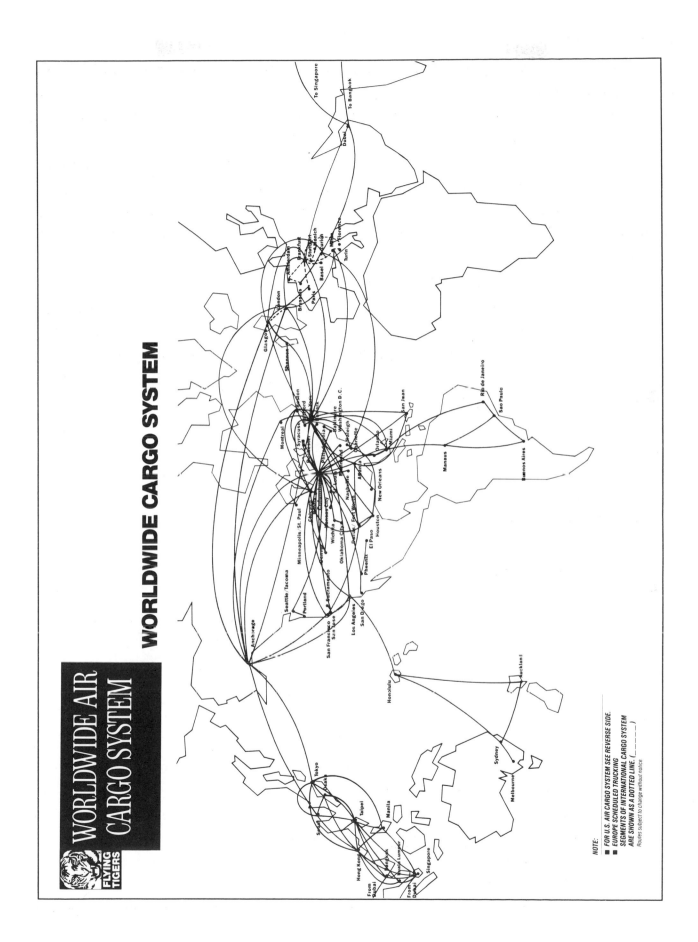

WORLDWIDE CARGO SYSTEM

WORLDWIDE AIR
CARGO SYSTEM

FLYING TIGERS

NOTE:
- FOR U.S. AIR CARGO SYSTEM SEE REVERSE SIDE.
- EUROPE SCHEDULED TRUCKING
  SEGMENTS OF INTERNATIONAL CARGO SYSTEM
  ARE SHOWN AS A DOTTED LINE. (_____)

Routes subject to change without notice

227

country), providing shippers with additional capacity and schedule flexibility in the Asia-to-Europe air freight markets.

The carrier continues to operate three west-bound Asia-to-Europe flights each week, and added another Asia-Europe flight in July, 1988. The carrier is presently seeking a Tokyo-to-Europe via Anchorage route requiring the Japanese government approval. Meanwhile, on January 8, 1989, Tigers expanded its Asia-to-Europe polar service offering B747 freighter flights six times per week on a Taipei-Seoul-Anchorage-Frankfurt routing, with daily service projected to commence in mid-February. In addition, the carrier will inaugurate four new polar flights weekly from Europe-to-Asia, operating on a Frankfurt-Anchorage-Seoul-Taipei routing.

Toward the end of 1987, Tiger representatives have also approached the Malaysian and New Zealand governments to discuss the possibilities of providing scheduled cargo service to those countries. Tigers have provided service into Kuala Lumpur, Malaysia, before. Subsequently, the carrier acquired authority to Kuala Lumpur, and incorporated that point on a Dubai-Singapore-Kuala Lumpur-Hong Kong routing. And scheduled service to Auckland, New Zealand, became a reality on March 7, 1988, following the west-bound routing New York-Los Angeles-Honolulu-Auckland, then proceeding onto Sydney, Australia, finally encircling into the Asia network. The integration of the South Pacific routes with previously existing trans-Pacific routes enables Tigers to generate additional revenue ton miles while positioning aircraft for the traditionally strong east-bound trans-Pacific market.

Increased volumes and more efficient use of capacity has warranted the flight frequency into New Zealand to two times weekly, and to Australia four times weekly, including a Melbourne stop. Service to New Zealand marked the only regularly scheduled B747 jetfreighter service to Auckland. The new inbound service provides shippers in North America, Latin America, and Europe direct access to New Zealand, while providing an outlet for New Zealand's export machinery and parts, electronics, and livestock.

After difficult negotiations, Flying Tigers instituted charter service into the People's Republic of China (Mainland China), including a number of livestock charters from New Zealand. In 1984, the carrier flew eight charters into Mainland China, and increased that number to forty-one the following year. The majority of cargo then being shipped into Mainland China was livestock and electronics. Seventy percent of the Tiger flights went into Beijing, while 30 percent were flown into the Guangzhou (Canton) and Shanghai areas.

The carrier also established interline arrangements for commercial air freight destined for China points. Traffic destined for Shanghai or Beijing were interlined with China's national carrier at the time, Civil Aviation Administration of China (CAAC), as well as Japan Airlines, United Airlines and Northwest Orient, all at the Tokyo airport. To serve points in southern China, Tigers established interline agreements with CAAC and Cathay Pacific Airways in Hong Kong. In addition, Tigers started an interline agreement with Air Hong Kong, providing service to Beijing, Shanghai, and Xiamen, on the southeast coast.

On September, 1987, a Flying Tiger delegation visited Beijing to discuss future prospects of scheduled air cargo service into China. A bilateral agreement between the U.S. and China allows a maximum of two carriers from each country, of which United Airlines and Northwest Orient Airlines are the two U.S.- designated carriers, irregardless of Tigers' all-cargo status. Therefore, Tigers' hopes rests on the possibility of negotiating a joint venture for scheduled all-cargo services similar to the venture which Tigers and Saudi Arabian Airlines had entered in previous years.

In that arrangement, Tigers provided the aircraft, crew and logistical support for the joint venture flight, while both carriers shared space. Such an arrangement with CAAC, now called Air China, or one of the regional carriers such as Shanghai East Airline, would be an extension of the Flying Tiger-CAAC joint venture on recent charters into and out of China, especially cattle charters. Tigers now handles about 25% of the China to U.S. airfreight market, serviced through Hong Kong.

In April, 1987, Flying Tigers entered into a joint venture with Canadian International Airlines to establish another round-the-world route, incorporating the major Canadian markets. Flight 80, as it is identified, uses a Flying Tiger aircraft with a Seoul-Anchorage-Montreal-New York routing employing a crew sharing arrangement. And plans are presently in the regulatory process to serve both Montreal and Toronto with direct flights through Tigers' principal hub near Columbus, Ohio (operational March, 1986), in the near future, it is anticipated. Start-up Toronto service has been approved by the U.S. government and is awaiting approval by the Canadian Transport Commission.

Military Contracts

Flying Tigers' MAC revenues have fluctuated during the 1970s and 1980s according to, primarily, its proportionate dedicated jetfreighter and PAX fleet contribution within CRAF, the carrier's proven experience and reliability, and other lessor considerations with respect to general MAC needs, year-by-year. However, prior to that period, qualifying factors were not always well-defined, and the process involved "open bidding" at times. Such an incident, as forementioned, occurred in 1959-60:

> "At the time of Tigers' CL-44D order (1959), the carrier was engaged in another rate war, this time with the descendants of the very airlines which had once been allies during the conflict with the big passenger airlines during the late 1940s. When the major trunk carriers moved into the jet age, they disposed of scores of old (and sometimes not so old) piston-engined equipment. Many of these perfectly sound aircraft were sold to the non-scheduled airlines for service under military contracts, in competition for which they cut their prices to the bone.
>
> On October 1, 1960, the CAB laid down minimum rates for military charters, and on July 1, 1961, the Military Air Transport Service negotiated three-year contracts, giving preference to those companies with modern, turbine-engined, convertible aircraft. This description fitted the CL-44D perfectly, and on July 16, 1961, Flying Tiger made its first trans-Pacific flight from Travis Air Force Base, near San Francisco, to the Far East".[3]

In a 1977 Defense Transportation Journal cover, General Paul Carlton, then retiring commander in chief of the Military Airlift Command (MAC), is viewed presenting a special plaque to Bob Prescott "in recognition of Flying Tigers' dedicated cooperation to national defense for the past 25 years." Only Tigers has pledged its entire fleet for immediate emergency airlift requirements since CRAF incipience; a tribute to Flying Tigers commitment in war and peace.

Bob on the Cover

In more recent times, MAC revenues for Tigers decreased 27% in 1983 from 1982 levels as the airline was in the process of selling off its DC-8 fleet, decreasing capacity. As a contribution factor, the lower MAC revenues was also a reflection of the military shifting its traffic to its own fleet. However, as forementioned, since 1975, Tigers has been the largest recipient of MAC funding among CRAF members, and has increased its share since the acquisition of Seaboard aircraft.

Flying Tigers' proportionate increase in MAC contracts has, in large part, been due to the fact that after the Vietnam airlift, many competing cargo carriers in the supplemental carrier class, either substantially decreased their fleet and/or service or phased out of operation. Meanwhile, in 1980, Tigers incorporated the Seaboard commitments and increased fleet capacity. In addition, many of the new cargo carriers which emerged after domestic air cargo deregulation have not become CRAF members, thus, not qualifying for MAC contracts.

The development of Flying Tigers' global network is to the carrier's advantage. The extensive international system of scheduled flights offers more leverage for better and more efficient deployment of its aircraft in MAC flights for purposes of repositioning and crew scheduling, and commercial charter requirements.

It may be noted that the MAC archives, located at Scott Air Force Base in Illinois, does not maintain any records of individual carrier participation in CRAF, although, historically, it is well known that Flying Tigers had contributed to the most significant mission associated with that organization. Included in those missions were the Berlin Blockade of 1948-49; the Korean War airlift in which about 60 U.S. airlines carried 67% of the passengers, 56% of the freight, and 70% of the mail to Korea; the Hungarian refugee airlift in 1956 from Germany to the U.S.; the Cambodian Resupply airlift in February to April, 1975, involving five commercial carriers to support Cambodian forces and citizens besieged in Phnom Penh by Communist Khmer Rouge insurgents; and **Operation Frequent Wind**, mid-April, 1975, in which three commercial carriers supported MAC transporting troops, cargo, and passengers in the final evacuation of U.S. personnel and other nationals from Saigon when the fall of that city to Communist forces was imminent.

A financial overview of Flying Tigers' MAC awards is revealing:

Fiscal year	Military Airlift Award	
June 1951	$7,492,469	Korean conflict to 1953
June 1952	9,278,571	
June 1953	12,358,940	
June 1954	4,689,452	
June 1955	1,043,996	

(Effective Dec. 31,1961, Company changed fiscal year ending June 30 to year ending Dec.31)

December 1961	13,305,366	
December 1962	38,394,750	Cuban crisis & Southeast Asia involvement
December 1963	27,465,723	
December 1964	23,151,385	Formal U.S. involvement in Vietnam crisis.
December 1965	30,237,475	
December 1966	48,074,385	
December 1967	53,413,028	
December 1968	43,255,211	
December 1969	49,386,000	
December 1970	30,629,000	
December 1971	34,091,000	
December 1972	32,862,000	
December 1973	15,579,000	Partly U.S. troop withdrawal in Vietnam.
December 1974	15,148,000	
December 1975	22,590,000	End of U.S. involvement in Vietnam with final airlift.
December 1976	19,753,000	
December 1977	23,915,000	
December 1978	35,112,000	
December 1979		
December 1980	86,035,000	Included Seaboard commitments to MAC

(Effective Oct. 1, 1980, MAC awards contracted from Oct. 1 to year ending Sept. 30)

October 1981	112,045,000	
October 1982	114,984,000	
October 1983	84,274,000	
October 1984	104,411,000	
October 1985	105,680.000	
October 1986	155,800,000	

Source: Flying Tiger Line Annual Statistics

U.S. POSTAL SERVICE

Although Flying Tigers has carried mail shipments since 1956, the carrier did not enjoy significant and consistent mail revenues until the initiation of international mail service in August of 1969. Primarily associated with the Vietnam airlift, none of the Tiger ramp people will ever forget the gruesome task of loading and unloading DC-8 belly loads of mail. However, the heavy outbound to Asia mail, in large part, complemented the developing Asia-to-U.S. imports inbound off the new scheduled route 163.

With the acquisition of Seaboard in 1980, the international mail revenues for the carrier climbed to $7 million for the Atlantic segment in 1981, and $17.3 million for the Pacific. Domestic mail revenues for that year exceeded $3.2 million.

Notes

1. "Chairman's Conference," **Tigereview**, Oct.-Nov., 1986.

2. Mark W. Lyon, "Cathay Pacific Redoubles Its Cargo Commitment," **Jet Cargo News**, Vol. 21, No. 4, August, 1988, p. 19, noting that:
    > "Tigers is selling its European service at HK $17/Kg. (98.6 cents/pound). That is less than the top tier market rate of HK $20 ($1.16/pound) charged by Cathay, Cargolux, Lufthansa, and Air France".

3. R.E.G. Davis, **Airlines of the U.S. Since 1914** (London: Putnam) 1972, p. 435.

14

The Heart of a Tiger

Domestic air cargo deregulation afforded the opportunity for Flying Tigers and several new air freight carriers to establish centrally-located air cargo hubs feeding a transcontinental route system through a "hub-and-spoke" arrangement. The system geographically encompassed all the major air cargo markets in the country. The hub-spoke system works by funneling traffic from multiple outlying service points along "spokes" to a central hub, where the freight is sorted, then transferred to go back out another "spoke via air or truck," to various destinations, systematically and sequentially. All flights arrive within a few minutes of one another to effect the transload, then depart with sorted and consolidated destination freight.

The alluring concept for freight carriers handling various sizes of air cargo was pre-empted by Federal Express' successful implementation of a small-scale air courier hub-and-spoke system centered at Memphis Airport during the years prior to deregulation. The express carrier, which started its operation on a precarious note in 1973, deployed smaller aircraft and was not constrained with CAB route restrictions to the degree that had straddled larger air freight carriers for years. Thus, the feasibility of an air cargo hub-and-spoke system complementing a successful operational overnight service with high volumes and consistency in high level service arose with deregulation.

With the coming of deregulation, air couriers and air freight operators began entertaining the idea of adopting a Mid-West hub and enjoying the advantages of uncongested night-sorting air freight and/or small-package operations distant from congested city airports. A distinct pattern emerged.

Emery Air Freight, a freight forwarder handling primarily air freight consolidation, began its air cargo charter hub operations in Dayton, Ohio, in 1977. Emery's charter services was called the **Emery Air Force**, and it was the harbinger to the scheduled hub operations. And, in 1979, Emery established a central sorting facility to accommodate its priority overnight package service at an airport near Smyrna, Tennessee. It may have been plan to emulate the successful implementation of a hub-and-spoke small package system of the dynamic Federal Express, but lacking scope and fleet infra-structure.

The opportunity to develop air cargo hubs away from busy urban airport traffic lanes, but within proximity to major highway systems, took into consideration the availability of obsolete Air Force bases and under-utilized commercial airports, many of which were located in the Mid-West, and centrally located with respect to possible continental hub activities. Each carrier could develop its own facilities and manage its own slot times with minimum interference from the hierarchy of government regulatory bodies.

Airborne Air Freight, through a merger in 1980, formed the **Airborne Express** as an air freight air carrier and established its fleet hub operations at Wilmington, Ohio. The site was an old Strategic Air Command Air Force base, which Airborne now owns. Airborne initiated scheduled flight hub operations serving primarily eastern United States, though extending into a continental system in a short span of time.

In 1981, competitor Emery Air Freight, offering both air cargo as well as air courier service, began its scheduled overnight service in continental scope. At this time, Emery made the decision to acquire its own jet aircraft fleet, including some DC-8 aircraft from Flying Tigers.

United Parcel Service (UPS), the long-established and extensive truck courier service, began its own air fleet operations in September, 1982, using, in part, DC-8s acquired from Flying Tigers. And, to remain competitive, a number of other former air couriers and air freight forwarders followed suit and started their air fleet operations, including **Burlington (BN) Air Express, CF, and Purolator.**

Concentration of Selected All-Cargo Carrier and Courier
Primary Sort Facilities with Scheduled Continental Service
by mid-1980s

Flying Tigers
Columbus Hub (LCK)

Airborne Express
Wilmington, Ohio

United Parcel Service
Louisville, Kentucky

Federal Express
Memphis, Tennessee
*Joint use with commercial
airport users

Burlington Express
Ft. Wayne, Indiana

CF Airfreight
Indianapolis, Indiana

Emery Air Freight
Dayton, Ohio

* Regional hubs not noted

In 1982, Flying Tiger engineers, architects and selected employees began designing their new hub complex, long before the company decided to locate at old Richenbacker Air Force Base, more recently a National Guard Base.[1] The area is commonly referred to as Lockbourne, being associated with a town of that name located just west of the old air base.

Within 500 miles of Richenbacker lies 58% of the U.S. population, 61% of U.S. manufacturing, 80% of headquarters of major U.S. firms, and 68% of all private and public sector research and development. The region produced 22% of the U.S. Gross National Product, and accounts for well over a fourth of the nation's value-added by manufacturing. Also within the 500-mile radius lies 53% of the disposable income in the country. Thus, applying certain air cargo marketing parameters, for Tigers the Hub is strategically located at the economic geographic continental center, being within one hour's flying time of 60% of the U.S. population, and at the junction of several Interstate highways, allowing easy accessibility for economical truck shipments to destinations in the Ohio Valley, Eastern Seaboard, southern U.S., and the Midwest.[2]

Tigers' previous hub operation at O'Hare in Chicago since 1969, involved numerous physical and operational constraints, including congestion and difficult winter conditions for operations. Diversions and delays were commonplace, especially during the winter months, Tigers' busiest season, which often, affected traffic on most segments of the carrier's hub system. With the increase in domestic guaranteed door-to-door traffic after 1982, Chicago's hub system became proportionately over-burdened as time constraints became critical. And, from 1977 to 1982, the period before the expansion of the door-to-door program, Tigers increased its primary station points from nine to twenty-one, forcing considerably more flight activity upon the Chicago hub.

At Chicago, the facilities were antiquated, and less than half the space at Richenbacker, and ramp space for only seven aircraft as compared to twenty at Richenbacker. Sometimes ten airplanes could be squeezed into the O'Hare facility, but extra ramps were also rented from airlines who didn't need them at night. Everything had to be completed and all planes out by 6 a.m. That was when "suddenly" the airport became active with one hundred flights or more.[3]

At Flying Tigers' new principal hub near Columbus, Ohio, often referred to by its employees as **Columbus** or **LCK**, its code name, there is space to accommodate the simultaneous loading and unloading of five B747 and sixteen DC-8 or B727 jetfreighters, and twenty-six trucks, with adjacent parking facilities for an additional eleven B747, DC-8 or B727 aircraft combination. Each plane from an origin and

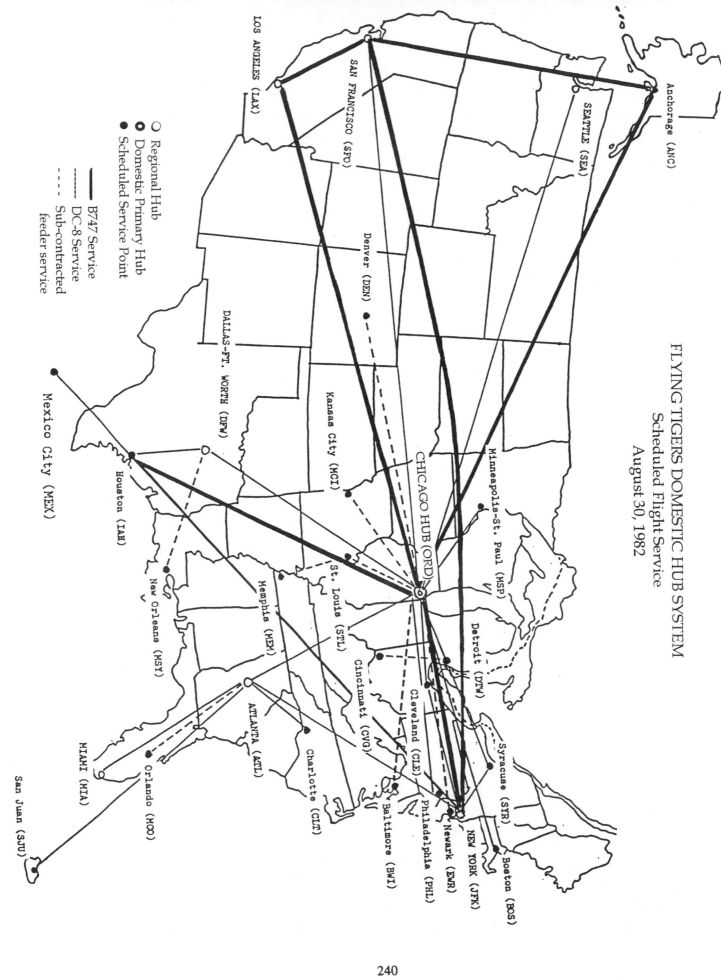

FLYING TIGERS DOMESTIC HUB SYSTEM
Scheduled Flight Service
August 30, 1982

Legend:
○ Regional Hub
◎ Domestic Primary Hub
● Scheduled Service Point

—— B747 Service
⸺ DC-8 Service
---- Sub-contracted feeder service
--- Scheduled feeder service

Anchorage (ANC)
SEATTLE (SEA)
LOS ANGELES (LAX)
SAN FRANCISCO (SFO)
Denver (DEN)
DALLAS-FT. WORTH (DFW)
Kansas City (MCI)
Minneapolis-St. Paul (MSP)
CHICAGO HUB (ORD)
Detroit (DTW)
Mexico City (MEX)
Houston (IAH)
New Orleans (MSY)
Memphis (MEM)
St. Louis (STL)
Cincinnati (CVG)
Cleveland (CLE)
Syracuse (SYR)
ATLANTA (ATL)
Charlotte (CLT)
Baltimore (BWI)
Philadelphia (PHL)
Newark (EWR)
NEW YORK (JFK)
Boston (BOS)
MIAMI (MIA)
Orlando (MCO)
San Juan (SJU)

destination city has its own bay, and, every night, the same plane is at the same bay. In complementary fashion, the same ground crew teams would enjoy the same regularity in offloading, loading, and transloading, aside from late aircraft, mechanical or infrequent weather problems.

Rickenbacker Air Industrial Park, controlled by the Port Authority since 1984, encompasses 1,642 acres adjacent to the airfield runways, featuring a 107-acre air freight building, equipment and ramps, all leased by Flying Tigers for a period of ten years with options. In March, 1986, when it became operational, Tigers was the only substantial tenant. The carrier received very favorable lease terms, and, in moving its hub from Chicago to Columbus, incurred no significant capital investment, which served as a blessing during its period of financial constraints. The center of Tigers' Columbus hub operations is the two-storied freight sorting building covering 4.5 acres, and housing almost two miles of conveyor belts criss-crossed with catwalks, tracks, platforms, and organized by sections to handle the breakdown and build-up for the respective regional flights and truck movements. Basic night sorting of the freighter domestic feed system occurs primarily between midnight and seven o'clock in the morning on weekdays and Saturday, averaging 1.1 million lbs. nightly through 1987, and 1.4 million lbs. some nights.[4] The facilities has a rated capacity of seven million lbs. a day. Using the most updated technological equipment to facilitate sorting, the hub has achieved an overall 99.6% accuracy standard in its sorting. The hub is staffed by approximately 350 employees, including many part-time college students.

The door-to-door air/truck shipments featuring three service levels for delivery are the mainstay of the domestic feed system, presently serving over 60,000 zip-coded U.S. destinations. There is also an emphasis to promote the time-guaranteed "priority airport-to-airport" program, as the carrier recedes from the lower yield airport-to-airport program to which it had been accustomed. The new hub is capable of handling virtually any size or type of shipment that moves via airfreight, and also features on-site U.S. Customs, constant surveillance service, and indoor storage, including refrigeration facilities. The Columbus facilities also has an integrated truck hub operation featuring fifteen economy and prime-time truck service to points radiating from the hub area in all directions to truck hub cities and other points within a day's ride.

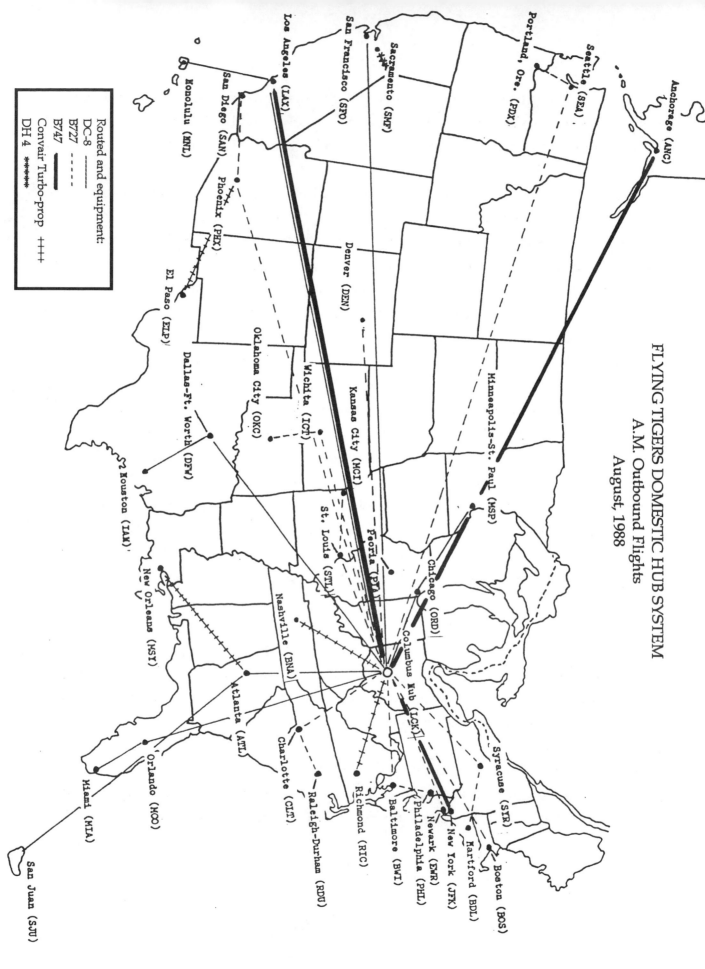

FLYING TIGERS DOMESTIC HUB SYSTEM
A.M. Outbound Flights
August, 1988

Routed and equipment:
DC-8 ————
B727 – – – –
B747 ██████
Convair Turbo-prop ++++
DH 4 ******

Anchorage (ANC)
Portland, Ore. (PDX)
Seattle (SEA)
Sacramento (SMF)
San Francisco (SFO)
Los Angeles (LAX)
San Diego (SAN)
Honolulu (HNL)
Phoenix (PHX)
El Paso (ELP)
Denver (DEN)
Dallas-Ft. Worth (DFW)
Oklahoma City (OKC)
Wichita (ICT)
Kansas City (MCI)
Minneapolis-St. Paul (MSP)
Peoria (PIA)
St. Louis (STL)
Chicago (ORD)
Columbus Hub (LCK)
Houston (IAH)
New Orleans (MSY)
Nashville (BNA)
Atlanta (ATL)
Charlotte (CLT)
Raleigh-Durham (RDU)
Richmond (RIC)
Baltimore (BWI)
Philadelphia (PHL)
Newark (EWR)
New York (JFK)
Hartford (BDL)
Syracuse (SYR)
Boston (BOS)
Orlando (MCO)
Miami (MIA)
San Juan (SJU)

242

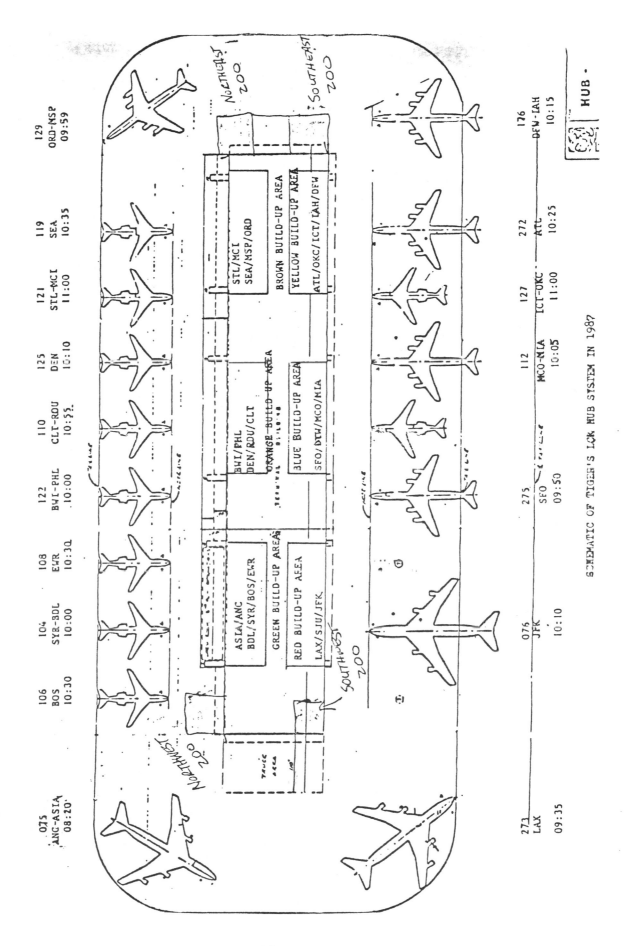

SCHEMATIC OF TIGER'S LCK HUB SYSTEM IN 1987

Tigers' Columbus Hub flight line scenes

Flying Tigers domestic and international air cargo hub at Rickenbacker Air National Guard Base near Columbus, Ohio is capable of handling up to seven million pounds of bulk, containerized and small package shipments a day.

Inside the LCK automated container controlled terminal.

246

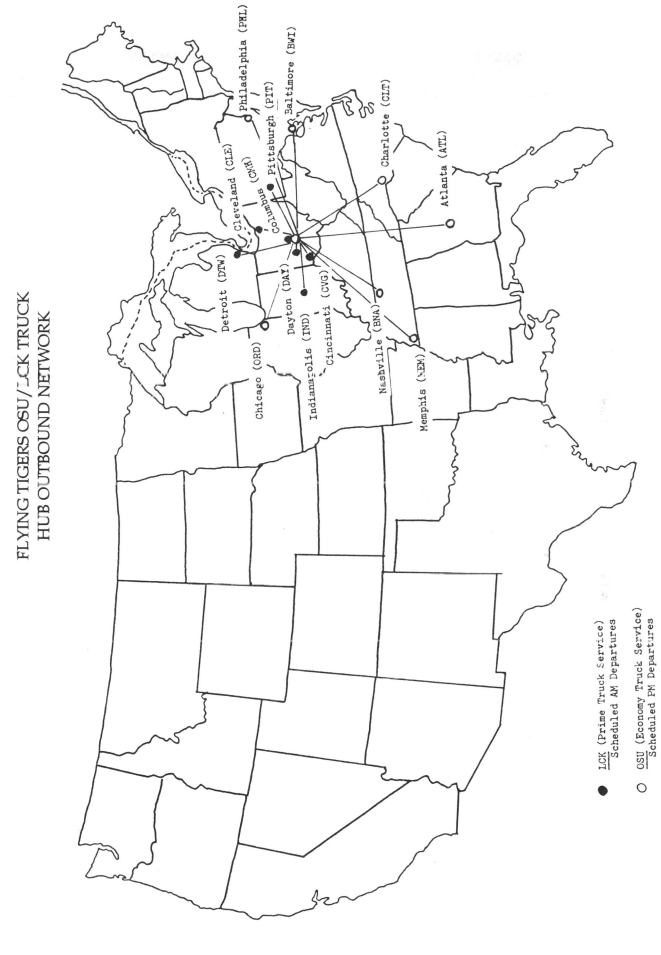

FLYING TIGERS OSU/LCK TRUCK
HUB OUTBOUND NETWORK

Philadelphia (PHL)
Pittsburgh (PIT)
Baltimore (BWI)
Charlotte (CLT)
Atlanta (ATL)
Cleveland (CLE)
Columbus (CMH)
Detroit (DTW)
Dayton (DAY)
Cincinnati (CVG)
Nashville (BNA)
Chicago (ORD)
Indianapolis (IND)
Memphis (MEM)

● LCK (Prime Truck Service)
  Scheduled AM Departures

○ OSU (Economy Truck Service)
  Scheduled PM Departures

Flying Tigers also positions its own Customs brokerage service which expedites clearance of customers' traffic, including support of two full-time U.S. Customs inspectors assigned to Tigers exclusively at the hub. U.S. Agriculture inspectors are also readily available. Thus, a system is derived whereas traffic arrives at the "inland gateway" from various international areas, quickly processed, then, if not warehoused, expeditiously transloaded to scheduled Tiger flights and trucks departing Columbus to various domestic points or gateways. Being the sole air carrier at the Columbus hub, besides U.S. Air Cargo, a small regional cargo operator, interlining is never a problem there as it is never an option inbound or outbound as it was in Chicago hub.

In large part through the carrier's efforts, in March 20, 1987, Rickenbacker Air Industrial Park was designated a **Foreign Trade Zone**, with attractive advantages for international shippers. A Foreign Trade Zone may be described as a secured enclave geographically within the U.S., but which is considered, as defined, to be legally outside U.S. Customs territory. There are presently over one-hundred-and-fifty FTZs in the U.S., including Dayton and Wilmington, Ohio, which are Emery's and Airborne's hub area, respectively. The primary advantage of using a FTZ is deferral of duty payments for goods brought into the U.S. to be assembled or processed. Duty is paid after the goods actually enter into the U.S. market, while still avoiding local taxes because of federal preemption. The importers can select the lowest duty to be applied, based on the entering merchandise's original foreign components or the final product. Other FTZ benefits include being able to store duty free goods until market conditions become more favorable, or being able to sample goods for quality, and returning those that do not meet customer standards, or holding merchandise until quota restrictions are lifted, or waiting until the next quota period begins. To enhance their services, Tigers has built a new international inbond warehouse. With the Columbus hub in operation, the carrier has a dedicated facility which offers controlled and centralized opportunities to complement its extensive geographic network.

As a logical move, on January 11, 1988, the international door-to-door service was moved from Chicago to the Columbus hub facility incorporating the conveniences for Customs clearance and expediency, if not warehousing. In addition, functioning as a full service International Distribution Center (IDC), the carrier provided a newly instituted system of using electronic transmission of documents, thus, obtaining customs clearance before the traffic arrives at the Columbus hub. Presently, about 80% of the non-textile freight arrives at the IDC already pre-cleared by Customs.[5]

In response to market demand for expedited freight service to the major U.S. interior markets, as well as gateways, Flying Tigers introduced a new International

Distribution Service (IDS) shipping program in May, 1988. Starting with Hong Kong and Taiwan in May, and Tokyo, Osaka, and Seoul in June, the program provides expedited one-and two-day airport-to-airport international freight service from these five major Asian gateways to fifty-five major U.S. markets utilizing Tigers' International Distribution Center in Columbus hub. Consequently, deliveries are two to three days faster than traditional airfreight shipments schedules.

The program involves expanding IDS delivery to the top one hundred U.S. markets, which account for about 98% of all international airfreight into the U.S., from all points that Tigers service globally, including twenty-four foreign countries. On November 1, 1988, the carrier began offering an airport-to-door option for its IDS shipments. Beginning 1989, Tigers will introduce IDS shipments from its European hub at Frankfurt, Germany, to over 70 major metropolitan centers across the U.S. as fast as one business day. Thus, the unique service integrates Tigers frequent around-the-world schedules with its domestic infrastructure at the IDC in Columbus hub.[6] The success of the IDS program may be measured by the increase of volume from 21,000 lbs. on May 1 to 600,000 lbs. per day in November, 1988.

The IDS program, in part, reflects Flying Tigers' direction of growth in its goal-oriented efforts to develop an international market niche:

> "Our marketing plan is based on building revenues and increasing customer satisfaction through the focused expansion of our global network and by providing consistently superior freight shipping and handling services. Our goal is to provide consistently reliable and cost-effective freight handling services to shippers worldwide regardless of their capacity, timing and destination requirements."[7]

With all the advantages at the Columbus hub, Flying Tigers may enjoy the opportunities of hub "warehousing." As an air industrial park, Tigers hopes to service nearby tenants who desire the carrier's services for transportation and distribution. The carrier has a separate sales and service facility at Columbus airport (CMH) nearby, called "Port of Columbus," and the city has over 21 million sq. ft. used for warehousing and distribution for companies such as Sears, J.C. Penney, K-Mart, The Limited, Gold Circle, Nissan, Radio Shack, Nestle, and other operating distribution centers ranging from 100,000 to four million sq. ft. in size.[8]

Tiger Connection at Chitose Airport

The success of the Columbus hub facility, and the endless frustrations related to Narita (Japan) airport problems such as congestion, curfew and regulatory constraints, has encouraged Flying Tigers to assist in developing an Asian international air cargo hub with certain key features similar to the Columbus operation, and favorable for Tigers' scheduling and marketing goals. In 1987, the Columbus hub handled 10,000 flight operations and more than 300 million lbs. of freight as compared with the carrier's major western Pacific base at Narita, which serviced 2,449 flight operations and handled 311 million lbs. of airfreight that year.[9] Therefore, Japan, being the pivotal point in Tigers' Asian route system, was the logical area of interest. **Chitose**, an obsolete Air Force base located on Japan's northerly Hokkaido Island, was selected as a suitable place for the hub.

In a turn of events, in December, 1987, a Japanese delegation, including Hokkaido officials, toured Flying Tigers' Columbus hub facility. The tour was made in conjunction with the Hokkaido Governor's plans for developing the Chitose Airport into an international air cargo airport. Tigers was working with Chitose Airport officials to provide air carrier input into their airport planning process.

The following month, a Flying Tiger delegation visited the Hokkaido facilities and, consequently, Tiger officials and the Governor of Hokkaido signed a "letter of intent" expressing the carrier's interest in participating in the development of the Hokkaido air cargo facilities. In the letter, Flying Tigers has agreed to explore potential uses of Chitose airport, and has set forth required conditions should it decide to utilize the planned facilities. Tigers intends to initially use the airport once a week as a technical fueling point, thus, avoiding congested Narita airport with a 2300 (11:00 p.m.) to 0600 (6:00 a.m.) curfew. The facility could eventually accommodate Flying Tigers' operations, acting as a support location to the airline's operations at Narita.

The new cargo terminal at the Chitose airport is currently in the planning and design stage and is scheduled to open in early 1990. Flying Tigers enjoyed its first charter flight to Chitose airport during the summer of 1988. The facility is anticipated to include 24-hour service and operations; reasonable cargo handling and fuel costs; expeditious on-site Customs clearance at all hours of airport operation; and facilities for handling the quarantine of cattle and other large animals.[10]

Central to its attractiveness and a primary geographic advantage of Chitose is that it is 408 miles closer to Anchorage than Narita, and 1,272 miles closer to Anchorage

Chitose Airport in Perspective

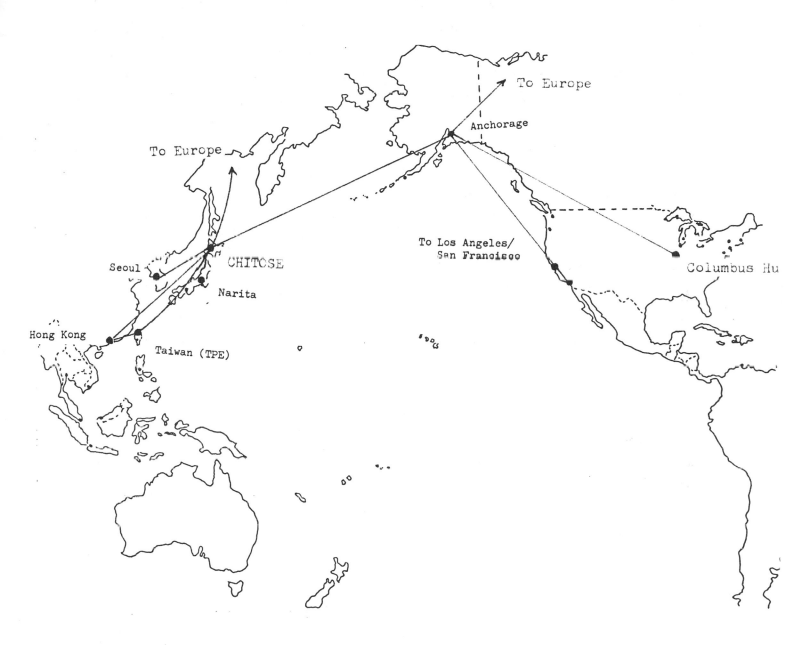

than Seoul, both of which offer significant advantages for trans-Pacific flights operating eastbound to the U.S. Thus, in consideration of the geographic advantages and increasing trans-Pacific payload capabilities, Flying Tigers hopes to initially use Chitose for technical stops such as re-fueling. Possible future uses include acting as a handling and/or fueling point for flights operating during Narita's curfew hours; accommodating charter flights and, eventually, a regular pattern of scheduled trans-Pacific flights that would bypass Narita; and becoming a gateway destination for Flying Tiger's trans-Pacific service.[11]

Tigers' usage of Chitose would require the approval of the Japanese government, and bilateral aviation issues between the U.S. and Japan have been less than amicable in the last few years. Under the U.S.-Japan air services agreement, Flying Tigers, in February, 1988, filed schedules for new all-cargo flights operating three times per week between Anchorage and Tokyo, with the aircraft continuing beyond Anchorage to and from Frankfurt, West Germany.[12] Japan has objected to the 'beyond rights' from Alaska to points in Europe, and refused initially to grant the application. Pressured by the U.S. government, it has been reported that the Japanese government finally approved the permit for only 179 days and with detailed reporting and requirements that no more than 50% of the payload be 'sixth freedom' freight from Japan to Europe. Tigers would be required to submit "data" on its flights after 90 days of operating that route. JAL and NCA, as well as Air France and Lufthansa, now offer air freight services between Japan and Europe via Anchorage. Meanwhile, the Japanese seek U.S. approval of Japanese carriers' intermodal operations in the U.S., moving cargo by trucks or other transportation modes between their authorized U.S. gateways.[13]

In the past, U.S. cargo carriers have not received the type of representation nor protection serving their interests in international air right agreements. Relegated a "back seat" position, these carriers have often been used as "trade off's" in bilateral negotiations for passenger or combination carrier flight rights. Unfortunately, certain foreign carriers have capitalized on the situation, and have grown at the expense of, in large part, U.S.-flag cargo carriers, many of which now are defunct. Thus, Chitose seems significant from a larger perspective in that it reflects Tigers' aspirations to overcome some of the regulatory and operational constraints as well as disadvantages in bilateral negotiations which have kept the carrier from **"spreading it's wings"** in the global setting which it is so capable should matters fall in place.

Notes

1. Robert Ruth, "Flying Tiger at Night," **Columbus Dispatch**, May 4, 1987, p. 1; and "Flying Tiger's Fortunes are Richkenbacker's Hopes," **Columbus Dispatch**, May 4, 1987, p. 3.

2. James A. Cronin, "Flying Tigers' Strategic Direction," **Flying Tigers Marketing Quarterly**, Inaugural Issue, 1988, No. 1, p. 1.

3. Tim Bradner, "Tigers Columbus Hub Super Terminal," **Air Cargo News**, Vol. 13, No. 10, Oct., 1988, pp. 14 and 16.

4. Ibid., p. 14.

5. Op. cit., "Flying Tigers' Strategic Direction."

6. "Tigers Offers Asian Next-Day," **Air Cargo World**, June, 1988, p. 22; and **Employee News Bulletin**, April 21, 1988; and **IDS Training Manual** (for Company employees).

7. "Tiger International Shareholders are Told of Company's Strong-Financial and Marketing Position," **Tigereview**, June, 1988, p. 2.

8. Op. cit., "Tigers Columbus Hub Super Terminal," p. 16.

9. Tiger International, Inc., **1987 Annual Report**, pp. 3 and 4.

10. "Chitose Airport Development," **Tigereview**, February, 1988, pp. 2-4.

11. Ibid.

12. **Air Cargo News**, Vol. 13, No. 9, Sept., 1988, p. 3.

13. "Flying Tigers Files Complaint Against Japan," **Flying Tigers Review**, Aug., 1988, p. 2, and George Elliott II, "Tigers To Tokyo is Conditional," **Jet Cargo News**, Vol. 21, No. 7, Nov., 1988, p. 11; and "DOT, Japan in Catfight," **Air Cargo World**, Oct., 1988, p. 8.

15

The Tiger Flight Plan into the 21st Century

Flying Tigers came out of the financial and operational "tail spin" in 1987, coincidentally, at the time when the international and the domestic air freight markets experienced a general upsurge. The carrier experienced a significant increase in volumes of traffic system-wide due to adjustments in marketing strategies, changes in fleet capacity and requirements, continual low aviation fuel prices, lower operating costs and competitive pricing, and the windfall effect of a general positive economic climate conducive toward the increase in air freight volumes. For Tigers, the turn-around was clearly pictured in business terms. The airline experienced a record pre-tax gain of $106.8 million in 1987 as compared with a 1986 pre-tax loss of $18.6 million.

The carrier's net profits were up 24% during the first half of 1988, with domestic revenues up 21% during the second quarter, while international revenues were up 31% during the same period. Revenues for the bread-and-butter Pacific area was up 48% for the first quarter.[1] Continuing the trend, Tigers' scheduled service third quarter revenues increased 14%, and were led by a 31% increase in U.S. export traffic. Consequently, at the end of the third quarter in 1988, Tigers reported a pretax profit of $78.4 million as compared to a pre-tax income of $71 million for the same period a year ago. As an important point, reflecting the carrier's strategy of expanding its global system, revenues from traffic not moving to or from the U.S., or sixth freedom traffic, more than doubled.

From an objective viewpoint, one may speculate that the prospective growth and success of Flying Tigers, or its demise, will arise from the interplay between exercising the carrier's comparative strength in the air cargo industry and its ability to manage growth determinants, including shifting markets, and limitations such as the potentially volatile aviation fuel costs. On the other hand, the carrier must deal with the growing collective competition both in the domestic and international marketplace. And, Tigers continually adjusts its operating and marketing emphasis on its international routes to improve the balance between inbound and outbound flights and to re-align capacity to serve markets where the greatest demand for service exists in order to achieve highest revenues.

Perhaps Flying Tigers' most apparent strength lies in its extensive scheduled geographic network, truly global in scope, together with the carrier's large fleet of twenty B747 jetfreighters, two B747 with passenger configuration, six DC-8-73s, and eleven B727 cargo aircraft. As an enhancing asset, the carrier has developed an efficient and high potential multi-functional primary hub system which services an extensive integrated global network, offering a significant advantage for Tigers over foreign carriers which have limited access to U.S. points other than certain gateways.

Aside from the more physical attributes is Flying Tigers' rich heritage as an air cargo leader for over four decades, persevering the oscillations which eliminated numerous competitors from the air cargo industry, and caused many of the major U.S.-based scheduled combination carriers to discard their cargo fleets prior to the 1977 deregulation. Tigers has been the number one IATA cargo carrier in terms of freight-ton miles for the past seven years. Flying Tigers' familiar name and image is widespread in the air freight industry world-wide, and the carrier is well-respected by the military and the U.S. Postal service.

However, the "shock" of the late 1986 order to take offers in preparation of "liquidating the carrier's assets" scared many customers, and offered competing carriers an opportunity to wrangle away from Tigers certain accounts. The "shock waves" are still felt to a variable degree in the recovery process, and, thus, formulates a moderating tone.

But to put other assets into play, Tigers has a well-qualified professional team, headed by a diversified and capable management group comprising of industry experts well-versed in most aspects of the air cargo industry and transportation, in general. The group includes an international marketing and legal staff responsible for promoting the company's objectives in developing an international marketplace niche.

The management team was put on place primarily by Stephen Wolf who assumed the position as Flying Tigers' CEO in early 1987, as well as chairman, president and CEO of Tiger International, the parent company. In his restructuring program, James A. Cronin, with a strong background in planning and marketing, was elected president and chief operating officer of the airline in September, 1987. Wolf retained his position as chairman and chief executive officer of the airline, but left the responsibility of implementing Flying Tigers' long range marketing strategy with the management team headed by Cronin.

Assisting Cronin, also with a strong marketing background, is Cyril D. Murphy, serving as VP-Market Planning, who had served in a variety of management positions in the marketing and government affairs departments. While the new management team included several new key administrators, to develop the carrier's international network and legal department, the company hired Vance Fort in September, 1987, a former DOT administrator. He assumed the position of VP-International and Government Affairs, serving under Larry Nagin, who was Tigers' General Counsel and Sr. VP of Administration.

In 1987 and 1988, strategies were formulated and implemented which placed the carrier in a positive posture for future growth into the 21st Century. As a strategic direction, Tigers focused on (1) further strengthening its financial position to allow for more capital expenditure, including decreasing its $470 million in long-term debt, (2) acquiring more aircraft and upgrading its facilities and ground equipment on a selective basis, (3) responding to potentially new and changing air cargo markets while balancing fleet and demand, and (4) enhancing its product service opportunities, among other matters. These major factors are congruent with the carrier's long-term objectives.

In defining its marketing niche, Tigers focuses its efforts on the customer base centered on the over-70 lb. air freight traffic with the geographic spectrum of the global economy covering primarily Asia, Europe, the South Pacific, North and South America. Statistically, Tigers' average international shipment weight is about 2460 lbs., while the average domestic freight weight handled by the carrier is 275 lbs.[2] Employing weight parameters, the carrier apparently feels a need to differentiate itself from the small-package air couriers such as Federal Express, UPS and DHL which, in the past, have serviced a different customer base. The international operations still depend primarily on freight forwarder and broker business, as it is the business trend which governs international air cargo. Tigers' domestic operations, however, has shifted from a dependency on freight forwarder business, and airport-to-airport shipments, to a predominantly direct door-to-door program.

Having an extensive geographic network allows for more flexibility and helps create opportunities for the Tiger fleet. The carrier has been in a position to accommodate guaranteed space to express carriers (air couriers) on certain high traffic segments not the latter's route system, or because of back-haul or aircraft repositioning problems. Or, in the case of UPS, fleet and facility limitations during their peak season demand in December has brought about an annual contract for Tiger lift just at the time that the latter's heavy season peaks off. And Federal Express was once a regular customer of Tigers, hauling its small-package full containers from Anchorage to Tokyo. Federal Express, which already competes with Tigers domestically, began small package (70 lb. maximum) service from Portland, Oregon, to Tokyo in early 1988. Fed Ex wants to increase that 70 lb. limit which would threaten Tigers' market share. In fact, Tigers is presently challenging Fed Ex's alleged infringement.

Entering the Asian air cargo markets, Tigers is seriously concerned over alleged practices of Fed Ex in selling above the 70 lb. weight limit on U.S.-Japan service, contrary to the spirit of the U.S.-Japan agreement on a small-package service to Japan that allowed Fed Ex in the route. Specifically, Tigers has complained to the U.S. Department of Transportation that Fed Ex carried 21,000 lbs. of fresh cherries on one of its summer westbound flights, and is carrying heavy general freight eastbound for Japanese shippers like Hitachi, Mitsubishi, Molex and Ricoh, weighing up to 7,088 lbs. per shipment. Fed Ex is also, purportedly, negotiating for a contract to carry 800,000 lbs. of cigarettes from the U.S. to Japan, and circulating rate sheets in Japan that offer services over the 70 lb. limit.[3] During a period in late summer of this year (1988), Fed Ex ran a weekly Seattle to Amsterdam charter carrying almost all if not exclusively ocean/air freight. Obviously, Fed Ex would enjoy "worldwide open skies," perhaps more so than Tigers.

On the other side of the coin, Tigers is also interested at this time to began another marketing program to increase its revenue and customer base with high-yielding dense freight outside its traditional domain. The carrier would like to develop an international hub for express freight at its Anchorage operation, sorting express freight en route to Europe, Asia, and South America, along the carrier's scheduled route system. It is hoped that the program will be operational within two years. With no surprise, Fed Ex has similar designs proposing a small-package shipment center which the company is building in Anchorage.[4]

In the growing global economy and increasing air cargo traffic which is accompanying such growth, Flying Tigers finds its marketing opportunities and competition meeting "head to head" at the same points. During the last three years or so, with the significant decrease of the U.S. dollar value relative to the Japanese yen, more so than other currencies, there has been a proportionate increase in U.S. exports to Japan. Consequently, Tigers' eastbound and westbound Asia traffic volumes are approaching 1½ to 1 ratio, respectively; whereas three or four years ago, the same ratio was approximately 2 or 3 to 1 with the trade imbalance. The carrier has profited from the opportunity to improve the westbound load factors across the Pacific route. And so has the host of other carriers serving the Pacific route, including JAL, NCA, Northwest, and United Airlines, some profiting as supplementary belly revenue loads on their passenger flights.

With so many freighters in its worldwide fleet, Tigers has the ability to rapidly adjust to changing market conditions whether in the form of increased Asian exporting to Europe, increased U.S. to Japan exports, or following a shift of northern Asian manufacturing to Southeast Asia and sub-continent points, such as Sri Lanka.[5] There has been an increase of air freight traffic within Asia, and from Asia to Europe, presently the most lucrative route in international air cargo. The market shift in the Pacific region may be, in large part, attributed to the foreign retaliatory trade legislation enacted by the U.S. in response to the mounting trade imbalance, and aimed primarily at Japan, China, and the four "Little Tigers" of Asia, namely Singapore, Taiwan, Hong Kong, and South Korea. January, 1989, will mark the end of duty-free status for the "Little Tigers" of Asia, involving an estimated $10 billion in imports to the U.S., thus, those countries will be removed from the nations that have received preferential trade treatment from the U.S.[6] In consideration of the punitive measures, the "Little Tigers" are attempting to shift their trade outlet to more affluent Japan as well as markets within Europe. Thailand, the emerging "Fifth Tiger" with an extraordinary growth rate, has also become a primary trade nation in Southeast Asia. Flying Tigers would like to capitalize on the forementioned market trends in the form of scheduled and commercial charter flights, exercising its extensive fleet flexibility in scheduling in regard to routing, frequency, and seasonal fluctuations.

Perhaps one of Tigers' greatest threat in the Pacific basin route is posed by the upcoming Nippon Cargo Airlines (NCA), which has experienced unprecedented growth since its incipience in 1985. As a result of hallmark changes in Japanese aviation policies of liberalization, in May, 1985, NCA, a new Japanese all-cargo airlines, initiated transpacific operations between Tokyo and San Francisco and New York. With four B747 jetfreighters, NCA is currently operating nine scheduled roundtrip all-freight flights per week between those points but is seeking unlimited New York-San Francisco flights, a co-terminus between San Francisco and Los Angeles, and rights into Chicago, an all-cargo point that has been a goal for JAL for some time. NCA's current scheduled service to the U.S. represents 12% of the total freight capacity provided by scheduled all-freight carriers transporting freight between Japan and the U.S.[7] In pursuing new horizons, NCA is also seeking the rights to scheduled service to Europe, certain Asia points, the South Pacific and Southeast Asia.

The majority of NCA is owned by Japanese steamship companies and air freight forwarders. In 1987, Flying Tigers estimated that NCA's freight forwarder owners originated more than 75% of Tigers' eastbound freight,[8] which is more than thought provoking.

In 1987, under pressure from Congress and the Flying Tigers, the Department of Transportation conducted a draft study elucidating the problems of U.S. air cargo policy and the impact of air cargo carriers in the international arena. The study concluded that "U.S. carriers were getting creamed by Fifth and Sixth Freedom foreign airlines in the competition for U.S. cargo traffic. It showed foreign airlines carry 69% of U.S. air cargo, and the U.S. airlines' share of world air cargo went down from 21% to 14% in a decade."[9] Finally, bringing the problems to the forefront, Flying Tigers is suggesting that there by an Air Cargo Department created within DOT to protect the interest of U.S.-flag carriers from both a political and economic standpoint. And, as a point of logic, Tigers would like to have air cargo rights negotiated as a separate issue in bilateral agreements, as the nature of passenger and cargo operations differ considerably.

Flying Tigers has a vested interest in protecting its integrated system linking its international network with its in-depth U.S. infra-structure:

> "The largest air freight market in the world is the U.S. domestic market. But if you add that also to the market that involves the U.S. on an export and import or re-export/re-import traffic, that market is by a magnitude of three or four times the largest airfreight market in the world."[10]

The pressure applied by Congress and Flying Tigers offers a new perspective and concern to strengthen the posture of the U.S. in the international arena. In early 1988, as a result of an aggressive stance by the U.S. in bilateral negotiations with Mexico, rights were acquired for three cargo airlines, from eleven U.S. cities to five Mexican cities, including temporary access for all-cargo companies to Mexico City's main airport until expansion at Toluca Airport, 40 miles away is complete.[11] Tigers, who have served Mexico City on a scheduled basis via Houston a few years ago, is awaiting the re-institution of its scheduled cargo flights into Mexico.

While Tigers seeks fair categorical representation at the bargaining table in aviation bilateral agreements, the carrier has virtually no control over potentially volatile aviation fuel prices. The carrier systematically negotiates annual contracts for aviation fuel on a regional or local basis for its scheduled services. "Tigers paid about 54 cents per gallon for fuel during the first quarter of 1987, with each penny per gallon increase representing approximately $3 million in additional cost per year. Fuel costs still represent about 18 percent of the carrier's total operating costs."[12] The average cost of aviation fuel was 85 cents per gallon in 1985, and dropped to 60 cents the following year. While capitalizing on the appreciable decrease in fuel costs, planning and budgeting is still at a critical point in the turn-around. From this perspective, the carrier must sustain its drive to increase its marketshare and revenue base irregardless of the cost of fuel. For Flying Tigers as well as other commercial carriers who do not operate on a government subsidy, they are required to seek other forms of leverage to remain competitive in the various international areas of operation.

The possibility of a reappearance of higher aviation fuel costs and/or spot scarcity is always a consideration, as Flying Tigers must consider possible hedges and alternatives. Viable alternative modes may include adjusting the air/truck system both domestically and in continental Europe to involve proportionately more trucking in place of air service, but still retain the marketshare. Another alternative may be to promote more sea/air intermodal services, especially between Asia to Europe, and Asia to South America, utilizing Tigers' west coast stations onto its scheduled routes. For instance, compared with the forty or so days required for an all-water move from Japan to Europe, sea-air has an obvious advantage with a 10- to 14-day transPacific transit to the Pacific Northwest, plus an additional one to two-days air move, combining both modes costing about $3 per kilo as compared with $7 per kilo direct by air.[13]

In 1982, the Port of Seattle began a promotional effort to solicit sea/air traffic from the Seattle docks direct to Europe over the short Polar Route. The Port originally sought a U.S. flag carrier for the cargo route, ensuring prospects of dependable manufacturing and shipping line accounts for the air segment. Martinair of Holland and Cargolux of Luxembourg, an established European cargo carrier, responded in place of any U.S.-based cargo carrier, and successfully developed scheduled service on that route. Martinair, unable to obtain cargo flight rights into Japan, started a joint venture with a shipping line to serve Europe via a Seattle gateway. "During its first few years, the sea/air cargo volumes grew by more than 70 percent a year. Those numbers have slowed in the last two years (1986-87) but, ironically, demand has outstripped capacity for outbound flights to Europe."[14] By 1987, the program was over-flowing the Seattle-Tacoma ports into the Vancouver, B.C., and other optional ports in the area. Cargolux increased its flight frequency on the Seattle/Europe route to three flights weekly using B747 jetfreighters, while Martinair has increased its frequency to twice weekly using a B747 and DC-10 cargo aircraft. Some of the overflow was trucked to Chicago for air transport to Europe. And the Port of Seattle also attempted to lure Europe-U.S. west coast backhaul air freight traffic with low attractive truck rates from Sea-Tac Airport to, purportedly, 60,000 cities and towns throughout the U.S.[15]

While considering optional revenue bases, Tigers continues to explore "promising new markets, and, in some cases, conducting 'in country' research, including India, China, Mexico and Canada. China's trading levels are expanding, while Mexico and Canada are both markets that are close to home and thus relatively easy to expand to, assuming regulatory rights can be obtained. And India, in addition to its longer-term economic prospects, offers seasonal advantages which complement Tiger's traditional Asian business."[16]

Still noticeable, MAC continues to be Flying Tigers' largest single customer, and receiving 40 percent of the total award made by MAC to all carriers in 1987.[17] For the first nine months of 1987, scheduled cargo operations accounted for 80% of revenues, with MAC accounting for 14%. In 1986, the figures were 82.3% and 11%, respectively.[18]

The role of commercial charters is also complementary. The primary role of the charter group is the utilization of idle resources during non-peak seasons in scheduled service where otherwise the aircraft would be parked, and positioning of aircraft to counter imbalances in the marketplace. From another aspect, charters allows the carrier to pioneer new markets for scheduled service, promotes visibility or exposure in the marketplace, and provides operating experience in the country with the ultimate objective of offering scheduled service into that country.[19] During recent years, commercial charters have constituted approximately 5% of the income revenues for Tigers. However, this sector offers high potential should the carrier experience more aircraft availability in order to commit to that sector, although scheduled service has been experiencing increased demand.

To meet its increasing needs, Flying Tigers wants to increase its fleet capacity, and is actively seeking the acquisition of B747 and DC-8 jetfreighters on an off-balance sheet, operating lease basis, and, perhaps, in a staggered lease basis. In this regard, among numerous recent Tiger tales, it has been mentioned that Emery Air Freight has been of interest to Tigers because of its fleet compatibility, complementary type of operation, and possible attractive terms while Emery is facing continual financial and operational problems brought about, in part, by its Purolator acquisition:

> "Now that Flying Tigers has $225 million in cash and a strong balance sheet...and feels that buying embattled Emery Air Freight Corporation might be ideal...expand its customer base to the international network, and link twenty new U.S. cities, including Buffalo, Salt Lake City, Manchester, N.H., to Tiger's overseas routes on top of the sixty now served."[20]

Emery experienced a $48 million loss in 1987 with mounting troubles integrating Purolator. The carrier's fleet mix includes seventeen DC-8s, which are no longer in production, although, as a cargo aircraft, is very cost-efficient.[21] As an added attraction, Emery has an air courier service, and a significant truck fleet.

Because of its extensive international routes and charter rights, among other various reasons, Tigers has been rumored to be of interest to UPS and United Airlines in recent times, after its impressive turn-around. Tigers also has passenger route authority to Japan. However, there is no clear evidence to substantiate the Emery, UPS, United Airlines or any other "Tiger Tales" in that respect.

However, displaying resilience and insight, Flying Tiger pilots formed a (ALPA) merger committee in 1987, which was exploratory in nature during the early formative period. Then, two particular events which occurred about October of that year forced the merger committee (MEC) to assume a different strategic posture. Firstly, investor Saul Steinberg, the significant FTL shareholder and influential Tiger International board member, suffered a severe loss in the devastating October stock market dive. Mr. Steinberg, whose Reliance Group Holdings, Inc., is the largest shareholder with 18.7% of Tiger's 32 million shares. Suggestively, potential manipulative strategies of an investor and possible shallow concerns for the carrier per se, sent strong negative signals to MEC.

Secondly, about the same time, Stephen Wolf accepted an offer to become CEO of United Airlines, which he assumed in mid-December, passing the leadership role as president at Tiger International to the 33-year old, James Cronin, who also retained his position as president of Flying Tigers. Meanwhile, the Corporation board named

Steinberg to head a three-member director group to select a chairman and chief executive officer to replace Wolf in those vacated positions.

The unsettling moves prompted MEC to take quick and strong measures in anticipation of a possible sale or merger of Flying Tigers in the foreseeable future. To protect pilot interest, MEC, under the Airline Pilots Association (ALPA) umbrella, approached the pilot leadership of various air carriers which were deemed to be prospective merger candidates holding an interest in FT, including American Airlines, United, Delta, Northwest, Federal Express and UPS.[22]

In an era of airline mergers, acquisitions, and joint ventures, the number of U.S.-based commercial carriers fell from 240 to 130 since deregulation. Many were forced out of business by the larger carriers, notwithstanding the impact of 38 airline mergers since 1983 in the United States. And since 1979, only four significant cargo carriers have been involved in that process. That involved the Emery-Purolator merger, and the Seaboard-Flying Tigers merger.

In January, 1989, the responsibilities of handling mergers and acquisitions will be transferred from the Department of Transportation (DOT) to the Department of Justice which may be much more stringent in qualifying its applicants. For the U.S. passenger airlines, the merger process has effectively eliminated or stymied competition in many areas, contrary to the original intentions of deregulation in 1978. Many areas have loss community air service once protected by CAB obligatory feeder service. Such the case has been the opposite with cargo carriers.

Flying Tigers continues to increase and improve its domestic service, and in 1987 and 1988, have began direct air service to Richmond, Virginia, Nashville, Tennessee, Peoria, Illinois, El Paso, Texas, Phoenix, Arizona, and San Diego, California, and re-opened direct air service to Portland, Oregon. In January, 1989, DC-8 service will be re-instituted in Seattle with a recently acquired aircraft.

But while Flying Tigers continues to strengthen its integrated global network, other carriers, both domestic and foreign, have not allowed the opportunities to go unnoticed. Competing carriers are forming alliances to gain market leverage. SAS and Continental have negotiated a joint venture using the Oslo and new Newark gateways. Singapore Airlines has linked with American Airlines, United Airlines with British Airways (BOAC), and Cathay Pacific with Lufthansa, which already has an extensive worldwide network spanning 169 cities in 83 countries. In the latter agreement, the Germans supply prime European landing rights and most of the B747 freighter equipment, while Cathay supplies the contracts in mainland China through Hong Kong, capitalizing on the Asia-Europe marketing opportunities.[23] More arrangements of this nature are forthcoming, and Tigers stays attuned to such challenges.

UPS, which is beginning to implement its courier service in six foreign countries in Asia, also needs the service of a dependable scheduled international air cargo carrier such as Tigers as a connecting agent in its international air express service. UPS does not have scheduled rights to fly its aircraft to those areas. And UPS lost its bid to win the Tokyo-U.S. route and authority, which was awarded to competing Federal Express in 1988.[24]

Through a contractual agreement in 1989, UPS still uses guaranteed space on Tigers' Anchorage to Japan flight to meet its needs. UPS also wants to extend its program to Europe and Latin America and, following its Hong Kong pattern, have set up possible local courier service. Tigers would appreciate the opportunity to be UPS's international carrier (airport to airport) as it would enjoy being everybody's preferred carrier, "**anything, anytime, and anywhere.**"

Notes

1. Tim Bradner, "Flying Tigers Roars Back," **Air Cargo News**, October, 1988, Vol. 13, No. 10, p. 47, and Perry Flint, "The Tiger is Smiling Again," **Air Transport World**, May, 1988, p. 47.

2. Bruce Johnson, "Changing Stripes and Making Money," **Air Cargo World**, Sept., 1988, Vol. 78, No. 9, p. 42.

3. Op. cit., "Flying Tigers Roars Back," p. 14.

4. Hal Bernton, "Cargo Carrier Plans Anchorage Hub," **Anchorage Daily News**, Friday, August 26, 1988, p. C2.

5. Op. cit., "Changing Stripes and Making Money," p. 38.

6. "Loss of duty-free status riles Singapore workers," **Seattle Times**, Feb. 6, 1988, p. B1.

7. **Tiger International, Inc., 1987 Annual Report**, p. 9, and Joan M. Feldman, "Japanese Liberalization Rapidly Opening Airline Opportunities," **Air Transport World**, July, 1987, pp. 27-34.

8. Op. cit., "The Tiger is Smiling Again," p. 47.

9. "Flying Tigers Appears Before Congress on Air Cargo Debate," **Tigereview**, Nov. 4, 1987, p.2., and Joan M. Feldman, "U.S. Airlines Eyeing International Cargo," **Air Transport World**, May 5, 1988, p. 54.

10. Op. cit., "The Tiger Is Smiling Again," p. 49.

11. James A. Cronin, "Growing Worldwide Air Freight Markets Need Regulatory Change," **Flying Tigers Review**, Feb., 1988, p. 2.

12. "Tom Barron Speaks on Financial Direction," **Flying Tigers Review**, Feb., 1987, p. 3.

13. Maggie Brown, "Sea-Air Shipping: Capturing the Best of Both Worlds," **Tradelines**, May-June, 1988, pp. 10 and 11.

14. Ibid.

15. Tim Bradner, "Cargo Floods Seattle," **Air Cargo News**, Vol. 13, No. 3, March, 1988, pp. 1 and 6.

16. James A. Cronin, "The Tiger Forum," **Flying Tigers Review**, Aug., 1988, p. 2.

17. Edwin H. "Ned" Wallace, "Ned Wallace Recaps International Divisions/MAC and Charter Operations," **Flying Tigers Review**, March, 1987, p. 3.

18. Op. cit., "The Tiger Is Smiling Again," p. 47.

19. Op. cit., "Ned Wallace Recaps International Divisions/MAC and Charter Operations," pp. 3 and 4.

20. **141 Messenger**, August, 1988 (Burlingame), Vol. 3, No. 11, p. 2.

21. Stewart Toy and Christopher, "Flying Tigers: Roaring, Soaring, and Prowling For Planes, **Business Week**, July 4, 1988.

22. FT Pilots Merger Committee, **FT Merger Report, January, 1989,** video report, and "Cronin Named Tiger President; Chief Is Sought," **Wall Street Journal,** Thursday, December 10, 1987, p. 34.

23. "Multinational airline networks may dominate industry," **The Seattle Times/Seattle Post-Intelligencer**, Sunday, October 23, 1988, p. D 10.

24. Mark W. Lyon, "Far East Hub for UPS," **Jet Cargo News**, Vol. 21, No. 4, August, 1988, p. 1.

16

The Legacy of Historical Airlifts Worldwide

Any history of the Flying Tiger Line would be amiss should it overlook the many historical airlifts throughout the carrier's years of service. Airlift relief flights have become a tradition, and the following will profile a handful of those missions.

In 1949, Tigers helped transport a significant number of the **35,000 Yemenite Jews** from the Arabian desert region to start their new lives in the newly created state of Israel. In a more difficult logistical project, in late 1951, Pan American Airlines subcontracted FTL to participate in the **Baby Berlin Airlift** in support of west Germany constrained by the blockade and counter blockade instituted in the confrontation with Soviet-occupied eastern Germany. The Communists had cut off the surface and water routes into Berlin, therefore an emergency airlift was needed. The over-surplus of goods in Berlin, in an unprecedented airlift, were flown to Bremen for export and Frankfurt for west Germany national distribution.

In another cold war-related event, in December of 1956, the airline flew its first flight of **Hungarian refugees** to the U.S. during an uprising that brought repressive measures by Soviet troops. And, the following year, Tigers began transporting **Korean War orphans** to adoptive parents in the U.S., comforted and nursed on the long transPacific flights.

Pictured to the right is a common scene, that is, a FTL flight attendant caring for a Korean orphan en route to a new home with an American family.

The occurrence of worldwide natural disasters and famine have on many occasions brought the "Tiger spirit" to the fore. In early February, 1953, the carrier sent medical and food supplies to assist in the **Holland flood relief effort**. In 1970, the carrier participated in the **Peruvian airlift** to aid earthquake victims.

Flying Tigers commitment and presence in global relief regarding human disasters and conflict is well known in the transportation industry and among numerous world governments. As aforementioned, in April of 1975, Tiger aircraft evacuated political refugees and employees from **Saigon** in dramatic fashion with the collapse of the South Vietnamese government, being over-run by communist North Vietnamese troops. And FTL flew 176 missions in the **Phnom Penh rice lift** to the beleaguered victims of the Cambodian holocaust. But perhaps the most memorable airlifts have been those in the 1980s involving employee planning and contributions, distinguishing itself from other carriers.

In 1985, the carrier scheduled two **Lifelift flights for Ethiopian famine relief.** The first Flying Tigers B747 jetfreighter arrived in Addis Ababa, Ethiopia, on January 29, carrying some 234,700 pounds of relief supplies. The humanitarian effort was conceived and accomplished by Flying Tigers employees throughout the carrier's worldwide system. After scheduling arrangements, Tiger personnel volunteered to load, fly and maintain the aircraft, and also contributed almost $20,000 toward the purchase of fuel for the operation. With the help of Interaction, a coalition of private and voluntary relief organizations, medical and food supplies most needed in Ethiopia were appropriated among relief organizations active in the east African nation.[1]

Lifelift was differentiated from other previous Tiger relief flights over the years in that it was wholly an employee-sponsored airlift from start to end. And, perhaps the most impressive fact of the project was that it took only three and a half weeks from the day a group of employees met for the first time at headquarters in Los Angeles to determine if the mission was possible to the afternoon when the big jet touched down at Addis Ababa. In that short span of time, an employee committee held a series of meetings at world headquarters in Los Angeles that planned and implemented the operational, legal, and public relations aspects of the famine-relief flight, and also coordinated the system-wide employee fund-raising efforts.

Flyers reading "Someone Must Care...Is That Someone You?" were prepared by the Flying Tigers print shop and distributed system-wide. To highlight the fund-raising, the contribution that put the total over the $20,000 mark came from Anne-Marie Prescott, the widow of Flying Tigers founder Bob Prescott.

The flight originated at Flying Tigers' JFK terminal where employees donated their time to build and load the relief freight. Two volunteer flight crews on board traded off on the flight to Addis Ababa-some 7,400 statute miles from JFK, including a fuel stop in Brussels, Belgium. Upon arrival at Addis Ababa airport, a mixture of military and civilian aircraft, some European and some Russian, were scattered about the airstrip, but none so impressive as the massive and inspiring red-and-blue striped Flying Tigers B747.

In appreciation by the United States Congress, during spring of 1985, Senator Alan Cranston of California put an account of the "Lifelift" flight into the Congressional Record of the 99th Congress.

FLYING TIGERS

We Were There....

TRIBUTE TO THE FLYING TIGERS LIFELIFT FOR ETHIOPIAN RELIEF

Mr. CRANSTON. Mr. President, today I would like to pay tribute to the Los Angeles headquartered Flying Tigers and its 6,000 worldwide employees for their contribution to the victims of the Ethiopian famine. In early February, the Flying Tigers' Lifelift for Ethiopian Relief flew a mercy flight of 7,400 miles from John F. Kennedy Airport in New York to Addis Ababa, Ethiopia, to deliver 234,771 pounds of medical supplies, food, and clothing valued at $1,066,537. The cargo was a gift from thousands of individuals and U.S. companies to the famine and drought-plagued people of Ethiopia.

Marilyn Folkes, a traffic agent for Flying Tigers at JFK was fundraising chairman of the Lifelift and integral to its success. She and dozens of other Flying Tiger employees, from cargo handlers to pilots, volunteered their time and energy without pay to coordinate the Lifelift. These people deserve our praise and recognition for their noble effort.

In reaching out to starving people thousands of miles away, Flying Tigers and its employees have set an admirable example for the rest of us. Their generous contribution of time,

effort, and money is well worth emulating.

I ask unanimous consent that an article from the Los Angeles Times regarding the Flying Tigers' effort be printed in the RECORD.

There being no objection, the material was ordered to be printed in the RECORD, as follows:

FLIGHT TO ETHIOPIA: FOOD, SUPPLIES, COMPASSION

FLYING TIGERS, OTHERS DONATE MONEY, TIME TO STARVING AFRICANS

(By Charles Hillinger)

ADDIS ABABA, ETHIOPIA.—The American Boeing 747 had been flying south over Ethiopia for more than an hour, covering 600 miles from the Red Sea at the nation's northernmost tip, across barren desert and bone-dry, rust-colored mountains indented with narrow, deep valleys.

Visible below were scattered settlements on high plateaus and in valleys where perhaps 200,000 people have died from famine in the last year alone, where thousands continue to starve and die each week in primitive huts or en route on the network of trails seeking help.

The incredible harshness of the landscape—not a sign of water or a patch of green—makes it remarkable that human life is possible there at all.

CAPITAL SIGHTED

"There it is! There it is! Addis Abada!" exclaimed Hal Ewing, 41, of Sumpter, S.C., captain of the Flying Tigers air freighter, as the 747 descended through puffy cumulus clouds. Ethiopia's 7,625-foot-high capital suddenly burst into view amid a patchwork quilt of dry, brown farms.

The plane was on a mercy flight sponsored by the Los Angeles-headquartered Flying Tigers and its 6,000 worldwide employees. The 747 carried 234,771 pounds of medical supplies, food and clothing valued at $1,066,537, a gift from thousands of Americans across the nation to vicitms of one of the greatest calamities of all times, Ethiopia's famine of the 1980s.

A few minutes later Ewing and his crew in the cockpit, First Officer Mick O'Connor, 32, of Key Largo, Fla., and Second Officer Paul Zahner, 31, of Danbury, Conn., landed the huge jet, using all but a few feet of the narrow, short runway with a hump in its middle. At the end of the airstrip lay the remains of wrecked Soviet planes that overshot the runway and ended at the bottom of steep cliffs, testimony to the airstrip's tricky nature.

The Flying Tigers Lifelift for Ethiopian Relief had flown 7,400 statute miles from New York's John F. Kennedy Airport to Addis Abada in 16 hours, 48 minutes counting a 3-hour, 50-minute refueling stop in Brussels.

For Marilyn Folkes, 35, traffic agent for Flying Tigers at J.F.K., who as fund-raising chairman for the Lifelift flight played a key role in its success, the arrival was one of enormous joy. During the stop in Brussels, while walking through the 185-foot-long main cargo deck loaded with tons of relief supplies, she commented:

"I am happy knowing the medicine will help save thousands of lives, prevent a lot of blindness and stop the spread of disease, that the food aboard the plane will provide needed nourishment, that thousands will be a little warmer because of these blankets and clothes. . . ."

For Marilyn Folkes, hunger is no stranger. She has worried about the starving people of Ethiopia for years. She has sponsored two Ethiopian children since 1976 at a cost of $60 a month. She has lectured about hunger in Africa in New York-area churches, primarily black churches, urging involvement in aid programs.

IMPACT OF BBC FILM

Then last November, not long after a BBC film crew jarred the conscience of the world with its startling footage of starving Ethiopians, Folkes decided: "The bottom line is I am my brother's keeper. I wouldn't want other people to ignore me." So, three months ago she took two weeks' leave from her job and flew to Ethiopia to do what she could in the camps set up for the victims of the famine.

During this, her second flight to Ethiopia, she told of the agony she witnessed: "I have not been the same person since. I feel absolutely miserable inside every time I think about it. I saw thousands of people lying on the dirt motionless, nothing more than skin and bones, obviously going to die. I saw physicians pick and choose who was going to live because of limited food supplies.

"I saw thousands of emaciated children, there faces covered with flies, staring into space. At Alamata in the refugee camp I saw the Mother Teresa Sisters of Charity comforting dying people, helping them to die with some sense of dignity. I have had nightmares ever since, waking up weeping." Folkes said as she wiped away tears.

Now, she was back to see firsthand the distribution of aid flown in by her fellow employees, back again to visit the sorrow, starvation, sickness and death at the refugee camps.

Within minutes after the 747 landed, cargo doors opened and the offloading operation began under the direction of Jochem Derschow, 29, of Amsterdam, Flying Tigers' European load master and charter operations supervisor who boarded the plane in Brussels.

Ethiopian cargo handlers moved the 86,751 pounds of medical supplies, 32,754 pounds of food and 115,266 pounds of clothing and blankets to a nearby section of the tarmac where trucks belonging to American-based relief agencies were waiting to transfer the material to famine camps 150 to 400 miles from the capital city. Some of the supplies would be airlifted.

In the boxes and fiber sacks were tons of vitamins, bandages, cotton swabs, emollient ointment, antibiotics, IV solutions, nutritional supplements for infants, butter oil, cereals, oral rehydration salts, blankets and warm clothing for the camps in the high mountains where temperatures are often below freezing.

The lifesaving items had come from humanitarian and church groups that had collected contributions from thousands of individuals and materials from several U.S. companies.

"Everything shipped here on this huge plane is needed desperately now," said Bekele Biri, 41, an Ethiopian who is president of the 35,000-member Ethiopian Union of Seventh-Day Adventists, as he met the plane. "The magnitude of the problem is so great resources will never be able to match it.

"The world came late. If it had come a little earlier perhaps things would have been much easier," said Biri with a sigh after each sentence, an idiosyncrasy of the Ethiopian melodious manner of speaking.

WIDESPREAD FAMINE

"Sad as it is, nearly every country in Africa is experiencing famine to varying degrees."

The Adventist Development & Relief Agency is one of several U.S. relief organizations active in Ethiopia shipping and receiving supplies on the Flying Tigers "Lifelift" flight. Others are Catholic Relief Services, Africare, Mennonite Central Committee, World Vision, MAP (Medical Assistance Programs) International, the Red Cross and Sudan Interior Mission.

Coordinating the assemblage of the 117-plus-ton shipment for the Flying Tigers flight was Interaction, headquartered at 200 Park Ave., New York, a coalition of 125 humanitarian and church relief groups, including those mentioned and others such as the American Friends Service Committee, Baptist World Aid and the American Jewish Joint Disaster Committee. Since last November, Interaction has shipped $40 million worth of medicine, food and clothing to Ethiopia for the consortium of voluntary groups.

"This airlift is of tremendous help. I hope this flight by Flying Tigers will have a domino effect and inspire other airlines to do likewise. The need is so urgent to get these vital items to Ethiopia as quickly as possible," said Julius Weeks, 31, of New York City, Interaction official aboard the Flying Tigers flight.

"It takes so long by ship, then by land once it arrives in an Ethiopian seaport. We have warehouses full of supplies in America waiting for ships and hopefully for planes destined for Ethiopia," added Weeks, a former Peace Corps worker who is a native of Liberia. His father was president of the University of Liberia and former secretary of state for Liberia.

It was an anonymous letter sent from an employee to Lewis Jordan, executive vice president of Flying Tigers, at the company's Los Angeles headquarters late in December that triggered the airlift.

While seeing the plane off in New York at the start of its mercy mission, Jordan recalled receiving the letter, which said: "We have a saying in our company. We care about people. We should do something about the victims of the Ethiopian famine."

Jordan mentioned the correspondence in the company's weekly newsletter. The response from employees was overwhelming. A committee was formed. Posters were printed and hung in all Flying Tigers offices showing an emaciated Ethiopian child and stating:

"Someone must care. Is that someone you? Give from your heart and save someone. You can help the famine and drought-plagued people of Ethiopia."

FUND DRIVE CONTINUES

Contributions poured in from throughout the company's worldwide system, from Japan, Taiwan, Australia, Hong Kong, Singapore, Europe, from across the United States.

"We're especially proud of this effort because to our knowledge no other air carrier employees have organized an airlift for the famine victims of Ethiopia," Jordan said.

The Flying Tigers company provided the airplane for the mercy flight without cost. Crew members volunteered their time to fly the 747.

The fund drive by employees, which is still going on, will offset a large part of the $95,000 fuel bill for the flight, the balance of which is being paid by contributions from four aviation fuel firms and by relief organizations that have goods on board. Flying Tigers employees in the Los Angeles office have already contributed $7,500.

To charter a 747 from the company to fly a comparable weight load the same distance would cost about $300,000. To get the plane back in the Flying Tigers system it was necessary to fly it empty from Addis Ababa to Taipei, another 6,000 statute miles.

Two crews alternated flying the big cargo jetliner on the long journey. Capt. Randy Patterson, 48, of Palm Coast, Fla., First Officer Charles Cozad, 37, of St. Helena, Calif, and Second Officer Charles Gallardo, 34, of Atlanta, flew the first leg to Ethiopia. Also aboard were mechanic Charles Millman, 41, of Long Island, N.Y., flight attendants Becky Rasmussen, 33, of Hermosa Beach, and Michele Rizza, 27, of Rancho Palos Verdes, Lifelift committee members Stephen Hanks, 40, of Fountain Valley, and Colleen Ferguson, 39, of Westwood, and a Times reporter.

"All 600 pilots in the system wanted in on it," said Capt. Hal Ewing, in charge of assembling the cabin crew for the mercy mission. A native of Long Beach, he has flown other disaster efforts in the past—including the Honduras hurricane and Cambodian famine.

For Hanks, director of labor relations at Flying Tigers and chairman of the Lifelift committee, it was hard to believe that only 25 days had passed since the company decided to set in motion the airlift to the famine stricken people of Ethiopia.

"It took the efforts of dozens of people within the company to make this all possible, to plan a way to free a plane from service for three days, to obtain landing permits and every so many other details," Hanks observed.

WORKED WITHOUT PAY

At Building 262, Tiger Corner at J.F.K. Airport Cargo Complex, a dozen volunteer cargo handlers led by Vince Buscarino, 30, worked through the night without pay loading the 747 with the relief supplies in preparation for the flight to Ethiopia. Typical comments from the cargo handlers:

Jerry Alston, 38: "My feelings, especially because I'm black, are I am so proud of everyone in this company for picking up on this great cause."

Jim Morrison, 38: "I have a 13-month-old daughter, Heather, at home. I see my daughter, how healthy she is. Then I see on TV those starving and dying kids in Ethiopia. It makes me sick at heart. I can picture my daughter in the same situation. I am saving money for my daughter's college education. I took some of that money and gave it for this flight."

Joseph Acanda, 54, truck driver who drove supplies to Flying Tigers from Maryland without charge: "I am a Comanche Indian. I got 13 children. I can't imagine people starving in this world of plenty. I got my health. Got a job. I'm giving to this cause because of the horror I saw in Ethiopia on TV."

The small airport at Addis Ababa was jammed with airplanes from various parts of the world, eight Soviet Antonov AN12 transports, two Antonov 26 (Russian made) Libyan Air Force planes, a French cargo plane, a Spanish Air Force Hercules, two British Royal Air Force Hercules, two West German Transall transports, an East German Interflug passenger jet, four Ethiopian Airlines passenger planes.

There are more planes moving in and out of Addis Ababa than ever in recent memory, said the airport manager, an Ethiopian who would not give his name but said he lived in Inglewood, while attending Northrop Institute.

The French plane was chartered by an organization of French doctors called Doctors Without Borders to bring in 36 tons of milk, medicine and blankets. The Spanish Air Force plane brought 15 tons of medical aid, food and clothing from the Spanish government.

A Libyan Air Force pilot said his country had been flying relief supplies in two planes to famine areas from Addis Ababa every day for two months. Aboard the two cargo

272

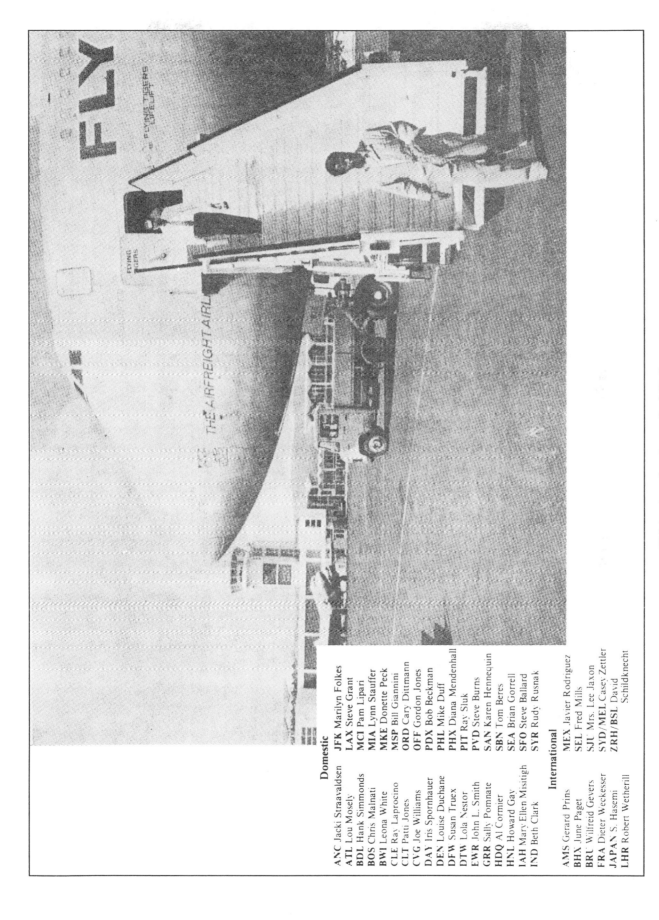

Domestic

ANC Jacki Straavaldsen	JFK Marilyn Folkes
ATL Lou Mosely	LAX Steve Grant
BDL Hank Simmonds	MCI Pam Lipari
BOS Chris Malnati	MIA Lynn Stauffer
BWI Leona White	MKE Donette Peck
CLE Ray Laprocino	MSP Bill Giannini
CLT Patti Jones	ORD Cary Dittmann
CVG Joe Williams	OFF Gordon Jones
DAY Iris Spornhauer	PDX Bob Beckman
DEN Louise Duchane	PHL Mike Duff
DFW Susan Truex	PHX Diana Mendenhall
DTW Lola Nestor	PIT Ray Sluk
EWR John L. Smith	PVD Steve Burns
GRR Sally Pommate	SAN Karen Hennequin
HDQ Al Cormier	SBN Tom Beres
HNL Howard Gay	SEA Brian Gorrell
IAH Mary Ellen Mistigh	SFO Steve Ballard
IND Beth Clark	SYR Rudy Rusnak

International

AMS Gerard Prins	MEX Javier Rodriguez
BHX June Paget	SEL Fred Mills
BRU Willreid Gevers	SJU Mrs. Lee Jaxon
FRA Dieter Weckesser	SYD/MEL Casey Zettler
JAPAN S. Hasemi	ZRH/BSL David
LHR Robert Wetherill	Schildknecht

Ethiopian famine relief flight

At FTL LAX, Ken Kragen, president of USA for Africa, Lionel Richie ,
and Quincy Jones give thumbs-up for the relief mission.
Flight was destined to Addis Ababa and Khartoum.

In June of 1985, Flying Tigers operated a special relief flight for **USA for Africa** carrying 231,463 pounds of food, medical, and clothing to Khartoum, Sudan and Addis Ababa, Ethiopia. The flight marked the year's sixth FT B747 jetfreighter mission to famine-stricken African nations. The June flight represented the first airlift of relief supplies by the highly publicized USA for Africa group, a non-profit organization formed by forty-five top American recording artists. Spearheaded by their hit recording "We Are the World," the group used funds from record sales, the sale of related merchandise, and other promotions to aid African famine victims.[2]

The **USA for Africa** flight operated on a Los Angeles-New York-Brussels-Khartoum-Addis Ababa routing, receiving major media attention along the way. In Los Angeles, Quincey Jones, Lionel Richie and Kenny Rogers watched the loading and departure of the flight Sunday night, June 9.

Marlon Jackson was on board the flight from Los Angeles to Addis Ababa, while Diana Ross was on hand at the carrier's new JFK facility Monday morning, June 10, and

USA for Africa group with Diana Ross.

participated in a press conference during the loading of additional freight on board the aircraft. Then Harry Belafonte and his wife, Julie, boarded the aircraft in Brussels, Belgium for the flight through to Addis Ababa.[3]

Flying Tigers' last significant international airlift was flown in **relief of Armenian SSR earthquake victims** in December, 1988, comprising of a volunteer flight crew, a company donated aircraft for the mission, and carrying volunteer relief workers. Amid local news media members, I recall the build-up and loading of that aircraft at Sea-Tac airport as it arrived from Los Angeles on its way through to New York for additional relief supplies. The coordination and mobilization between Tiger "volunteerism" and local "volunteerism" untied the political strings to effect the extraordinary mission.

On December 7, 1988, a devastating earthquake, registering 6.9 on the Richter scale, struck Soviet Armenia, the mountainous province bordering eastern Turkey. The quake cut a wide swath across the Transcaucasus, simultaneously crippling communications and transportation in the region, delaying disaster relief. It was reported that the quake left an estimated 60,000 dead and up to half million homeless.

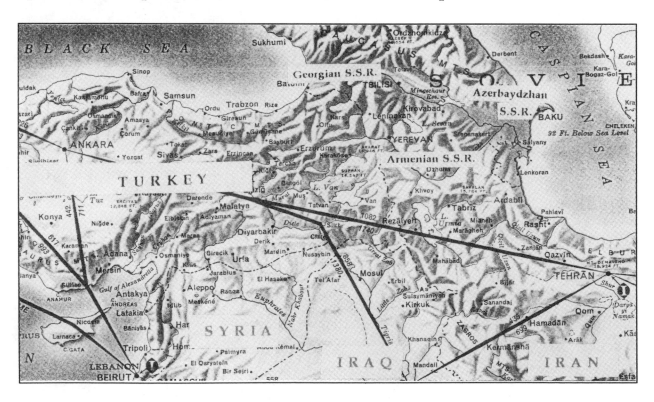

Collapsed building at a disaster site.

Tiger pilot, meeting Soviet counterpart, and displaying
picture of impressive Soviet super aircraft.
(Photos courtesy of Steve Castello,
Seattle-King County Disaster Team)

Leninakan, the largest Armenian city with a population of 250,000, was reportedly ²/₃ destroyed, while Kirovakan, with a population of 150,000, had half of its buildings destroyed. Spitak, the Armenian regional center of 30,000 was leveled, killing over half the population. In Spitak, seven of the eight schools were flattened while children were attending school, causing instant graveyards.[4] Immediate airlift relief was imminent.

Upon learning of the disaster, the Seattle-King County Medical Disaster Team of physicians, paramedics and nurses volunteered their services. The organization had sent an experienced team to Mexico in 1985 and El Salvador in 1986 after their respective earthquake tragedies. The group's efforts to give aid to Armenian SSR had been stymied by the Soviet authorities before the successful intervention by Bob Walsh, president of the Seattle Organizing Committee of the 1990 Goodwill Games. Walsh, who previously had extensive dealings with the Soviets because of the Games, helped secure permission and a waiver on visas. As such, they are believed to be the first and only private American medical group allowed into the Soviet Union to aid in earthquake relief efforts.[5]

Meanwhile, Flying Tigers donated an aircraft and assembled a volunteer flight crew, and scheduled the flight. Their planning coordinated with local efforts to collect donations and to meet the transportation needs of the Pacific Northwest medical team consisting of a 30-member relief team organized by the Seattle-King County Disaster Team and a 16-member contingent from Portland, both including surgeons, emergency physicians, emergency nurses, and a pharmacist.

In the sequence of events, the medical group assembled at our Sea-Tac station and boarded the B747 just before midnight on December 13th. Nearly all of the supplies loaded on the plane were donated by local hospitals and individuals, including medicine, diagnostic machines, two portable operating rooms, generators, tents, food, clothing, and a team of rescue dogs from Alaska. From JFK airport, the flight proceeded to Frankfurt, then directly to Yerevan, the capital city of Armenia.[6] On the second day of arrival, the Portland contingent stayed in Yerevan and worked in an undamaged hospital, while the Seattle-King County Disaster Team established a 24-hour a day field clinic in Leninakan, as well as conducting search and rescue operations. The time frame for the mission was set for seven to ten days.[7]

Within that time frame, a system-wide news bulletin was to shake Flying Tigers' very own foundation!

Notes

1. "We Did It! 'Lifelift' a Great Success," **Flying Tigers Review**, March, 1985, pp. 1 and 2.

2. "Employees Join Forces, Fight Famine in Big Way With 'Lifelift," **Flying Tigers Review**, May, 1985, pp. 3-5.

3. "USA for Africa Flight's A Big Event, Big Success," **Flying Tigers Review**, June, 1985, p. 1.

4. Ibid.

5. "Armenia Quake," **Seattle Times**, Dec. 12, pp. A1 and A12, and "Spitak Wiped Out," **Seattle Times**, Dec. 10, pp. A1 and A7, and "Seattle-King County Medical Disaster Team Prepares," **Seattle Times**, Dec. 11, pp. A5 and A7.

6. "Pacific Northwest Medical Team Leaves for Armenia Quake Site," **Seattle Times**, Dec. 13, p. A10.

7. Per conversation with Steve Castello, paramedic with Seattle-King County Disaster Team on their mission.

17

What Would Cause the Proud Tiger to Turn Purple?

On December 14, 1988, a Flying Tiger system-wide bulletin was released noting that "Tiger International, Inc., today announced that it has been approached by an unrelated third party interested in acquiring the company."[1] It was a response to matters which occurred a week or so earlier when Reliance Holding Group, which had a vested interest in the Corporation since 1979, had advanced a proposal to acquire the outstanding common stock of Tiger International at premium over the current market price ($12^{3}/_{8}$). Saul Steinberg, chairman of the investment group, and principal shareholder of Tigers, expressed his consideration to take the Company private. It was carefully worded to imply a "consideration" and may have been an obvious business gesture to quickly boost the stock value of Tiger International, to which Steinberg was also an influential board member. Quite succinctly, it appeared to be a well orchestrated move to entice potential parties who might be interested in acquiring Flying Tigers.

The following day, December 15, Tigers scheduled a special meeting of its Board of Directors to consider any offer which might be forthcoming from such a third party. The next day, it was learned that the party in question turned out to be the foremost air express carrier, Federal Express, tendering an offer (via Steinberg) for all of Tigers'

.HDQSR 170211

     - - - - - S P E C I A L   B U L L E T I N - - - - -

     .///// IMPORTANT ///// IMPORTANT ///// IMPORTANT /////

            PLEASE POST ON ALL BULLETIN BOARDS

THE FOLLOWING PRESS RELEASE WAS ISSUED TODAY--

            FEDERAL EXPRESS TO ACQUIRE
            TIGER INTERNATIONAL
            FOR APPROXIMATELY USD 880 MILLION

     MEMPHIS--DEC. 16 CMA 1988-- FREDERICK W. SMITH CMA CHAIRMAN
AND CHIEF EXECUTIVE OFFICER OF FEDERAL EXPRESS CORPORATION
/NYSE-FDX/ CMA AND SAUL P. STEINBERG CMA CO-CHAIRMAN OF TIGER
INTERNATIONAL CMA INC. /NYSE-TGR/ JOINTLY ANNOUNCED TODAY THE
EXECUTION OF A DEFINITIVE AGREEMENT PROVIDING FOR THE MERGER
OF TIGER INTERNATIONAL WITH A WHOLLY-OWNED SUBSIDIARY OF
FEDERAL EXPRESS.

     UNDER TERMS OF THE AGREEMENT CMA APPROVED BY BOTH
COMPANIES/ BOARDS OF DIRECTORS CMA FEDERAL EXPRESS WILL MAKE A
CASH TENDER OFFER FOR ALL OF TIGER/S COMMON STOCK AT A PRICE
OF USD 20.875 PER SHARE. THE TENDER IS EXPECTED TO BEGIN ON
TUESDAY CMA DEC. 20 CMA 1988. THE OFFER WILL BE CONDITIONED UPON CMA
AMONG OTHER THINGS CMA THE TENDER OF AT LEAST 50.1 PERCENT OF
THE TIGER SHARES ON A FULLY-DILUTED BASIS. TIGER HAS
APPROXIMATELY 40.8 MILLION SHARES OF COMMON STOCK ON A
FULLY-DILUTED BASIS.

     IN CONNECTION WITH THE MERGER CMA TIGER HAS GRANTED
FEDERAL EXPRESS AN OPTION TO PURCHASE AUTHORIZED AND
UNISSUED SHARES OF TIGER COMMON STOCK AMOUNTING TO 22
PERCENT OF THE OUTSTANDING FULLY-DILUTED SHARES AT A PRICE
OF USD-20.875 PER SHARE. IN ADDITION CMA FEDERAL EXPRESS WAS
GRANTED AN OPTION TO PURCHASE THE TIGER SHARES OWNED BY
RELIANCE GROUP HOLDINGS CMA INC. AMOUNTING TO 14.8 PERCENT OF
THE OUTSTANDING FULLY-DILUTED SHARES AT THE SAME PRICE BEING
OFFERED TO ALL OTHER SHAREHOLDERS.
     CONSUMMATION OF THE MERGER WILL BE SUBJECT TO APPROVAL
BY THE U.S. DEPARTMENT OF TRANSPORTATION AND DEPARTMENT OF
JUSTICE

     SMITH SAID -- //THE COMBINATION OF TIGER/S
INTERNATIONAL ROUTE AUTHORITIES CMA HIGHLY EFFICIENT CARGO
FLEET AND STRATEGICALLY LOCATED AIRPORT FACILITIES WILL
ENABLE FEDERAL EXPRESS TO ACCELERATE THE DEVELOPMENT OF ITS
GLOBAL DISTRIBUTION NETWORK. WHILE OUR TWO BUSINESSES HAVE
TO DATE SERVED DIFFERENT MARKETS CMA WE BELIEVE THE MERGER WILL
RESULT IN SIGNIFICANT OPERATING EFFICIENCIES WHICH WILL
BENEFIT OUR RESPECTIVE CUSTOMERS. //

     SMITH FURTHER STATED CMA //THE FACT THAT FEDERAL HAS ON
ORDER OVER 60 ADDITIONAL AIRCRAFT IS CLEAR EVIDENCE THAT
THERE WILL BE FUTURE GROWTH OPPORTUNITIES FOR THE EMPLOYEES
OF BOTH FEDERAL AND FLYING TIGERS. //

common stock at a price of $20.875 per share.[2] Shortly thereafter, a Federal Express system-wide bulletin announced the acceptance of a merger between the two Corporate giants, and that FedEx, being the surviving party, intends to continue operating Flying Tigers as a separate subsidiary pursuing its regular operations until the actual merger can be effected.[3] The merger is subject to approval by both the U.S. Department of Transportation and Department of Justice.

For those of us who had experienced a considerably amount of sacrifices in order to achieve a successful turn-around, and had enjoyed many years working for Flying Tigers, the surprising situation prompted many mixed emotions. Observing one of our recent organizational slogans, we thought that we had "recaptured the jungle."

But, taken in perspective, the final merger of Flying Tigers into Federal Express, and the integration of their collective capabilities promises the opportunity for a premiere world-wide air freight/air express carrier offering a full range of services almost anytime and anywhere in significant air cargo markets.

But, in the distant background, one could hear the sound of a P-40 echoing into the night!

```
ATTN    ALL EMPLOYEES              ----- 5/26/89 -----
FROM    CORPORATE COMMUNICATIONS DEPARTMENT

COPY - OFFICERS / GEN MGRS / CHIEF PILOT / TERM SVC DIRS /
       REG SLS DIRS / DIST MGRS / MAINT DIRS/SUPVS / CUST SVC DIRS

       - - - - - -  S P E C I A L    B U L L E T I N  - - - - - -

       /////  IMPORTANT  /////  IMPORTANT  /////  IMPORTANT  /////

                 PLEASE POST ON ALL BULLETIN BOARDS

THE FIRST SESSION OF THE 101/ST CONGRESS ANNOUNCED ON MAY 18
THAT IT HAD PASSED SENATE CONCURRENT RESOLUTION 39 WHICH COMMENDS
THE GROUP OF AVIATORS KNOWN AS THE //FLYING TIGERS//.   THE
RESOLUTION IS AS FOLLOWS --
```

Congressional Record

United States of America

PROCEEDINGS AND DEBATES OF THE *101st* CONGRESS, FIRST SESSION

Vol. 135   WASHINGTON, THURSDAY, MAY 18, 1989   *No. 64*

SENATE CONCURRENT RESOLUTION 39—SUBMISSION OF A CONCURRENT RESOLUTION COMMENDING THE "FLYING TIGERS"

Mr. WILSON submitted the following concurrent resolution, which was referred to the Committee on the Judiciary:

S. CON. RES. 39

Whereas the merger of Tiger International with the Federal Express Corporation led to the transfer of the international air cargo routes from Flying Tiger Line, Inc., a subsidiary of Tiger International, to the Federal Express Corporation, will bring to a close one of the most remarkable and distinguished chapters in United States aviation history;

Whereas the pilots of the Flying Tiger Line, Inc. bear a name which represents members of a proud and distinguished group of aviators (properly known as the "Flying Tigers");

Whereas approximately 50 years ago the Flying Tigers initially operated in the jungles of Burma, with the operations of the American volunteer group under the command of General Clair Chennault;

Whereas the tradition of proud and distinguished service by the Flying Tigers to the United States began under the direction of Robert W. Prescott;

Whereas for more than 4 decades such proud and distinguished group of aviators has steadfastly served the specialized air transportation needs of the United States; and

Whereas the Flying Tigers have provided assistance with rescue efforts in Korea, Hungary, Vietnam, Cambodia, and Ethiopia, and have conducted many other humanitarian missions: Now, therefore, be it

Resolved by the Senate (the House of Representatives concurring), That Congress commends the group of pilots that bear the name Flying Tigers, a distinguished group of aviators, for nearly 50 years of valued and competent service to the United States.

Mr. WILSON. Mr. President, along with my colleague from California, Senator CRANSTON, I rise today to introduce a resolution commemorating the proud and distinguished service of the pilots of the Flying Tigers.

This group of pilots, first organized by Gen. Clair Chennault, has provided the American public and people all over the world with continuous service for almost 50 years. Their heroics on behalf of our Armed Forces and humanitarian relief efforts are well documented and merit our recognition.

Mr. President, we all know of the heriocs performed by these courageous pilots in the defense of freedom. What is less known is how 12 members of the famed group of World War II combat pilots, the Flying Tigers, formed what was once a small airline. They were at once pilots, mechanics, and shippers.

In the days following World War II, the pilots of Flying Tigers flew the largest airlift ever performed by a single contractor—the supply of General MacArthur's occupational forces in Japan. Ever since that time, these pilots have given great service to the Armed Forces for cargo and passenger services.

The pilots of Flying Tigers have risked their lives many times on behalf of the world's underprivileged and oppressed. During the 1970's, the airline participated in several mercy charter flights flying supplies to needy Cambodian refugees. On Thanksgiving Day in 1979, history was made when the pilots delivered $1.5 million in food and medical supplies in the first direct mercy flight from the United States to Phnom Penh—4 years after the famed "ricelift" to Cambodia in 1975.

Life saving supplies were also delivered to refugee camps along the Thailand/Cambodian border, and passenger charter flights were commissioned to carry refugees to the United States. In March 1982, the Flying Tigers flew a charter flight into Warsaw, delivering over 40 tons of medical supplies, staple foods, and relief goods—the first airlift of relief supplies to reach Poland since the imposition of martial law the previous November.

Clearly, Mr. President, the pilots of Flying Tigers deserve the recognition of this Congress. They have performed valiantly and with great skill during both war and peace. I urge the Senate to consider this commemorative legislation quickly and to ensure its passage.

Notes

1. Flying Tiger Employee Bulletin dated Dec. 14, 1988.

2. Flying Tiger Employee Bulletin dated Dec. 16, 1988.

3. Federal Express Corp. Employee Bulletin dated Dec. 16, 1988.

BIBLIOGRAPHY

Books

Bender, Marylin, and Altschul, Selig. **The Chosen Instrument: The Rise and Fall of an American Entrepreneur.** New York: Simon and Schuster, 1982.

Bond, Charles R., Jr. and Anderson, Terry H. **A Flying Tiger's Diary.** Texas A & M University Press, 1984.

Brewer, Stanley H. **Military Airlift and Its Relationship to the Commercial Air Cargo Industry.** Seattle: Graduate School of Business, Univ. of Washington, 1967.

---------------- **Air Cargo Comes of Age.** Seattle: Graduate School of Business, Univ. of Washington,

--------------- **Air Cargo – The Big Breakthrough.** Seattle: Graduate School of Business, Univ. of Washington, 1959.

---------------- **The Gold is in the Terminals.** Seattle: Graduate School of Business, Univ. of Washington, 1962.

---------------- **Vision in Air Cargo.** Seattle: Graduate School of Business, Univ. of Washington, 1957.

---------------- **The Complexities of Air Cargo Pricing.** Seattle: Graduate School of Business, Univ. of Washington, 1967.

---------------- **The Environment of International Air Carriers in the Development of Freight Markets.** Seattle: Graduate School of Business, Univ. of Washington, 1967.

----------, and Decoster, D.T. **The Nature of Air Cargo Costs.** Seattle: Graduate School of Business, Univ. of Washington, 1967.

----------, Kast, Fremont E.; and Rosenzweiz, James E. **The North America-Asia Marketing for Air Freight.** Seattle: Graduate School of Business, Univ. of Washington, 1963.

Building the Seattle-Tacoma Air Gateway. Developed for the Washington Parties; By and Under the Direction of Stanley H. Brewer. Seattle: Graduate School of Business, Univ. of Washington, July, 1968.

Cameron, Frank J. **Hungry Tiger, the Story of the Flying Tiger Line.** New York:McGraw-Hill Book Co., 1964.

Cook, John C. **International Air Cargo Strategy.** Philadelphia: Freight Press, Inc., 1983.

Corke, Alison. **British Airways: The Path to Profitability.** New York: Martin's Press, 1986.

Davies, R.E.G. **Airlines of the United States Since 1914.** London: Putnam, 1972.

Frederick, John H. **Commercial Air Transportation.** 4th ed., Homewood, Ill: Richard D. Irwin, 1955.

Gill, Frederick W., and Bates, Gilbert L. **Airline Competition.** Cambridge: Harvard U., 1949.

Green, William; Swanborough, Gordon; and Mowinski, John. **Modern Commercial Aircraft.** New York: Portland House, 1987.

Hotz, Robert, edit. **Way of a Fighter; The Memoirs of Claire Lee Chennault.** New York: G.P. Putnam's Sons, 1949.

Leary, William H., Jr. **The Dragon's Wings.** Athens: Univ. of Georgia Press, 1976.

Lewis, Howard T.; Culliton, James W.; and Steele, Jack D. **The Role of Air Freight in Physical Distribution.** Boston: Graduate School of Business, Harvard University, 1956.

Morrison, Steven, and Winston, Clifford. **The Economic Effects of Airline Deregulation.** Wash., D.C.: Brookings Institution, 1986.

O'Connor, W.E. **An Introduction to Airline Economics.** New York: Praeger Publishers, 1978.

Ray, Jim. **The Story of Air Transport.** Philadelphia: John C. Winston Co., 1947.

Rosholt, Malcolm. **Flight in the China Air Space, 1910-1950.** Rosholt, Wi.: Rosholt House, 1983.

---------------- **The Education of Anna.** Rosholt, Wi.: Rosholt House, 1972.

Schneider, L.M. **The Future of the U.S. Domestic Air Freight Industry: An Analysis of Management Strategies.** Boston: Harvard Business School: Harvard U., 1973.

Strazheim, Mahlon R. **The International Airline Industry.** Wash., D.C.: Transport Research Program, Brookings Institution, 1969.

Taneja, Nawal K. **The Commercial Airline Industry: Managerial Practices and Regulatory Policies.** Lexington, Mass.: D.C. Heath, Lexington Books, 1976.

-------------- **The U.S. Air Freight Industry.** Lexington, Mass.: D.C. Heath, Lexington Books, 1977.

-------------- **Airlines in Transition.** Lexington, Mass.: D.C. Heath, Lexington Books, 1981.

Thayer, Frederick C., Jr. **Air Transport Policy and National Security.** Chapel Hill: Univ. of North Carolina Press, 1965.

Ulanoff, Stanley M. **MATS: The Story of the Military Air Transport Service.** New York: Franklin Watts, Inc., 1964.

Whelan, Russell. **The Flying Tigers.** New York: Viking Press, 1942.

Wyckoff, D.D., and Maister, D.H. **The Domestic Airline Industry.** Lexington, Mass.: D.C. Heath, Lexington Books, 1977.

Young, Arthur N. **China and the Helping Hand, 1937-1945.** Cambridge: Harvard U. Press, 1963.

Thesis (Unpublished)

Day, Robert Lee. **The Present Competitive Position of Air Cargo.** MBA Thesis, Graduate School of Business, Univ. of Washington, 1958.

Dissmore, Elbert Newell. **A Trenchant Analysis of Post-War Developments in Air Freight Transportation.** M.A. Thesis, Graduate School of Business, Univ. of Washington, 1955.

King, John Philip. **The Global Pattern of Wide-Body Jet Routes: A Study of Network Determinants.** M.A. Thesis, Geography Dept., Univ. of Washington, 1974.

Woolley, John Vernon. **Development of Aviation in the Pacific.** M.A. Thesis, Graduate School of Business Administration, Univ. of Washington, 1969.

Yamanaka, Judy Hamaka Matsubu. **The Geography of the U.S. Air Cargo Industry.** M.A. Thesis, Geography Dept., Univ. of Washington, 1979.

Periodicals and Newspaper articles and other publications

"A Fifth Tiger Shows Signs of Joining the Fast-Charging Asian Menageries," **The Seattle Times**, November 13, 1988, p. K3.

"Air Freight Case (Docket 810, decided July 29, 1949)" **Civil Aeronautics Board Reports**. Wash., D.C.: U.S. Government Printing Office, 1951.

"Air Freight Certificate Renewal Case (Dockets 4770 and 5016, decided March 12, 1956) **Civil Aeronautics Board Reports**. Wash., D.C.: U.S. Government Printing Office, 1957.

"Airlift Plans Strong Air Freight Emphasis," **Aviation Week & Space Technology**, August 31, 1970, pp. 34-36.

"Air-Trade Gold on the Pacific Horizon," **Cargo Airlift**, July, 1973, pp. 4-5

Bernton, Hal. "Flying Tiger Hopes to Open International Express Routes," **Anchorage Daily News**, August 26, 1988, p. C2.

"Bigger Asian Market for Tiger?" **Air Cargo Magazine**, January, 1977, p. 12.

Bowie, Beverly M. "MATS, America's Long Arm of the Air," **National Geographic Magazine**, March, 1957, pp. 283-86.

Bradner, Tim. "Cargo Floods Seattle," **Air Cargo News**, March, 1988, pp. 1 & 7.

------------. "Flying Tigers Roars Back," **Air Cargo News**, October, 1988, pp. 1 & 14.

Brown, Maggie. "Sea-Air Shipping: Capturing the Best of Both Worlds," **Tradelines**, Port of Seattle, May-June, 1988, pp. 10-11.

"Cargo Carrier Plans Anchorage Hub," **Anchorage Daily News**, August 26, 1988, p. C2.

Carter, Harry A. "A Bigger Jetfreighter Family...And Why," **Air Transportation**, July, 1965, pp. 11-12.

"Chairman's Conference Highlights," **Flying Tiger Review**, October-November, 1986.

"Commercial Carrier Augmentation," **Military Air Command Directives (dated 6 Jan 82)** and other information provided by John W. Leland, Deputy Command Historian, Scott Air Force Base, Illinois, Department of Air Force, MAC Headquarters.

Cotter, Marion. "BA - United Linkup May Be a Trend-Setter," **Journal of Commerce**, June 15, 1988, p. 3.

Cronin, James A. "Global Trends Seen Promising for Pure Air Cargo Operators," **Traffic World**, November 16, 1987, pp. 3-5.

"Deregulation Domestic System," **Air Cargo Magazine**, November 9, 1978.

Donoghue, J.A. "Emery's Versatility, Flexibility and Global Distribution System Makes it a Potent Competitor," **Air Transport World**, October, 1984, pp. 46-51.

"Douglas DC-6A Airfreight Study," **Douglas Aircraft Company**, April 3, 1952.

Dunphy, Stephen H. "Bumpy Ride," **The Seattle Times**, February 28, 1988, pp. J4-5.

"Emery Surveys the Scene," **Air Cargo Magazine**, July, 1977.

"Enter the Corvair-Freighter," **Air Transportation**, October, 1954, pp. 17-18.

Feldman, Joan M. "Flying Tiger and Seaboard: After 32 Months Finally a Merger," **Air Transport World**, January, 1981, pp. 40-46.

--------------. "Japanese Liberalization Rapidly Opening Airline Opportunities," **Air Transport World**, July, 1987, pp. 27-34.

--------------. "Megacarriers Expand Abroad Slowly but Steadily," **Air Transport World**, October, 1987, pp. 18-22.

--------------. "U.S. Airlines Eyeing International Cargo," **Air Transport World**, May 5, 1988, pp. 53-54.

Finn, Edwin A., Jr. "21st Century Truckers," **Forbes**, April 4, 1988, pp. 1-3.

Flint, Perry. "The Tiger is Smiling Again," **Air Transport World**, May, 1988, pp. 1-5, 47-49.

"Flying Tiger at Night," **Columbus Dispatch**, May 4, 1987, p. 1.

"Flying Tiger Plans to Expand; Earnings Could Hit $70 Million," **(IAM) 141 Messenger**, August, 1988, p. 10.

"Flying Tiger Line," **Air Cargo Magazine**, February, 1964, p. G6.

"Flying Tiger: Roaring, Soaring-and Prowling for Planes," **Business Week, July 4, 1988,** Transportation Section, p. 1-2.

Flying Tigers Marketing Quarterly, Inaugural Issue, 1988, p. 1.

"Flying Tiger's New Domestic Liability Rules," **Cargo Airlift**, March, 1973, p. 16.

"For Emery Another Kind of Tomorrow," **Cargo Airlift**, February, 1973, pp. 4-11.

Gardner, Hugh. "A Life With Tigers," **Air Cargo News**, October, 1988, p. 18.
Gellene, Denise. "Flying Tiger Faces Strong Head Wind on Its Course Back to Profitability," **Los Angeles Times**, May 11, 1987, pp. 5-6.

Hagen, Paul. "Chartering a New Course to the Far East," **Air Cargo World**, August, 1987, pp. 36-41.

Hackney, L.R. "Mike." "The Jet Train---For Strategic Distribution," **Air Transportation**, June, 1964.

Hardy, M.J. "The Vickers Vanguard," **Air Freight**, November, 1958.

Harris, Roy J., Jr. "Cronin Named Tiger President; Chief is Sought," **The Wall Street Journal**, December 10, 1987, p. 34.

----------------. "Eligible - But Not Eager - for United Job," **The Wall Street Journal**, July 23, 1987.

Healy, Joseph J. "Marketplace Should Determine Domestic Rates, Routes, Healy Says," as entitled testimony on Regulatory Reform Hearings before U.S. Senate Subcommittee on Aviation, March 24, 1977.

------------. "Will Air Cargo Take Off Again in 1972," **Cargo Airlift**, January, 1972, pp. 12-14.

Higdon, Dave. "4 May Survive Air Cargo Shakeout," **Journal of Commerce**, August, 1988.

Holmgren, T.W. "The Case For the All-Freight Airlines," **Pacific Air and Truck Traffic**, February, 1954, pp. 5-7.

"How Tigers Staged a Comeback," interview with James Cronin, **Air Cargo News**, October, 1988, pp. 15 & 18.

"JAL Cargo Rides Westward Updraft as Dollar Slips Down," **Air Transport World**, March, 1988, pp. 69-73.

Johnson, Bruce. "Changing Stripes and Making Money," **Air Cargo World**, September, 1988, pp. 36-42.

Kingston, Rick, (Capt.). "People, Planes & Phnom Penh," **Tiger Tracks**, March, 1989, pp. 3, 9-11.

Laurenzano, Nicholas. "More Heft in the Air," **Air Transportation**, November, 1964,pp. 32-34.

Lefer, Henry. "Recession and Deregulation Posing a Stiff Test for Flying Tigers," **Air Transport World**, February, 1983, pp. 34-38.

------------. "Seaboard is Flying Less, But Enjoying it More," **Air Transport World**, March, 1978, pp. 56-58.

Loebelson, Robert M. "MATS Broadens Military Airlift Role," **Air Transport World**, May, 1965, pp. 81-82.

"Loss of duty-free status riles Singapore workers," **The Seattle Times**, February 6, 1988.

Lyon, Mark W. "Approval Pending For a New Asian Airline," **Jet Cargo News**, October, 1988, pp. 1 & 7.

------------. "Cathay Pacific Redoubles Its Cargo Commitment," **Jet Cargo News**, August, 1988, p. 19.

Marcial, Gene G. "It's Time to Grab Tiger by the Tail," **Inside Wall Street - Business Week**, May 2, 1988, p. 117.

Maturi, Richard. "Wolf Works Another Airline Industry Turnaround With Tiger International," **Investor's Daily**, November 25, 1987, p. 1.

"Multinational Airline Networks May Dominate Industry," **The Seattle Times/Seattle Post-Intelligencer**, October 23, 1988, p. D10.

Murphy, Joseph S. "New Terminal Plan, Profit Orientation Shape Flying Tigers for Jets," **Air Transport World**, July, 1968, pp. 19-21.

Nagatani, Diana Smith, and Sharon Schleis. "Flying Tigers Passenger Operation '45-'89," **Tiger Tracks**, March, 1989, p. 13.

Perrault, William D. "New Planes Show Cost of Speed and Size," **American Aviation**, November, 1948, pp. 9-10.

Plous, F.K., Jr. "Sea-Air: A Winning Compromise of Cost and Speed," **Intermodal Age: Ports/Shipping**, November-December, 1987, pp. 36-39.

Pustay, Michael W. "Airline Competition and Network Effects," **Transportation Journal**, Summer, 1980, pp. 63-72.

Reuters, Walter. "Asian Trade Shift May Herald Change in Political Landscape," **The Seattle Times**, June 28, 1988, p. D2.

Ruth, Robert. "Flying Tiger's Fortunes are Rickenbacker's Hope," **Columbus Dispatch**, May 4, 1987, pp. 1, 4-5.

"SAS - Texas Air Sign Pact," **The Seattle Times**, October 4, 1988, p. C2.

"Seaboard Gets out of IATA and into 747s - Expecting Growth in Atlantic Volume Freight Markets," **Air Transport World**, June, 1973, pp. 20-24.

"Seaboard World Airlines - The Only Intermodal Air Service Between the U.S. and Europe," **Air Cargo Magazine**, June, 1977.

"747s Impact Upon Global Air Cargo," **International Business**, November-December, 1976.

Stephensen, Frederick J., and Stephensen, J. Beier. "The Effects of Airline Deregulation on Air Service to Small Communities," **Transportation Journal**, Summer, 1981, pp. 54-62.

Stone, Mark. "First Flying Tigers to NZ," **Jet Cargo News**, June, 1988.

Taylor, Eugene C. "Jet Freight Triggers Ground Revolution," **Air Transportation**, February, 1964, p. 24.

"The Air Force Emery Would Rather Not Have," **Air Cargo Magazine**, August, 1977, p. 10.

"The Air Cargo Airplane," **Handling and Shipping**, July, 1968, pp. 47-54.

"The Flying Tiger Line, Inc. - Mercury General American Corporation Acquisition," **Civil Aeronautics Board Reports**, Docket 16387, December 30, 1965, pp. 467-69.

"Tiger Does It in a Big Way," **Cargo Airlift**, October, 1974, pp. 32-33.

"Tiger to Own Flying Tigers," **Air Cargo World**, May, 1988, p. 18.

"Tiger Wins its Stripes," **Cargo Airlift**, October, 1972, pp. 6-7.

"Tigers Asia," **Air Cargo Magazine**, January, 1977.

"Tigers Columbus Hub Super Terminal," **Air Cargo News**, October, 1988, pp. 14 & 17.

"Tigers Offers Asian Next-Day," **Air Cargo World**, June, 1988, p. 22.

"Tigers Show Biggest Cat, Biggest Lair," **Air Transport World**, October, 1974, pp. 48-49.

"Tigers is Off to Fast Start in Deregulated Cargo Arena," **Air Transport World**, February, 1979, pp. 34-39.

"Tigers to Tokyo is Conditional," **Jet Cargo News**, November, 1988, pp. 1 & 7.

Tour 364. Published by Headquarters, U.S. Military Assistance Command, Vietnam, Winter Issue, 1971.

"Transpacific Route Investigation (Docket 16242, adopted July 21, 1969)" **Civil Aeronautics Reports**, June-July, 1969.

"Transports 251-500 Miles Stage Length," **Aviation Age**, March, 1954, p. 11.

"U.S. Loses Grip on Global Air Cargo Market," **Air Cargo World**, December, 1987, pp. 44-45.

"Water Down Air Freight Costs with Ocean Shipping," **Air Cargo World**, September, 1987, pp. 29-33.

Woolsey, James P. "Flying Tiger Line gains financial stability after years of struggle as pioneer all-cargo airline," **Air Transport World**, June, 1972, pp. 18-21.

GENERAL REFERENCES

Air Cargo Magazine

Air Cargo News

Air Cargo World

Air Transport Facts and Figures (Air Transport Assn. of America)

Air Transport World

Air Transportation

Airline Executive

Airline Management and Marketing

Aviation Week & Space Technology

Daily's Airline Statistical Annual, 1974-77 (Wash., D.C.: The Ziff-Davis Publishing Co.)

Business Week

Cargo Airlift

Civil Aeronautics Board publications (Wash., D.C.:U.S. Government Printing Office:

      Air Carrier Analytical Charts and Supplemental Carrier Statistics.
      Handbook of Airline Statistics (Annuals).
      CAB Reports (Regulatory Decisions).
      CAB Statistical Reports:
        1946-49 Re-current Reports of Mileage and Traffic Data
        1955-64 Certificated Air Carriers
        1953-   Air Carriers Operating Factors
        1965-77 Summary Form 242 Reports, submitted by individual carriers
      Trends in Scheduled All-Cargo Service: Selected U.S. Certificated Route Air
      Carriers.

Flying Tigers Review

Flying Tigers Sales and Service Alerts

Handling and Shipping

Jane's All the World's Aircraft

Jet Cargo News

Journal of Commerce

Moody's Transportation Manuals

Newsnet (Flying Tigers employee bulletins)

Traffic World

Transportation and Distribution Management

Transportation Journal

The Wall Street Journal